CW01670351

YOUR FIRST VEGETABLE GARDEN UK

starting on the right foot for success

Paperback ISBN 978-1-7397793-8-2
eBook ISBN 978-1-7397793-9-9

First Paperback Edition April 2023

Cover art and layout by SpiffingCovers.com
Images by Tony O'Neill

Publisher Simplify Gardening LTD
publisher@simplifygardening.com
simplifygardening.com

YOUR FIRST VEGETABLE GARDEN UK

starting on the right foot for success

TONY O'NEILL

Author of *Composting Masterclass: Feed the Soil, Not Your Plants*

DEDICATION

To my dearest wife, Tina,

I am filled with gratitude and appreciation as I dedicate this book, 'Your First Vegetable Garden,' to you. Your support and encouragement have been unwavering, and without you by my side, this book would not have been possible.

From the moment we met, you have been my rock, my biggest fan, and my source of strength. Your love and belief in me have allowed me to pursue my passions and follow my dreams, and for that, I am forever grateful.

You have always been my partner in every sense of the word, standing by me through all the ups and downs and cheering me on every step of the way. Your love and support have been invaluable to me, and I am so grateful to have you by my side.

Thank you, babe, for being my everything. I love you more than words can say. With love and appreciation,

ACKNOWLEDGMENTS

Dear Reader,

I would like to express my deepest gratitude to my beautiful wife Tina, for her unwavering support and encouragement throughout the writing of this book. Your love and patience have been a constant source of motivation for me, and I am forever grateful for your partnership.

I am also grateful to my daughters Caitlyn and Amber and my son Wayne for their understanding and kindness as I spent countless hours at my desk working on this project. Your enthusiasm and your willingness to help me test out various techniques have been invaluable.

In addition, I would like to thank my parents, Elaine and Edward, for their love and support throughout my life. Their guidance and encouragement have played a significant role in my development as a writer, and I am forever grateful for all that they have done for me.

I would also like to extend my heartfelt thanks to the team at Simplify Gardening for their hard work and dedication to this project and managing other aspects of our network. Your expertise and guidance have been invaluable, and I am grateful to have had the opportunity to work with such a talented group of individuals.

I hope that the readers of this book will find value in the information and techniques presented within its pages. It has been a labour of love to research and write, and I am passionate about sharing my knowledge and experience with others. I hope this book will serve as a helpful guide and resource for those interested in gardening and inspire and enable readers to pursue their passions and interests.

I also hope that the readers will simply enjoy reading this book. Whether used as a reference or simply for leisure, I strive to make my writing engaging and enjoyable. I appreciate the time and attention readers have given to it and trust it will bring them some enjoyment and fulfilment.

Finally, I would like to thank the readers for your support and encouragement. Whether you have followed along on our website or YouTube channel or by purchasing my books, your enthusiasm for gardening and your willingness to learn has inspired me to continue sharing my knowledge and love of this wonderful hobby we all enjoy.

Thank you all for your love and support. I couldn't have completed this book without you.

Sincerely, Tony O'Neill

CONTENTS

INTRODUCTION

The most challenging part of realizing any goal is the first step. Congratulations on starting one of the most rewarding projects one could undertake – growing a vegetable garden. After decades of gardening, I can promise you that becoming a gardener has been one of my better decisions – I'm sure it will be for you too.

Appropriately, gardens are often used as a symbolic backdrop to essential encounters and life-changing decisions. In love or betrayal, gardens seem to be an anchor point, a place of reflection, an opportunity to become grounded or uproot what isn't working. Gardens are endlessly cooperative with the gardener's need for new beginnings, generously responding even if they've been ignored for a while. Your garden will respond in abundance when taken care of, nurtured, listened to, and loved. Nothing quite matches plucking a fresh carrot from the ground, rinsing it under nearby running water, and taking that first bite from the season's harvest! It's a taste of nature's bountiful response to your efforts.

Working with nature, caring for it, knowing and meeting its needs will be amply rewarded – even if the reward is a learning opportunity. For me, my garden reflects my relationship with nature, and it's a healthy relationship of give-and-take, of listening and being sensitive to nature's needs and responding appropriately. Nature has been waiting for you – are you ready?

My name is Tony O'Neill, and I'm passionate about gardening. From early childhood with my grandfather and throughout my life, gardening has been a constant feature, providing endless satisfaction and a sense of well-being. If you're familiar with my *Simplify Gardening* website and my YouTube channel, you'll know that I love sharing my discoveries. In writing this book, I want to help vegetable growers flourish, improving the availability of nutritious food at local levels. The book is a companion to my online course of the same name – *Your First Vegetable Garden Course.*

In writing Your First Vegetable Garden, I wanted to produce a guide for first-time and experienced gardeners. The book is a culmination of years of work, research, and experimentation, and I'm proud to put my name to it. While my website, SimplifyGardening.com, focuses on all things gardening, this book is dedicated to helping gardeners grow vegetables, herbs, and fruits packed with nutrients.

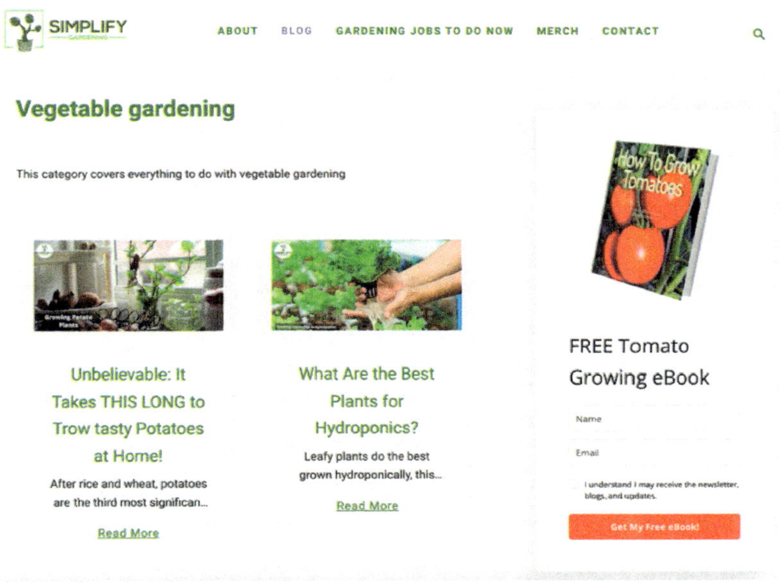

I like to think of gardening as an orchestra, with the gardener positioned as the conductor of various players. Your orchestra can be a trio, small ensemble, or a complete, 80-member symphony orchestra – the choice is yours. If you lean into the relationship with soil and all the microorganisms in it, with the different plants and their needs, it becomes addictive. You will want to learn more, try new things, and explore different approaches, not merely for production's sake but to strengthen the relationship.

I wish I'd had a similar book to start my gardening journey. The fact is that gardening is ever-evolving. Much of the knowledge reflected herein includes recent discoveries as society returns to regenerative gardening. For several decades farming and gardening were about killing pests and using fertilizers to boost growth. In the process, we destroyed much of nature's potential to outperform any pesticide or fertilizer (yes, it's possible). But the tide is rapidly turning, and even large-scale farmers realize that working in harmony with nature is more economical and productive than was initially thought. It's a fascinating world we'll explore together.

Chapter 1 – ***Why Grow Your Own Vegetables*** explores 25 reasons why gardening, in its various forms, is an excellent idea. This book is unapologetically biased towards regenerative practices, and we'll explore the benefits of cooperating with nature in a regenerative process – for improved taste and better plant resilience and performance. Regenerative gardening, or biodynamic gardening as it's also known, is healthier for the soil and plants – and healthier for you.

The great thing about gardening is that it can be practised in various environments. Even with limited space, you can produce a substantial crop.

Chapter 2 – ***Gardening Spaces*** explores the spaces where gardening is or could be, practised – from herbs in the kitchen to polytunnels and everything in between. We also explore community gardens, setting them up and running them – or merely being part of a community garden. If you're a compulsive gardener, we'll look at all the ways you can get your fix. If you prefer pottering, your explorative spirit can be well satisfied.

I wish everyone, even those with packed schedules, could reap the benefits of gardening – and harvesting is only a tiny part of that benefit. Most of us know what's healthy to do, but ambivalence prevents us from initiating and sustaining the proper habits. Gardening allows different involvement levels, with benefits that far outweigh our efforts. Getting started is always the biggest challenge.

Not over-committing yourself initially will benefit the process of starting your first vegetable garden. Start small and consider doing it with a friend who starts their own garden in the same season. A word of caution – gardening isn't a competitive sport. For me, gardening has been a place of solitude. My gardening friends are good friends because they stay in their gardens, and I am in mine. Still, they help me with advice, and I reciprocate – we're all continually learning. As a tandem effort, we encourage each other and share discoveries.

Chapter 3 – ***Plant Health***, explores plant biology, a broad overview of the needs of different plants, and how to satisfy those needs. As a fundamental building block of healthy plants, we explore photosynthesis processes and sugar levels in plants. We also explore the biodynamic role of these sugars in strengthening symbiotic relationships with soil-borne microorganisms.

Water is an essential ingredient for all of life. In this third chapter, we review the role of water, improving its quality, and how to preserve it without damaging your crop. While water is essential for healthy plants, more gardens are damaged by too much water than vice versa. Plants need air, and when you keep your soil too wet, they can't breathe. Nature has provided all the solutions; we merely must cooperate.

Chapter 4 – Weather Considerations examines how regional climates affect our gardening efforts. I have summarized regional information from the Met Office to help gardeners make climate-informed decisions.

Chapter 5 – *Preparing the Ground,* looks at how microorganisms benefit gardening and how to become a microorganism farmer by making your own compost. I provide 25 reasons why adding aerobic compost to your soil is essential for gardeners and farmers. Healthy aerobic compost is pivotal in transforming dirt into soil vibrant with life.

We'll also explore soil structures, amendments, and how to test your soil. Depending on the scale of your garden, testing your soil should be about more than mineral content or basicity (pH). Knowing the diversity of the microorganisms in your soil is invaluable to reaching ultimate plant health. Plants with the highest level of health can resist pests and diseases, a product of a healthy soil biome. Nature enables gardeners to raise crops that are ultimately healthy and productive – without added chemicals.

The soil food web should be a balanced predator-prey environment of microorganisms, organisms, and small animals. This fifth chapter reviews the role players in the soil food web and their effect on keeping your soil healthy and productive. We also examine what can be done to boost specific population groups to meet our plants' needs and control soil and plant pathogens.

Chapter 6 – *Propagation* provides plans and methods to create your garden. From indoor vertical gardens to polytunnel plans, the book contains all the guidance you need to avoid making some of the mistakes I made – like using cedarwood planters. While trees like cedar and black walnut are beautiful, they are poisonous to fungi, and their use to make planters should be avoided.

The chapter also examines bed types, locations, benefits, and drawbacks. Many of you will have seen my videos on YouTube, showing my successes (and failures) at growing record-breaking vegetables in containers. I gladly share the learning these challenges have afforded me, making them available for you to use.

If you're considering establishing a greenhouse or a polytunnel, I will give you my opinion on which one is better in which situation and how to maintain both. Growing in different structures allows you to mitigate climatic risks, but mistakes can cost you. The book provides experience-based knowledge on using various systems to help you avoid some of the pitfalls.

So, you have a growing environment and healthy, weed-free soil; now for the planting.

In **Chapter 7 – *Growing Vegetables***, we review planting and caring for 48 plants – from asparagus to watermelons.

Chapter 8 – *Growing Herbs*, provides guidelines for growing 32 different herbs. For those botanically pedantic folks, please pardon my including some fruits in the vegetable section, such as tomatoes, cucumbers, and other vine fruits. I've provided growing and caring references for more than a hundred plants.

Chapter 10 – *Managing Pests and Diseases*, reviews the most common causes for failure, though, in gardening, we don't fail; we learn. I cover all the uninvited teachers I've met in my almost 40 years of gardening (as well as some I have yet to meet). We also explore ways of avoiding those lessons in the future.

The final chapter, **Chapter 11 – *Monthly tasks***, reviews monthly to-do lists for UK gardeners. A monthly gardening to-do list can help you stay on track and plan your time better. It helps me, so I've included it.

I've provided an addendum at the back of the book to help new gardeners familiarize themselves with uncommon terms. Happy reading, learning, and growing – growing for you, your family, and your plants.

CHAPTER 1

WHY GROW YOUR OWN VEGETABLES

Growing your own vegetables, herbs, and fruit has several benefits beyond having access to ultra-fresh produce. There are hundreds of studies exploring the advantages oflocalisedfood production – below, I have listed the top 20.

Physical Activity

Stress, anxiety, and depression are all reduced by regular physical activity. Still, many of us don't have time to fit it into our already hectic schedules. One of the best things about gardening is that it doesn't require you to hurriedly walk past the gym with your head down, feeling guilty about the money you're spending on a membership you never use.

Gardening offers you the recommended 150 minutes of moderate exercise per week required for maintaining a healthy lifestyle; this is especially true for those who enjoy gardening for its simple pleasures. Even a leisurely stroll through the garden or watering the plants can burn calories, and the more time you spend tending to your green space, the more you'll be exercising your body. In addition, gardening is a full-body workout that targets all major muscle groups.

Strengthening your upper body and thighs can be achieved by pushing the lawnmower into those hard-to-reach corners and shifting wheelbarrows full of soil or compost. Hands-on activities, such as gardening, can help prevent arthritis and other debilitating conditions later in life by keeping your joints supple and lubricated (as well as strengthening your back). Gardening is a physical activity; pulling weeds, planting, and digging can burn up to 400 calories per hour. Gardening is also an excellent mental exercise and helps keep your mind sharp.

You can benefit from regular bursts of garden exercise, which will raise and increase your cardiovascular rate without the need for jogging or pedalling on an exercise bike. Walking around the garden in gardening boots can help older people maintain their sense of equilibrium and balance, significantly reducing the risk of falls in other homes or public areas.

The best part is that gardening offers a valid reason to invest in garden furniture and a comfortable space to take a break from work and relax. You'll be able to enjoy the tranquillity of your garden while you survey your handy work, taking a break with a fresh lemonade – maybe with lemons from the garden you cultivated.

Nutritional Advantage

Homegrown vegetables are packed with vitamins, minerals, and antioxidants, and they are tastier and healthier to eat in their most natural state. Since most supermarket vegetables are picked before fully mature, they lack the nutrients we imagine vegetables contain. Distributed produce may sit on the shelf or in storage for an extended time before reaching the supermarket shelves, losing nutritional value along the way.

The fact is that plants start dying the moment they're taken off life-support. While in the soil, a carrot can absorb moisture and nutrients to support its life – pluck it from the ground, and it starts losing moisture and nutrients from that moment. The same applies to all herbs, vegetables, and fruit.

Boosting our immunity requires regularly consuming an abundance of immune-boosting vitamins and minerals like vitamins C and E, iron, and zinc, as well as foods rich in B vitamins. Some examples include:

- Vitamin C – Citrus fruits, dark leafy greens such as spinach and kale, bell peppers, Brussels sprouts, and strawberries
- Vitamin E – Almonds, peanuts, spinach, broccoli, and avocado
- Vitamin B6 – Chickpeas and potatoes
- Iron – Beans, peas, dark green vegetables, raisins, and legumes
- Zinc – Beans, peas, wholegrain cereals

Localized Production

Sustainable diets prioritise responsible food production, processing, and distribution, focusing on minimising environmental impacts and supporting local economies. This concept is based on the belief that food should be grown, processed, and distributed as close to the point of consumption as practically possible. The following points further expand on this idea and highlight the benefits of this approach:

Environmental sustainability: Producing food near where it is consumed reduces the need for long-distance transportation, lowering fuel consumption and greenhouse gas emissions. Minimising the distance that food travels reduces the overall carbon footprint of food production.

Economic viability: Supporting local farming and food production promotes the financial well-being of local communities. More money stays within the community when consumers purchase food from local producers, stimulating regional economic growth and job creation.

Enhanced food quality and safety: When food is produced and consumed locally, it is often fresher and more nutritious due to reduced transportation times and fewer opportunities for nutrient degradation.

Social benefits: Sustainable diets prioritising local food production can strengthen community ties by fostering direct connections between farmers, producers, and consumers. This can lead to increased collaboration, improved communication, and a greater sense of shared responsibility for the community's well-being and environment.

Improved food security: Localised food production can contribute to greater food security by diversifying food sources and reducing dependence on global supply chains. This makes communities more resilient to disruptions in international trade, extreme weather events, or other factors that can impact the availability and affordability of food.

Cortisol Inhibitor

Cortisol is a hormone produced by the body in times of stress, and its function is to provide you with the resources to deal with a crisis – like when faced with a bear. Cortisol in the bloodstream causes your pupils to dilate, air passages to open, and heart rate to increase – all in preparation to fight, flee, or freeze. Continued exposure to cortisol, caused by living in a stressful environment, can badly affect your health. According to health officials, cortisol is public enemy #1 for mental health concerns, indicating its risks.

When we spend time gardening, the active distraction of connecting with nature can measurably reduce cortisol levels. Focussed activity unrelated to the source of anxiety, mindfulness, and stress reduction all help reduce cortisol levels and benefit physical and mental health enormously. Extended exposure to cortisol in the bloodstream can alter your DNA – gardening is a proven antidote. The mental health benefits of gardening cannot be overemphasized. It is the type of activity that can change the chemistry in your body, improving your health directly.

Vitamin D Exposure

There are numerous health advantages to spending time outside, including the opportunity to soak up the sun's rays (remember to apply a UV-blocker and wear a hat). The benefit stems from the vitamin D the sun helps generate, which is good for us in so many ways! What better way to learn about vitamin D than to look at your cat or dog and see how happy they are when basking in the rays of the sunshine?

However, despite the name, vitamin D is not an external vitamin that must be ingested as a supplement. When the sun's rays bounce off our skin, our bodies produce vitamin D as a chemical reaction. The health benefits this reaction provides are numerous.

Vitamin D helps produce calcium, an essential mineral to keep bones and teeth strong and healthy. Vitamin D also boosts the immune system, helps regulate the flow of insulin throughout the body, drastically reduces the risk of developing a condition like diabetes, maintains the health of the heart and lungs, and even reduces the risk of cancer. One of the essential benefits of increasing your direct exposure to the light of day is its ability to alleviate symptoms of stress, anxiety, and depression.

Scientists describe vitamin D deficiency as an epidemic in countries in the North. Many of these countries now have *Sunlight Clinics* to make extended (artificial) daylight available to people living in short-day winter areas. Gardeners are fortunate to have free access to a natural source of light – the sun. Spending time in the garden, tending to your flowerbeds, or relaxing on a bench under the sun can significantly improve your well-being.

Bacteria Exposure

Our awareness of the risks of viruses has been piqued since the onset of COVID. In the process, antibacterial sales have rocketed. While good hygiene is essential, our ability to produce antibodies to common pathogens is only possible if exposed to some risks. Antibodies form in defence of our health, but only if activated by bacteria and fungi. Trying to create a sterile world creates more risks than benefits – the only organisms that develop resistance to the antibacterial used are the harmful ones.

Of course, a few diseases and conditions can be contracted while spending time outdoors. Still, these can easily be avoided with education and due diligence. Despite what you may have been taught, getting your hands dirty is a good thing. It is harder for bacteria to invade your body and make you sick if your body is allowed to build defences. Effective defences require some exposure to the bacteria – it sounds wrong, but it's a scientific fact. If we insulate ourselves, we are more vulnerable – more exposure equals an increased potential for resilience.

If your immunity system is depleted, it's strongly advised that you seek professional medical advice before you start gardening. If your body is already fighting invading viruses or diseases, adding additional stress to the system is ill- advised.

Personal Creativity

Creativity at any level is a proven stress-buster, and it takes a mere 45 minutes to reduce your cortisol levels. Of all the creative exercises, those done outdoors offer the most significant benefits – think of a Zen garden. Repetitive motions, like raking or digging, increase focus on the present and interrupt an overactive awareness of the past and the future. Everything doesn't have to be perfect – instead, strive for simplicity and inner contentment in your gardening.

You can't get any more creative than creating your own private oasis and private garden based on your preferences. Gardening provides a chance to work on something that will fill your heart with joy as you watch it maturing and producing a harvest.

Few things are more satisfying than taking an idea and making it a reality in your backyard, creating an oasis of tranquillity and production – and you needn't be an expert. Merely add action to your dreams to make them a reality.

Executive Function

Executive function is a mental skill set that includes mental agility, working memory, and self-control. We use these daily skills to learn, work, and manage daily life. Difficulties with executive function can make it hard to focus, follow directions, or regulate our emotions. Developing executive function is a precursor to a more fulfilling life. People with high executive function can:

- Plan, prioritize and organize
- Remain focussed amidst distractions
- Complete projects they start
- Understand and accept varied opinions on a topic

- Know what they believe and why they believe it
- Regulate their emotions
- Keep track of their progress over time – self-manage

We all occasionally fail at managing our lives effectively. Keeping all the plates spinning can be challenging when there are added factors such as complicated relationships or perceived threats. Gardening helps in that it is a tactile, forgiving, and tranquil activity. Planning a garden, planting seedlings, and caring for them during their limited life, is a fantastic way of developing executive function. For me, gardening is a space where I can shut the noise out and focus on the task at hand. That skill is transferable to other situations in my professional life as a fireman.

Mindfulness

Mindfulness is the practice of being present in the *now* – a conscious decision to embrace the moment. The practice of mindfulness is becoming increasingly popular as a tool to still our racing minds. Mindfulness is a proactive way to keep our overactive minds from getting in the way of enjoying the small moments of happiness. There is no better place for this than in a garden where you can stop and smell the roses – and enjoy the moment.

The underlying principle of mindfulness is being present in the here and now. While working in your garden, feel the breeze on your skin, see the bee moving from flower to flower, and appreciate the living space you've made possible. Breathe in and breathe out, focusing on the air entering and leaving your body. It's not an exercise of ignoring reality but rather a shift in focus to the present realities. If your mind wanders to thoughts of yesterday's mistakes or tomorrow's challenges, gently refocus on your breathing, the smell of garden air entering your body, and the tension leaving your body.

Sitting still and doing nothing isn't an option for some people. However, you can still cultivate a sense of mindfulness in the garden while engaging in physical activities. Planting, weeding, and lawn mowing are all excellent opportunities to practice living in the moment. You'll likely never run out of things to do in the garden. Use your gardening time to heighten your awareness of your senses – your hand on the spade, your feet in the soil, the different smells and textures.

Our minds are ever busy but have limited bandwidth. Suppose we choose to focus on our senses. In that case, our minds can be trained to think thoughts other than the tired reruns of self-lambasting reproaches and fearful imaginings. Give yourself a break – feel the textures, imagine your olfactory glands respond to the smells, and experience the air entering your lungs. I know we're addicted to the drama, but just for a moment, change the channel – just another example of how a well-tended and cherished garden can positively impact your mental health.

Being Grounded

At the risk of introducing too many alternatives to pharma-promoted remedies, please can I add one more – grounding, also known as earthing. Grounding means being in contact with the earth to support the specific functions of the organs in your body. According to Laura Koniver (M.D.), grounding supports the body's organs at a cellular level[1]. Dr James Oschman, a biophysicist in energy medicine, believes a lack of "direct physical contact of the human body with the earth's surface" is associated with the rise of modern diseases.

Reducing stress, muscle tension, and hormonal imbalances are just a few of the benefits of grounding on the body's ability to function better. According to Oschman, our separation from the soil has caused physical damage to our bodies.

According to some earthing experts, health benefits can reportedly be seen in as little as half an hour per day. Even though many people remain sceptical of earthing's purported benefits, I feel a lot healthier when I've spent some time in the garden in contact with Mother Earth. It makes perfect sense; we're electrically charged beings, and electrical units are legally required to have an earth-leakage system. Why would it be different for people?

The studies are conclusive – getting your body in contact with the earth has real benefits for your health. A healthy body has other spin-offs, such as improved libido, weight loss, and better resilience. Finding half an hour a day to spend in your garden is easy, fun, and healthy – especially if you can spend it in contact with the soil.

Youth Involvement

It's encouraging to see that an increasing number of young people are adopting farming, gardening, and even compost production as an occupation. An interest in gardening bodes well for our planet, especially for a generation facing challenges we couldn't imagine. In my opinion, the increased use of artificial intelligence will result in a growing need for people to express their connection and unity with all that is natural.

---

[1] https://www.youtube.com/watch?v=44ddtR0XDVU

A survey by The Sun found that 58% of individuals aged 18 to 34 have been cultivating fruits and vegetables at home in the past year, surpassing other age groups in this activity.

Furthermore, a coalition of specialists, including a famous gardener, an international athlete, and a major supermarket, have joined forces to promote fruit and vegetable cultivation in schools. Studies indicate that over 96% of children do not consume sufficient fruits and vegetables. Still, those attending schools that grow their own food consume more than one and a half additional portions of their recommended five-a-day servings.

Positive Modelling

My grandfather was an avid gardener, and some of the best years of my life were spent with him in the garden, where he mentored me. He played a crucial role in my continued gardening, establishing my *Simplify Gardening* YouTube channel and all the platforms I use to promote *Simplify Gardening*.

Involving others, children, or neighbours in gardening can trigger a response. You may focus on vegetables and a neighbour on herbs or fruit. That way, you can barter or swap your handiwork with them. Maybe donating a pack of seedlings can get the process going.

Financial Benefits

Growing your own food can offer significant financial benefits for individuals and families. You can reduce your grocery expenses by cultivating vegetables at home, as homegrown produce is generally cheaper than store-bought alternatives. Additionally, growing your own food can lead to healthier eating habits, potentially saving healthcare costs in the long run. Moreover, excess produce can be shared with friends and family or sold at local markets, generating a small income. Growing your own food is an economical way to promote a healthy lifestyle and save money.

Skill Development

Attachment, self-regulation, and competencies are essential to a happy, productive life. I used the work with disadvantaged youths, helping them develop these three facets of being human. Those who adopted and developed the skills improved their chances of an ever-improving future. Sadly, in the absence of any desire to change, everything keeps going as it always has.

Attachment is a function of predictability, and routines add predictability. Having a daily, weekly, monthly, and annual routine significantly improves our sense of order and control.

Self-regulation is aided when we understand that our emotions are signposts of what we like, what threatens us, and our values. Emotions should be triggers to thought processes, not unconsidered actions. Gardening can have mishaps – some we cause, some are out of our control. While we could vent and dig it all up, taking failure as a learning opportunity is healthier.

Competence is a product of sufficient learning opportunities, and gardening offers plenty. High competency levels have saved many lives—think of some football stars. Many of them would have very different lives without the opportunities to shine.

Improve flavour and nutrition

Synthetic fertilizers often lack macro and micronutrients found in compost, and these soilborne nutrients increase the nutritional value of the produce. Composting enriches the soil with nutrients, reducing the need for pesticides and fertilizers. Pesticides and fertilizers require fossil fuels for their production, and some are potentially harmful to your health.

Comparative studies of homegrown organic crops show they have a significantly higher presence of antioxidants. These include flavones (+26%), stilbenes (+28%), flavonols (+50%), phenolic acid (+19%), flavanones (+69%), and anthocyanins (+51%).

Concentrate and retain growth forces essential to growth and health

Soil health is critical to preserving (and remedying) our waterways. Increased water retention and reduced runoff are two benefits of composting. Effective microorganisms have demonstrable effectiveness at remediating polluted water sources. Cultivating vegetables can improve soil quality and fertility through composting and crop rotation.

Social Connections

Gardening can foster community connections, such as sharing produce or participating in community gardens. Gardening is an engaging activity that can involve the whole family, teaching children about nature and responsibility.

Reduce packaging waste

Store-bought vegetables are often packaged in plastic bags, containers, or cling wrap to protect and preserve them during transportation and storage. Growing your own vegetables eliminates the need for such packaging, reducing plastic waste generation.

Many packaging materials used for store-bought produce are single-use and end up in landfills or contribute to pollution in natural environments. Growing vegetables minimizes the demand for these materials, reducing overall waste.

To improve environmental hygiene

Growing your own vegetables can contribute to improved environmental hygiene in several ways. Cultivating produce locally reduces the need for transportation, lowering greenhouse gas emissions and air pollution. Moreover, home gardening allows for more sustainable and targeted use of resources like water and fertilizers, preventing excessive runoff and contamination of nearby water sources. Additionally, composting kitchen waste and plant materials from your garden can enhance soil fertility while reducing the amount of organic waste sent to landfills, which helps in mitigating methane emissions.

Limits wastage of valuable resources

Reusing freely available resources such as leaves, weeds, and grass trimmings to produce compost, a substance with known benefits, makes perfect sense. Sending these resources to landfills creates unmanaged anaerobic conditions that pour methane and hydrogen sulfides into the atmosphere. Not only does dumping these resources have no benefit, but it also causes environmental harm.

CHAPTER 2

GARDENING SPACES

Before grabbing gardening gloves and planting seeds, consider the types of vegetable gardens that will work best for your lifestyle. Consider your family size, the crops you want to cultivate, the soil's health, and how much time and money you can devote to a vegetable garden.

You can create a traditional in-ground vegetable garden with a spacious backyard with ample sunlight and good soil. However, if your soil is not ideal, consider using raised beds for cultivation. Front yards, often underused, can also provide space for growing food in a communal setting. Many vegetable plants are aesthetically pleasing, so if your landscape already has limited room for a formal vegetable garden, incorporating vegetables into your ornamental beds could be a suitable option. While interplanting offers numerous advantages, choosing your plants thoughtfully is essential.

Many veggies grow well in containers; container gardening is perfect for people with limited space. Vegetables cannot thrive indoors without supplementary light, although hydroponically cultivating plants indoors is a developing trend. Hydroponics allows the gardener to manage temperature, light, and nutrients while avoiding disease pressures that would otherwise be present in plants cultivated outside, and it can need significant initial investment. Therefore, it may not be the best option for someone new to plant cultivation.

These approaches aren't necessarily mutually exclusive. Cucumbers and maize, for example, might be grown in a standard in-ground garden bed in the backyard, while carrots and broccoli are grown in raised beds suitable for your front yard. At the same time, you could interplant kale and Swiss chard in a perennial border, grow herbs in pots on your patio, and grow microgreens hydroponically indoors.

Selecting a Suitable Garden Site

Choosing the right location for your vegetable garden is crucial for its success. Here are some key factors to consider when selecting a suitable site:

Sunlight: Most vegetables require at least 6 to 8 hours of direct sunlight daily. Choose a spot that receives adequate sunlight throughout the day to ensure healthy growth and good yields.

Soil quality: Healthy, well-draining soil is essential for successful vegetable gardening. Test the soil to determine its pH, nutrient levels, and composition. Amend the soil as needed with organic matter, such as compost or well-rotted manure, to improve its structure and fertility.

Accessibility: Your vegetable garden should be easily accessible for regular maintenance, watering, and harvesting. Choose a location close to your home, preferably with easy access to water sources and tools.

Drainage: Vegetables need well-draining soil to prevent waterlogging and root rot. Avoid low-lying areas or spots where water tends to pool after heavy rainfall. If drainage is an issue, consider using raised beds or containers to improve soil drainage.

Protection: Select a site that offers some protection from harsh winds, which can damage plants and reduce yields. Consider using natural barriers like hedges or trees or building a windbreak to shield your garden.

Space: Plan your garden according to the area available and the size of the vegetables you intend to grow. Ensure there is enough room for plants to grow without overcrowding, and allow easy access to all areas for maintenance and harvesting.

Crop rotation: To maintain soil fertility and prevent the build-up of pests and diseases, practice crop rotation in your vegetable garden. Divide your garden into sections, and rotate the types of vegetables grown in each bed every year.

By carefully considering these factors and selecting an appropriate site, you can create a thriving and productive vegetable garden that will reward you with fresh, homegrown produce.

Garden Types

There are various types of vegetable gardens to suit different needs, preferences, and available spaces. Traditional in-ground gardens involve planting vegetables directly into the soil in rows or beds, making it a popular choice for those with ample backyard space and good soil quality. Raised bed gardens, on the other hand, consist of soil-filled frames or containers elevated above the ground, providing improved drainage, better soil control, and easier access for those with mobility issues or poor native soil. Container gardens are an excellent option for those with limited space, such as apartment dwellers.

Vegetables can be grown in pots, planters, or even repurposed containers on balconies or patios. Vertical gardens take advantage of vertical space by growing vegetables on trellises, walls, or other vertical supports, making them suitable for urban environments or small yards.

Finally, allotments are shared spaces where people collectively grow vegetables, offering a valuable resource for those who lack the space or resources to establish their own garden while fostering social connections and community involvement. Allotment gardening isn't unique to the UK, but it is one of the first countries to have legislation that obliges local councils to provide sufficient space to meet demands.

In-Ground Gardens

In-ground vegetable gardening is a traditional and popular method of cultivating produce directly in the soil. It involves selecting a suitable site with well-draining soil, ample sunlight, and adequate space for plant growth. Preparing the ground is crucial, including tilling, amending with compost or other organic matter, and ensuring the proper pH balance for optimal plant health. In-ground gardening allows vegetables to establish deep and rebust root systems, enabling them to access nutrients and water efficiently. This method also promotes natural interactions with beneficial organisms in the soil, such as earthworms and microbes, which contribute to overall plant health and growth. In-ground vegetable gardening can be a cost-effective and rewarding way to grow a wide variety of vegetables while enhancing the beauty and productivity of your outdoor space.

Raised Bed Gardens

Raised beds are garden areas typically 15 to 20 cm above the general ground level. They are linked to the native soil underneath them and may or may not have built sides. They can be created of simply piled-high earth with a flattened top, or they can be framed with logs or boulders or built with wooden boards or straw bales. Raised beds with just enough width to reach the middle are great for producing veggies. Defined beds make a garden more appealing and minimize cross-contamination caused by foot traffic, compacting the soil. Above-ground beds generally drain better and can warm up faster.

Raised beds come in various shapes and sizes, and the soil used inside the beds may be reused. Use dirt from surrounding walkways, mixed with existing soil and organic matter, for shallow beds with no support. Soil can be stacked and compacted to create a raised bed less than 6 inches tall. To avoid soil erosion, slightly slope the bed's sides.

You may need more soil if you build a taller raised bed or one in a framed box. If your soil is of excellent quality loam, you may screen it into the raised bed and mix it with 50% compost. Raised garden soil mixtures can also be purchased bagged from a nursery. Alternatively, dirt can be purchased by the cubic yard from a landscaping business. Consider that 1 cubic yard of dirt equals 27 cubic feet when calculating how many cubic yards you require.

To calculate the volume of growing medium required, multiply the length by the breadth and depth of your raised bed. A raised garden bed measuring 1.2 m wide, 3 meters long and 45 cm deep will need 1.2 x 3 x 0.45 m growing medium, i.e., 1.65m^3 or 1650 cubic decimeters (litres).

Make sure to inquire about the blend's components. Topsoil, compost, and a soilless mix, such as vermiculite, make up a high-quality combination. Are the materials natural? What is the origin? Does the mix include manure of animals fed on treated grass? Is the compost cured, damp, and less than six months old? Is the topsoil guaranteed free of contaminants, weeds, insect pests, illnesses, and harmful nematodes? Buying a raised bed mix isn't enough to keep a garden going for the long haul. After each growing season, raised beds must be treated with a 10 cm layer of organic material to maintain high nutrient levels.

If the sides are made of wood, avoid cedar and walnut, as both will negatively impact your soil's microorganism populations. While these woods are more rot-resistant, they will negatively affect your crops. Do not use treated pine either – such as wood from pallets. Wrapping your lumber in weed cloth can extend its life by up to ten years, and untreated lumber should last six years.

Container gardens

Growing edibles in containers is a standard food production method for the household. Many vegetables can be planted in deep enough pots to sustain their roots. Container size is connected to gardening ease and success – the larger the container, the better. The following plants grow well in containers:

Vegetable	Minimum Container Depth
Beans	20 cm
Beets	20 cm
Bok choi	46 cm
Collards	32 cm
Cucumbers	20 cm
Eggplant	40 cm
Green garlic	15 cm
Kale	20 cm
Lettuce	20 cm
Mustard greens	15 cm

Peas	32 cm
Peppers	40 cm
Potatoes	32 cm
Radishes	10 cm
Scallions	15 cm
Spinach	10 cm
Squash	46 cm
Swiss chard	20 cm
Tomatoes	40 cm

These plants flourish in containers and are an excellent option for gardeners with limited space, soil issues, or animal pressure. Containers can be installed on a rooftop, balcony, patio, deck, entranceway, or pathway. Containers should be positioned in areas that promote crop development. For example, if producing tomatoes, a container may be relocated to a sunny place, a partly shady area for growing lettuce, or a sheltered microclimate during the winter for growing year-round kale. Edible container gardening provides more flexibility than traditional gardening and is ideal for children, renters, beginner gardeners, those with physical disabilities, or seasoned gardeners looking to downsize. Container gardening has no digging or tilling, and crops are essentially weed-free. Container gardening may also keep aggressive herbs, such as mint, from taking over typical garden settings. Container- grown vegetables require more attention than plants cultivated in regular garden beds in the ground.

Container Selection

Selecting suitable containers for vegetable gardening is essential for ensuring your plants' healthy growth and development. Here are some factors to consider when choosing containers for your garden:

Size: The size of the container will determine which vegetables you can grow and how many plants you can accommodate. Generally, choose containers with a minimum depth of 20-25 cm for shallow-rooted vegetables like lettuce and radishes, 30-40 cm for medium-rooted vegetables like peppers and tomatoes, and 45-60 cm for deep-rooted vegetables like carrots. The container's width should also provide ample space for plant growth, with at least 30-60 cm of diameter for most vegetables.

Material: Containers can be made from various materials, including plastic, terracotta, ceramic, wood, and metal. Each material has its advantages and disadvantages. For example, plastic containers are lightweight and affordable but may deteriorate under UV exposure. Terracotta and ceramic containers are attractive and breathable but can be heavy and prone to cracking in cold temperatures. Wooden containers are durable and provide good insulation but may rot over time. Metal containers can heat up quickly in the sun, potentially harming plant roots, but are generally durable and long-lasting.

Drainage: Good drainage is essential for preventing waterlogged soil and root rot. Ensure your container has multiple drainage holes at the bottom to allow excess water to escape. If necessary, drill additional holes to improve drainage.

Weight: Consider the weight of the container when filled with soil and water, especially if you plan to move it regularly or place it on a balcony or deck with weight restrictions. Lightweight containers like plastic or fabric pots are ideal for easy transport or weight-sensitive areas.

Style and aesthetics: Select containers that suit your personal style and complement your outdoor space. A wide range of colours, shapes, and designs allow you to create a visually appealing and cohesive garden.

By carefully considering these factors and selecting appropriate containers, you can create a thriving and productive vegetable garden that maximizes the available space and caters to your specific needs.

Container materials for vegetable gardening can be classified into several categories based on their characteristics and properties. Here are the main classifications:

Plastic containers: Lightweight, affordable, and widely available, plastic containers come in various shapes and sizes. They retain moisture well but may degrade under UV exposure. Look for high-quality, UV-resistant plastic to ensure durability.

Terracotta and ceramic containers: These traditional, porous materials allow for good airflow and moisture evaporation, promoting healthy root growth. They can be heavy and may crack in cold temperatures, so they may not be ideal for all climates. Glazed ceramic containers are less porous, retaining moisture better but potentially reducing breathability.

Wooden containers: Wooden containers, such as boxes, barrels, or planters, provide good insulation and a natural aesthetic. Avoid chemically treated wood that may leach harmful chemicals into the soil.

Metal containers: Durable and long-lasting, metal containers can add an industrial or modern touch to your garden. They can heat up quickly in the sun, potentially harming plant roots, so consider lining them with insulation or placing them in a shaded area. Galvanized steel or aluminium containers are good options for rust resistance.

Fabric containers: Also known as grow bags, fabric containers are made from breathable materials like geotextile or felt, allowing excellent drainage and air circulation. They are lightweight, easy to store, and can prevent root circling. Fabric containers may require more frequent watering as they lose moisture through the material.

Recycled or repurposed containers: Innovative gardeners can transform various items into unique and sustainable planters, such as old tires, buckets, or furniture. Ensure these containers have proper drainage and are made from non-toxic materials that won't harm your plants.

Each container material has advantages and drawbacks, so it's essential to consider your gardening needs, climate, and personal preferences when selecting the most suitable materials for your vegetable garden.

Gardening Techniques

Most of the yields specified in this book refer to 3.6 square meter beds (1.2 m wide and 3 meters long). More intensive gardening will have more abundant plants but necessarily greater yields. The famous *square-foot garden* is a form of intensive gardening, and another method of maximizing yields is to plant a vertical garden. Let's review each of these separately.

Row Gardening

Vegetable gardening in rows is a traditional and practical method for organizing and planting vegetables in a garden. It involves planting vegetables in parallel rows with designated pathways in between, allowing for easy access and maintenance. Row gardening promotes efficient use of space and simplifies the process of planting, watering, weeding, and harvesting.

To create a successful row garden, start by preparing the soil and planning the layout based on the specific needs of each vegetable type. Consider factors such as sunlight requirements, plant size, and growth habits to ensure that each plant receives adequate light and has enough room to grow. Be mindful of the spacing between rows, leaving sufficient space to walk and work without disturbing the plants. Plant taller vegetables, such as corn or tomatoes, on the north side of the garden, to prevent them from shading smaller plants. Additionally, practice crop rotation in your row garden to maintain soil fertility and reduce the risk of pests and diseases. By carefully planning and maintaining your row garden, you can create a productive and organized space for growing a variety of vegetables.

Intensive Gardening

An intensively planted garden aims to get as much food as possible from a small space. Intensive gardening has been popular as cities have become more populated and yards have become smaller. Many house settings are too small for a classic row garden; intensive gardening has become the most viable option. Intensive gardens improve yield by optimizing area utilization and succession planting, but they require careful design. Although intensive gardens are commonly seen on raised beds, they can also be found in-ground or in big containers.

"Square Foot Gardening" is a style of intense planting popularized by Mel Bartholomew in his 1981 book *Square Foot Gardening.* The French already used these intense gardening techniques in the late 1800s, but Bartholomew popularized the concept. In a raised bed, vegetables are grown in squares of 30 cm (1 foot) each. Beds are made to be no wider than 1.2 m across to be managed from the outside. The gardener never steps on the soil where the veggies grow; therefore, the earth is never compacted or cross-contaminated. Gardeners may use the available area to arrange their square-foot beds in various configurations.

Beds are delineated in 30cm squares using a wood lattice or twine, helping delineate planting areas and making following planting density guidelines simple. Many veggies may be cultivated inside each square, and the final size of the veggies growing within that square determines the spacing.

Large plants, such as broccoli or tomatoes, may need numerous squares for each plant to reach maximum growth. Smaller plants (such as beets) can have up to 16 plants per square, whereas smaller plants (such as carrots) can have up to 32 plants per square. Unlike typical row gardens, where there is as much vacant space as plant-occupied areas, a square-foot garden has no wasted space. Fertilization, irrigation, and control activities are centred on the planting beds in intensive gardening.

Interplanting is another intensive gardening technique that involves growing two or more types of vegetables close, maximizing space utilization and productivity. This method can provide various benefits, such as improved pest control, enhanced pollination, and better nutrient use. However, it requires careful planning and consideration of the following factors:

Compatible plants: Choose combinations that complement each other's growth habits, nutrient requirements, and pest resistance. Companion planting can help create a balanced ecosystem where plants support each other's growth.

Plant size and growth rate: Combine plants with different sizes and growth rates to ensure they do not compete for space, sunlight, or nutrients. For example, fast-growing, shallow-rooted plants can be interplanted with slow-growing, deep-rooted ones.

Sunlight requirements: Interplant vegetables with similar sunlight needs to avoid shading issues. Taller plants should be positioned so they do not block sunlight for shorter plants, ensuring that each plant receives adequate light for optimal growth.

Root depth: Combine plants with different root depths to maximize nutrient use and minimize resource competition. Shallow-rooted plants can be interplanted with deep-rooted ones to better use the soil profile.

Succession planting: Incorporate succession planting in your interplanting strategy by replacing harvested crops with new plants or sowing seeds regularly. This practice ensures continuous production and efficient use of space.

Pest and disease control: Interplanting diverse crops can help minimize the spread of pests and diseases by disrupting their life cycles and habitats. Combining plants with natural pest-repelling properties can further enhance this benefit.

Soil fertility and nutrient management: Interplanting plants with different nutrient requirements or those that contribute to soil fertility, such as nitrogen-fixing legumes, can help maintain and improve soil health.

When planning your interplanted vegetable garden, consider these factors to create a highly productive and efficient space that maximizes available resources and promotes a healthy, diverse ecosystem.

Intensive Planting Distances

Produce	Plant Separation (cm)	Produce	Plant Separation (cm)
Artichokes (globe)	142 - 152	Kohlrabi	10
Asparagus	38	Leek	7 - 10
Bean, bush	5 - 8	Lettuce, head	25
Bean, lima	10 - 15	Lettuce, leaf	10 - 15
Bean, pole	15 - 30	Mustard	10 - 15
Beets	5 - 8	Okra	30 - 45

Broccoli	45 - 60	Onion	5 - 10
Brussels sprouts	36 - 46	Parsley	30
Cabbage	23 - 30	Parsnips	30
Cantaloupes	122	Pea	8
Carrot	5 - 8	Pepper	24 - 30
Cauliflower	15–18	Potato	25 - 30
Celery	24	Potatoes (sweet)	60
Chard, Swiss	38 - 46	Pumpkin	60 - 91
Chinese cabbage	60	Radish	2 - 5
Chives	30	Rhubarb	122
Collards	30 - 38	Rutabagas	60
Corn, sweet	30	Southern pea	7 - 10
Cucumber	30	Spinach	10 - 15
Dill	60	Squash, summer	45- 60
Eggplant	45 - 60	Squash, winter	60 - 91
Endive	20 - 30	Tomato	45 - 60
Garlic	30	Turnip	7 - 10
Kale	15	Watermelons	150

Vertical Gardening

Vertical gardening involves trellises, poles, tiered beds, and strings to support growing plants and is ideal for gardeners with limited gardening space or arable land. Tomatoes, cucumbers, melons, pole beans, and other vining plants are suitable for vertical planting. Some plants weave themselves onto the framework, while others require tying.

Vertical plants throw a shadow, so put them on the north side of a garden bed to avoid shadowing and grow shade-tolerant crops nearby. Vertically grown plants take up considerably less space, and while the yield per plant is lower, the yield per square foot is significantly higher.

Vertically growing plants are more exposed to the elements, causing them to dry out faster – remember to compensate for the loss by watering more regularly. This rapid drying is beneficial to plants that are prone to fungal infections. Raised beds, tiered beds are typically used in vertical gardening.

Optimizing Available Garden Space

A diagram can help you plan your garden once you've decided on the size and style of garden that will best fit your needs. When drawing a garden diagram, there are various factors to consider.

To correctly design the dimensions of the garden bed and plants, use graph paper or a scale.

- Draw a north arrow and record the sun's position throughout the day.
- Make a note of where you can get water and where you can compost.
- For each variety of vegetables, choose a distinct colour or form.
- Review each crop's planting dates to help you plan for succession throughout the growing season. Ideally, after harvesting one crop, another crop is ready to be planted in its place.
- Plant from north to south to make the most of the available sunshine.
- To prevent shadowing shorter plants, group tall crops (corn, okra, sunflowers) and trellised vines (peas, beans, squash) together on the north side of the garden. Crops such as leafy greens are a good stopgap for shady spots against a perimeter wall or near a tree (not under).
- Leave walkways to access the plants or beds from all sides.

- Display the plant's mature size to ensure appropriate space is allocated.

For those with the space, an area of 58 square meters should be sufficient for a family of four to meet most of their produce needs throughout the growing season. Begin small and gradually grow your garden as time and interest allow. Start with a small area; it's easy to become overwhelmed by the weeds and labour of starting a new garden. It is simple to expand once you get started.

CHAPTER 3

PLANT HEALTH

We're all part of a complex symphony of life, and none of it depends on humans' presence. It all fits together from the smallest microorganisms to the largest mammals, each playing a leading role. Without plants, life on Earth would not be possible. They supply nourishment to all animal life, either directly or indirectly. Their roots hold the earth and prevent erosion, while their leaves produce oxygen. Their branches shade and chill the ground, and their unique forms, colours, textures, and aromas provide beauty to our surroundings. Botany is the study of plants as a science. This chapter covers vegetable plant classification, structural and reproductive components, development processes, and environmental influences. The aim is to help you understand how plants grow, their needs, and proper management approaches to navigate challenges.

Four fields of study are of interest, though the scope of this book will restrict us to the fundamentals of each discipline:

1. *Taxonomy* – how plants are classified, grouped, and named
2. *Anatomy and Morphology* – plant structures and adaptations
3. *Physiology* – internal functioning and development
4. *Ecology* – their interaction with their environment

Plant Taxonomy

More than 350,000 different types of plants are on Earth, with this number continuously changing as new species are discovered and others become extinct. There is an international system by which plants are classified based on characteristics, natural habitat, and reproduction forms. These are grouped in a hierarchal structure, with each tier subdivided into further groupings as follows:

- Kingdom
- Phylum

- Class
- Order
- Family
- Genus
- Species
- Variety, or cultivar

An example would be the Brassicaceae Family, with approximately 338 genera and 3,700 species. One of those 338 genera is the genus Brassica, in which we have:

- Broccoli (Brassica oleracea var. italica)
- Brussels sprouts (Brassica oleracea var. gemmifera)
- Cabbage (Brassica oleracea var. capitata)
- Cauliflower (Brassica oleracea var. botrytis)
- Kale (Brassica oleracea var. acephala)
- Kohlrabi (Brassica oleracea var. gongylodes)
- Rutabaga (Brassica napus var. napobrassica)
- Turnips (Brassica rapa)

Other genera and variants in the Brassicaceae family are:

- Horseradish (Armoracia rusticana)
- Radish (Raphanus sativus)

Plant Anatomy and Morphology

Plants are distinctly divided into two main parts – roots and shoots, the one visible and the other generally below the surface of the pedosphere. What happens above the ground affects what happens below and vice versa.

Roots

Roots usually grow from the bottom of a plant or cutting. Roots' primary roles are to absorb nutrients and water, anchor the plant in the soil (or other growth media), give physical support for the stem, and act as food storage organs. Roots are used as a propagation technique in some plants, either naturally or through human intervention. Roots interact with microorganisms, forming symbiotic partnerships for mutual benefit. Root structure and growth patterns significantly impact a plant's size and vigour, propagation mode, adaptability to certain soil types, and response to cultural techniques and irrigation. Certain vegetable crop roots are also essential food sources.

Root growth influencing factors include:

- Roots thrive in soil that has a good mix of moisture and air.
- Soil richness and pH determine the pace and depth of root development.
- A lack of oxygen in the soil restricts growth, reducing total water and nutrient absorption.
- Root development is hampered by soil compaction.

Stems

Stems are the structures that hold buds, flowers, and leaves in place. The vascular tissue system, which comprises the xylem, phloem, and, in most plants, the vascular cambium, is a stem's most crucial internal component. The plant's vascular tissue system carries food, water, and nutrients while providing support. Water and minerals are transported by the conducting elements in the xylem, whereas the conducting elements in the phloem transport food. Hormones can be carried by both xylem and phloem.

Buds

A bud is an immature branch from which new leaves or flower components emerge. Temperate zone tree and shrub buds generally grow a protective outer coat of tiny, leathery bud scales.

Annuals and herbaceous perennials have bare buds with outer leaves that are green and succulent. Buds are named based on where they appear on the stem surface. Terminal buds grow at the very tip of a stem, and lateral buds form on the stem's sides. Axillary buds are lateral buds that grow in the axil of a leaf (the narrow- angle between the plant's stem and the leaf attachment).

In rare cases, more than one bud forms. Adventitious buds appear in locations other than the terminal or axillary positions. Adventitious buds can form from the internode of a stem, the edge of a leaf blade, callus tissue at the cut end of a stem or root, or laterally from the roots of a plant. A leaf bud is a small stalk with immature leaves, and these buds grow into green stalks. Leaf buds are frequently more pointed and plump than flower buds. A flower bud comprises a short stem and embryonic floral components.

Leaves

The fundamental purpose of most leaves is to collect sunlight to produce plant sugars through photosynthesis (more on this in the next section – ***Plant Physiology***). Each leaf grows into a flattened surface with a significant area for effective light energy absorption. A stem-like extension called a petiole supports the leaf away from the stem. At the node, the petiole's base connects to the branch.

Flowers

Flowers are appreciated for their beauty and perfume, yet their primary function is sexual reproduction. Wind-pollinated plants, such as grasses and pines, have no need to attract an insect or animal, so they invest minimal energy in aesthetics and instead generate vast amounts of pollen for the wind to disseminate. On the other hand, other plants have evolved fragrant, pale, night-blooming blooms to attract pollinating moths.

Most fragrant, showy flowers with landing platforms (or nectaries) have developed to attract insect pollinators to secure the plant's reproductive success and survival. Insects can tell how to approach and where to land by the markings on the petals. Flowers fertilized by bees reflect ultraviolet light, which humans cannot see. Flowers that look and smell like females of an insect species fool certain male insects into sharing pollen. Bees, butterflies, moths, and other insects are drawn to fragrant flowers. Flowers with unpleasant scents attract flies, beetles, and other insects. Flowers are also pollinated by other creatures, such as birds and bats. Some flowers contain nectaries at the ends of long tubes that correspond to the body sections of the pollinators.

Fruit

Fruits are essential for human sustenance and frequently take centre stage in a garden. A fruit is an ovary that has matured and contains one or more seeds, and the fruit protects the seed until it is mature enough to disperse. Because many fruits appeal to animals, a fruit's seed can be eaten, transit through a digestive tract, and end up far away from the parent plant, distributing genes and assuring the plant's long-term survival. Some fruits, such as dandelion fluff and maple-winged samara, use wind to disseminate their seeds.

Seeds

A flower's final result might be seeds. A seed is comprised of three parts:

- An embryonic plant (miniature plant) that remains dormant.
- The endosperm is a food supply for the embryo that is stored in proteins, carbs, or lipids.
- A seed coat or covering surrounds the seed and protects the embryo from illnesses, insects, and moisture until germination.

Germination occurs when the right temperature, moisture, oxygen, and light conditions are fulfilled. The radicle is the first portion of the seed to develop as water is taken in through the seed coat. The radicle will grow into the primary root, from which root hairs and lateral roots will shoot. The hypocotyl develops into the stem in due course.

Plant Physiology

Photosynthesis, respiration, and transpiration make a plant's growth and development possible. Like all living organisms, including you and I, well-being is an environmental factor – our environment's influence and interaction with us. Weather conditions, temperature levels, day length, soil conditions, and systemic threats contribute to plants' health. Studies have shown that a healthy plant is pest and disease resistant – a combined product of healthy photosynthesis, optimal hydration, and soil that consists of a beneficial biota.

Photosynthesis

Photosynthesis is a process used by plants, algae, and some bacteria to create energy from sunlight. It's essential for life on Earth, as it allows these organisms to convert sunlight into energy, which is then stored in the form of glucose. This energy is used for growth and other life processes.

During photosynthesis, plants absorb light using a green pigment called chlorophyll, found in chloroplast structures. They also take carbon dioxide (CO_2) from the air and water (H_2O) from the soil. Through a series of chemical reactions, these ingredients are combined to produce glucose ($C_6H_{12}O_6$) and oxygen (O_2). The plant stores and uses glucose for energy, while the oxygen is released into the atmosphere as a waste product.

In summary, photosynthesis is a vital process that allows plants to harness sunlight to produce energy and release oxygen, supporting life on Earth.

Respiration

Plant respiration is a crucial process that allows plants to release energy from stored glucose, and it is a continuous process that happens in all living plant cells, both day and night. While photosynthesis produces glucose and oxygen by converting sunlight, carbon dioxide, and water, respiration breaks down glucose. It converts it into usable energy, essential for growth, maintenance, and other vital functions within the plant.

There are two main types of respiration in plants: aerobic and anaerobic. Aerobic respiration occurs when oxygen is present and is the most common form of respiration. During this process, glucose is broken down in plant cells through a series of chemical reactions, producing carbon dioxide, water, and a molecule called adenosine triphosphate (ATP). ATP is the primary energy source used by the plant for various cellular functions. In anaerobic respiration, which occurs in the absence of oxygen, glucose is broken down into different byproducts, such as ethanol and lactic acid. This process is less efficient and provides less energy compared to aerobic respiration.

Transpiration

Transpiration is the process through which plants lose water in the form of water vapour, mainly from their leaves, to the surrounding atmosphere. This process is essential for the proper functioning of plants and serves multiple purposes, including nutrient uptake, temperature regulation, and maintaining water balance within the plant.

Water is absorbed by plant roots from the soil and transported upward through specialized tubes called xylem vessels. This movement is made possible by a combination of root pressure, capillary action, and water's cohesive and adhesive properties. Once water reaches the leaves, it evaporates into the surrounding air through tiny pores known as stomata. Stomata are primarily found on the underside of leaves and can open and close, allowing the plant to regulate the transpiration rate.

Transpiration is closely linked to photosynthesis, as the opening of stomata also allows for carbon dioxide intake, which is necessary for that process. While transpiration can lead to water loss, it also helps plants cool down on hot days, similar to how humans sweat to regulate body temperature. Water movement through the plant helps distribute essential nutrients and minerals from the roots to various parts of the plant.

Plant Ecology

To grow and reproduce, plants must balance their core life activities of photosynthesis, respiration, and transpiration. Light, temperature, humidity, water, carbon dioxide, and oxygen levels can all impact how plants accomplish essential biological tasks. Understanding how these environmental elements impact plants enable us to improve yields, prevent risks and provide better plant management.

This section will go through how the following environmental elements can have an impact on plants:

- Light
- Temperature
- Water

- Oxygen
- Carbon dioxide
- Soil microorganisms

Light

Three major factors are essential for effective photosynthesis: quality, duration, and amount. Duration is the exposure time, and light amount refers to the intensity or concentration of sunshine, which fluctuates depending on the season. Summer has the most powerful light, and winter has the least.

Light quality is the colours or wavelengths of light that reach the plant surface. A prism separates sunlight into red, orange, yellow, green, blue, indigo, and violet. The colours at either end of the spectrum, red and violet, impact photosynthesis most. Plants primarily reflect green light, resulting in the green hue we see and associate with them. Blue light is largely responsible for fostering vegetative development. Infrared and ultraviolet (UV) are the non-visible waves on either side of the visible spectrum.

Fluorescent and incandescent plant lights, sometimes known as 'grow' lights, use a combination of red and blue wavelengths to mimic sunshine as nearly as possible. Fluorescent light, particularly cool-white tubes, can promote foliage development. This type of light is ideal for germinating seeds. Incandescent light has a high red-orange wavelength range yet creates a lot of heat.

Temperature

Temperature influences flowering and fruit set, photosynthesis and respiration, water usage, and plant dormancy. Thermoperiodism is the term used to explain the time plants need to be exposed to particular temperatures to promote or inhibit certain developmental phases in their life cycle – as described below:

- *Flowering and Fruit Set* – Cool-season crops like spinach can blossom prematurely (bolt) rather than grow the necessary leaves if temperatures are high and the day is long. Temperature extremes can also result in stunted growth and poor quality. High temperatures, for example, cause bitterness in lettuce and cucumbers. Furthermore, pollen may become ineffective at high temperatures, inhibiting fruit sets. Temperatures that are too low for warm-season crops, such as tomatoes, will, on the other hand, impede fruit set. Temperature adjustment, either alone or in conjunction with day duration, can influence when particular flowers bloom.

- *Photosynthesis and Respiration* – Photosynthesis and respiration rates typically increase as the temperature rises. However, high nighttime temperatures can cause respiration to outpace photosynthesis. When this happens, the plant consumes food quicker than it can generate it. Photosynthesis occurs at its maximum rate for most plants in the 18 to 29°C range and diminishes when temperatures are higher or lower than this range. As a result, when day temperatures are 5 to 10°C higher than night temperatures, plants have the most effective thermoperiod (day temperature range). This temperature range allows plants to photosynthesize and respire (break down food) during the day but decreases respiration at night when there is no light, and the plants cannot manufacture food.
- *Water Use* – Temperature extremes can harm how plants use water. Plants lose moisture quicker than they can absorb in hot weather, producing withering and limiting development. Extremely low temperatures can cause the soil to freeze, significantly restricting the passage of water into the plant. Plants continue to transpire (give up water) on a windy, bright winter day and may become dry (dried out). In addition to dehydration, freezing temperatures can promote the development of ice crystals within and between plant cells, which can cause considerable physical damage.
- *Dormancy* – Plant dormancy is affected by temperature. Many plants' buds require a certain number of days below a critical temperature (chilling hours) before they resume growth in the spring. Peaches are an excellent example. Most cultivars require 700 to 1,000 hours of dormancy below 7°C but above freezing point (0°C) before breaking dormancy and growing. The period varies depending on the variety. Buds can endure extremely low temperatures when dormant. However, buds become more vulnerable to late cold or frost once the rest phase is through and are readily injured by these circumstances. While frigid temperatures can hurt nonhardy plants, unusually high winter temperatures can trigger premature bud break in some plants and subsequent bud-freezing damage when temperatures drop.

Water

Water has several critical roles in photosynthesis. It keeps a plant's turgor, or the firmness or fullness of plant tissue, stable for starters. Turgor pressure in a cell is comparable to the pressure of an inflated balloon, and plant cells require water pressure, or turgor, to retain form and enable cell development. Second, the solar energy collected by chlorophyll in the plant's leaves splits water into hydrogen and oxygen. Oxygen is emitted into the environment, whereas hydrogen is employed to produce carbohydrates. Third, water dissolves soil minerals and carries them upward from the roots and throughout the plant, where they serve as raw materials for creating new plant tissues. The soil moisture around a plant should alter – before re-irrigating, the soil should be left to dry before rewetting it.

Oxygen

Plants need oxygen for respiration to generate energy by breaking down the carbohydrates produced during photosynthesis. The aboveground sections of a plant have an abundance of oxygen, but soil oxygen can be a plant growth-limiting factor.

Soils with a healthy soil biota have extensive pore spaces that allow air and water to circulate readily. Well-aerated soils offer the oxygen that seeds and roots need to sprout and flourish. Some soils are poorly drained, resulting in little or no pore space for oxygen and anaerobic conditions. Soils that are oversaturated with water or compacted might prevent oxygen from reaching the roots and induce root death. For more information on ensuring optimal soil oxygen levels, see ***Chapter 5: Preparing the Ground***.

Carbon Dioxide

Carbon dioxide is an essential component of photosynthesis. Carbon dioxide is abundant, and its concentration in the atmosphere is rarely a limiting factor for plant development. During the day, when sunlight is available and photosynthesis is active, most plants take in carbon dioxide through open stomata. If the plant does not open its stomata throughout the day, carbon dioxide can be a limiting factor. When stomata shut, photosynthesis slows and even halts entirely. If the plant is drought-stressed, the stomata may shut down to reduce water loss throughout the day.

Soil Microorganisms

One of the most neglected elements of ensuring an environment optimal for plant growth is the soil life cycle (or soil biota). Because this is often the missing ingredient to successful vegetable gardening, I have given this factor a chapter of its own (see ***Chapter 5: Preparing the Ground***).

CHAPTER 4

WEATHER CONSIDERATIONS

Global climate changes require gardeners to become more agile in their approach to the craft. We all need to draw alongside nature, forming a symbiotic relationship to help both flourish, even in challenging times. Extended droughts, higher temperatures, colder winters, floods – nature has an appropriate response for them all, but humans need to listen. The global average temperature in 2019 was about 0.95°C warmer than the 20th-century average. This places 2019 as the second warmest year on record, just behind 2016, the warmest year observed at that time. It's important to note that these figures might have slight variations depending on the data source, but they all indicate that 2019 was significantly warmer than the 20th-century average.

Like any healthy relationship, we need to be attuned to the changing needs of our partners. In the absence of regular rain, our soil needs better water-holding capacities. In floods, our soil needs improved cohesive strengths. While nature is often remembered for its tempestuous display of force, the trick to becoming an effective gardener is to listen to her whispers. We need to be present in the relationship, listening and responding – and nature will do the same; she always does. What are the plants and soil saying, the birds and the bees? Are there earthworms in the soil? Is the colour of my plants' foliage changing year-on-year? Are you attentive and finely sensitive to your garden's needs?

A healthy relationship is one where the needs are met with finesse. Is it better to water more, or is it better to add microorganisms, mulch, and organic matter to help address the thirst? Do you rush in, adding nitrogen, insecticides, and everything you think your plant needs, or do you approach your garden with love and understanding? Nature loves natural solutions. In managing changing weather patterns, we need to work with nature, implementing subtle adjustments that prevent a pendulum swing from one extreme to the next.

Most people's lives are filled to capacity, so I'm hesitant to add more to your to-do list. However, your relationship with your garden requires some experiential understanding. You need to know what your plant is experiencing – when last it had some unchlorinated water, sunshine, soil biota population, and the pests it is fighting. I have a simple chart to record the rainfall, full sun days, and pest prevalence. It's the only way to recognize patterns and devise appropriate responses.

United Kingdom Climate Zones

Several blogs use the USDA plant hardiness zones (PHZ) to indicate which plants can grow where. The UK has a similar system called the Royal Horticultural Society (RHS) hardiness ratings. It classifies plants based on their ability to tolerate various climatic conditions, particularly the minimum temperatures they can withstand.

The RHS hardiness ratings are divided into six categories, ranging from H1 (the least cold-hardy) to H6 (the most cold-hardy). These categories are:

- H1a: Warmer than 15°C (PHZ 13) - suitable for tropical plants and indoor use.
- H1b: 10°C to 15°C (PHZ 12) - suitable for subtropical plants and unheated greenhouses.
- H1c: 5°C to 10°C (PHZ 11) - suitable for frost-tender plants and heated greenhouses.
- H2: 1°C to 5°C (PHZ 10) - suitable for plants that can tolerate mild frost, typically found in the warmer areas of the UK.
- H3: -5°C to 1°C (PHZ 9) - suitable for plants that can tolerate moderate frost, common in many parts of the UK.
- H4: -10°C to -5°C (PHZ 8b – 9a) - suitable for plants that can withstand cold winters, found throughout much of the UK.
- H5: -15°C to -10°C (PHZ 7b to 8a) - suitable for plants that can tolerate frigid winters, found in colder areas of the UK.
- H6: -20°C to -15°C (PHZ 6b – 7a) - suitable for plants that can withstand extreme cold, found in the coldest regions of the UK.
- H7: Colder than -20°C (PHZ 5b to 6a) - suitable for plants that survive harsh winter conditions.

The RHS hardiness ratings are helpful for gardeners in the UK to choose plants that are suitable for their specific climate and ensure the plants' survival and growth in their gardens.

Comparatively, the growing conditions in the UK are less severe than those in North America's northern regions. While the two systems are not directly interchangeable, they can still provide helpful guidance for gardeners. For example, if you know the USDA zone for a plant, you can find the equivalent RHS rating by comparing the minimum temperatures for each category. Similarly, if you know the RHS rating, you can find the approximate USDA zone by comparing the temperature ranges. However, it's essential to consider other factors, such as soil type and precipitation, when selecting plants for a specific location.

Small heat islands, such as those created by blacktop and concrete, or cool spots created by small hills and valleys are examples of microclimates, minor variations in climate on a fine scale. The microclimates of individual gardens may also be very localized. Because your yard is sheltered or exposed, it may be warmer or cooler than the rest of the neighbourhood. Your garden may also have warmer or cooler areas than the general climate in your area or the rest of your yard, such as an area in front of a south-facing wall or a low spot where cold air settles (because cold air is heavier than warm air). No map of hardiness zones can replace the in-depth knowledge gardeners gain from working in their gardens.

As the days grow shorter and the temperature drops in the autumn, many plants develop a greater tolerance to cold. This hardiness fades away as temperatures rise and daylight lengthens in late winter. An early autumn freeze can harm plants even if temperatures don't autumn below your zone's average low temperature. In the same way, hot weather in the middle of the winter, followed by a sudden change to cold weather, can harm plants.

All recommendations are nothing more than a set of guidelines. As a result, they are based on average low temperatures rather than the record-breaking lows. With an extreme cold snap lasting only a few days or even hours in the most frigid zone, plants that thrived for years could be destroyed in a year if grown there.

OTHER FACTORS

In addition to plant hardiness suggestions, many other environmental factors play a role in the success or failure of plants. Wind, soil type, soil moisture, humidity, pollution, snow, and winter sunshine can all significantly impact the survival of plants in the winter. Several other factors may influence a plant's survival, including where it is planted, how large it is, and how healthy it is.

Plants need the right amount of light to grow and prosper. For example, during the winter, plants that need partial shade may be damaged by too much sunlight because it could cause rapid temperature changes. Depending on the season, plants may have different needs for soil moisture. Typically hardy plants in your area may be damaged if soil moisture levels autumn too low in the late autumn, causing them to go into dormancy.

Wind

Wind factors that affect the UK climate

The United Kingdom's climate is significantly influenced by various wind factors due to its location, surrounded by the Atlantic Ocean to the west and the North Sea to the east. These factors help create the UK's temperate maritime climate, characterized by mild winters, cool summers, and frequent rainfall. The main wind factors that affect the UK's climate are:

Prevailing Winds: The UK is predominantly affected by south-westerly prevailing winds originating from the Atlantic Ocean. These winds bring relatively mild, moist air, resulting in milder winters and cooler summers compared to regions at similar latitudes. The south-westerly winds also contribute to the UK's generally high levels of rainfall throughout the year.

Jet Stream: The UK's climate is influenced by the position and strength of the jet stream, which is a strong, high-altitude wind that flows from west to east. The jet stream separates cold polar air from warmer tropical air and influences the formation and movement of weather systems. The jet stream's position can result in extended periods of wet, windy weather or cold, dry conditions, depending on whether it is positioned to the north or south of the UK.

North Atlantic Drift: Also known as the North Atlantic Current, this warm ocean current is an extension of the Gulf Stream. It transports warm water from the Gulf of Mexico towards the British Isles, which helps to moderate the UK's climate, keeping it warmer than other regions at similar latitudes. The North Atlantic Drift affects the UK's coastal regions, particularly in the west, making them milder in winter.

Polar and Tropical Maritime Air Masses: The UK is also affected by polar and tropical maritime air masses, which can significantly influence the country's weather. Polar maritime air masses originate from the cold polar regions and bring cold, moist air to the UK, leading to cooler temperatures and precipitation. On the other hand, tropical maritime air masses originate from warmer equatorial regions, bringing milder temperatures and higher humidity.

Continental Air Masses: Occasionally, the UK experiences winds from the east or northeast, which can bring continental air masses from mainland Europe. These air masses can result in cold, dry weather during the winter months or hot, dry conditions in the summer, depending on the season.

These wind factors interact with other meteorological and geographical factors, such as altitude and distance from the coast, to create the UK's distinct climate. The varying influence of these wind factors can lead to significant regional differences in weather and temperature across the country.

Rain

Water

Plants, and any form of living organisms, cannot live without water. Water constitutes between 80 and 90% of the plant cell in plants. The amount of water in different plant parts varies:

- The apical portion of root and shoot >90%
- The stem, leaves, and fruits 70–90%
- Woods 50–60%
- Matured parts 15–20%
- Freshly harvested grains 15–20%

Water is the base material for all plant metabolic and biochemical activities. Water plays a critical role in the plant's respiration and transpiration systems and is essential for photosynthesis. Without water, there can be no germination, growth, or fruit. Water serves as a plant nutrient solvent and microorganisms sustainer in the soil. A plant's ability to remain erect (turgidity) is water-dependent – in its absence, the plant wilts.

Water helps to maintain soil temperatures and balance salinity and pH. Water is essential for microbial life, and microorganisms, in turn, enhance water efficacy. Water, like microorganisms, helps improve the soil's tilth. The effectiveness of all the gardener's labour is dependent on water.

Soil Moisture

In this book, as in most planting guides, we refer to soil moisture levels as hydric, mesic, and xenic – high moisture habitat, medium moisture habitat, and arid habitat. Each descriptor has ranges within that are hard to pin down, and as far as possible, we will explain these.

CHAPTER 5

PREPARING THE GROUND

Creating Healthy Soil

There's a growing understanding of microorganisms' role in sustainable, productive, and healthy farming. We're finding harmony between ourselves and all living creatures, allowing nature to become its best self. Your garden can be a space where nature thrives – resistant to pests and diseases, super healthy, and able to produce nutritious food. Isn't it what we all want for ourselves too?

According to the United Kingdom's Office of National Statistics, cost of living insights - food[2], food prices have risen a staggering 18%, and more people are buying cheaper food. The trend is expected to continue as input costs increase. Much of those input costs are linked to fuel and fertilizers. But there's a gradual shift to doing things differently, better, more sustainably. Much of the solution lies in cooperating with nature and using soil biology to our advantage. If you are starting a garden, you can do it right from the outset. If you already have a vegetable and herb garden, adopting some new habits will surely improve your gardening experience.

Six soil-related elements are essential for effective traditional gardening:

- Soil structure
- Soil nutrition
- Organic matter
- Soil biology
- Water and oxygen

Soil Structure

---

[2] https://www.ons.gov.uk/economy/inflationandpriceindices/articles/costoflivinginsights/food

Mineral Portion of Soil

The inorganic part of the soil consists of deconstructed rock, tiny mineral particles called clay, silt, and sand, each identified by their particle size. Imagine a grain of sand is the size of a cricket ball; comparatively, a particle of silt would be a size of a pea and a particle of clay the size of a pinhead. Depending on the representative ratio of each of these, soil texture could be defined as:

- Clay
- Silty Clay
- Silty Clay Loam
- Clay Loam
- Sandy Clay
- Sandy Clay Loam
- Sandy Loam
- Loam
- Silt Loam
- Silt
- Loamy Sand
- Sand

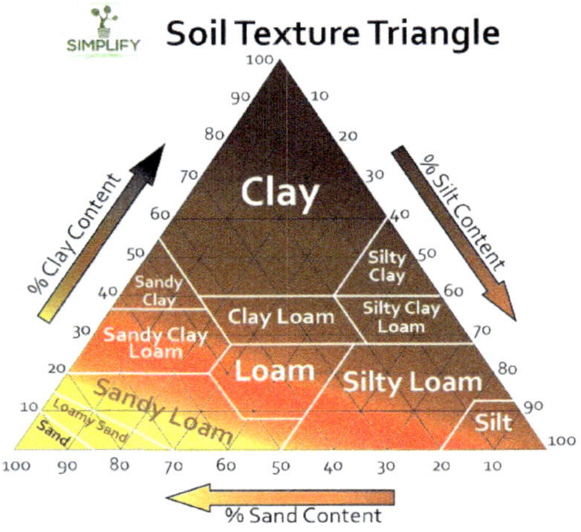

If you wish to test your soil texture, a jar test will give you an accurate assessment.

a. Fill a clear glass jar about one-third full with your soil sample.

b. Fill the jar with water until it's about two-thirds full.

c. Add a teaspoon of dishwashing liquid to help disperse the soil particles.

d. Seal the jar tightly and shake vigourously for several minutes, allowing the detergent to mix with the soil and water.

e. Set the jar on a flat surface and allow the soil particles to settle for at least 24 hours.

f. Once settled, the soil particles will form distinct layers: sand at the bottom, silt in the middle, and clay at the top.

g. Measure the thickness of each layer and calculate the percentage of sand, silt, and clay in your soil sample.

h. Use a soil texture triangle or chart to determine the soil texture class based on the percentages of sand, silt, and clay.

Below are the characteristics of the different base textures:

Characteristic	Clay	Silt	Sand
Looseness	Poor	Fair	Good
Water and Air Space	Poor	Fair	Good
Water Management	Poor drainage	Fair	Poor water retention
Clod-Forming Inclination	Good	Fair	Poor
Workability	Poor	Fair	Poor
Fertility	Fair to Good	Fair	Poor
Cation-Exchange Capacity (CEC)	Good	Poor	Poor

Soil Nutrients

The 17 Essential Plant Nutrients

Sourced from Water

Carbon (C)
Oxygen (O)

Sourced from the Air

Hydrogen (H)
Oxygen (O)

Sourced from the Soil

Primary Nutrients	*Secondary Nutrients*	*Micronutrients*	
Nitrogen (N)	Calcium (Ca)	Boron (B)	Manganese (Mn)
Phosphorous (P)	Magnesium (Mg)	Chrorine (Cl)	Molybdenum (Mo)
Potassium (K)	Sulfur (S)	Copper (Cu)	Zinc (Zn)
		Iron (Fe)	Nickel (N)

Soil nutrients are essential for plant growth, development, and overall health. They play a crucial role in various biological processes and are categorized into macronutrients and micronutrients based on the quantity plants require. Here is a summary of the primary soil nutrients and their roles in plant growth:

Macronutrients:

Nitrogen (N): Nitrogen is a vital component of chlorophyll, which is responsible for photosynthesis. It is also a key element in amino acids, proteins, and nucleic acids (DNA and RNA), all essential for plant growth and reproduction. Nitrogen deficiency can lead to stunted growth, yellowing leaves, and reduced yield.

Phosphorus (P): Phosphorus is necessary for energy transfer within plant cells, root development, and the formation of flowers, seeds, and fruits. It also plays a role in synthesising nucleic acids and ATP (adenosine triphosphate). Phosphorus deficiency can cause slow growth, weak root systems, and poor fruit and seed development.

Potassium (K): Potassium is essential for regulating plant metabolism, water uptake, and the opening and closing of stomata. It also helps in the activation of enzymes, the synthesis of proteins, and the development of strong cell walls. Potassium deficiency can result in weak stems, reduced resistance to pests and diseases, and poor fruit quality.

Calcium (Ca): Calcium is crucial for cell wall structure, cell division, and the proper functioning of cell membranes. It also plays a role in the activation of certain enzymes and the regulation of nutrient uptake. Calcium deficiency can lead to weak cell walls, poor root development, and leaf tip burn.

Magnesium (Mg): Magnesium is a vital component of chlorophyll and plays a role in photosynthesis. It also helps in the activation of enzymes and the synthesis of proteins. Magnesium deficiency can result in yellowing leaves, poor fruit development, and reduced photosynthesis.

Sulfur (S): Sulfur is an essential component of certain amino acids, proteins, and vitamins. It also plays a role in the formation of chlorophyll and the synthesis of oils and plant hormones. Sulfur deficiency can cause slow growth, yellowing leaves, and reduced yield.

Micronutrients:

Iron (Fe): Iron is necessary for the synthesis of chlorophyll and the activation of certain enzymes, and it also plays a role in electron transport during photosynthesis. Iron deficiency can lead to chlorosis (yellowing) of leaves and reduced growth.

Manganese (Mn): Manganese is involved in photosynthesis, activating enzymes, and synthesising chlorophyll. Manganese deficiency can result in interveinal chlorosis and reduced growth.

Zinc (Zn): Zinc is essential for the activation of enzymes, the synthesis of proteins, and the regulation of plant growth hormones. Zinc deficiency can cause stunted growth, reduced leaf size, and poor fruit development.

Copper (Cu): Copper is necessary for the proper functioning of certain enzymes, photosynthesis, and lignin synthesis in cell walls. Copper deficiency can result in stunted growth, leaf curling, and poor fruit development.

Boron (B): Boron is essential for cell division, cell wall formation, and the proper functioning of cell membranes. It also plays a role in the transportation of sugars within plants. Boron deficiency can lead to poor root development, deformed leaves, and reduced fruit quality.

Molybdenum (Mo): Molybdenum is necessary for the proper functioning of certain enzymes involved in nitrogen metabolism and also plays a role in the synthesis of amino acids.

Organic Matter and Soil Biology

In my opinion, knowing how to develop healthy soil should be a life skill taught at schools. Composting is nature's preferred method of ensuring productive soil – nothing is better. Creating healthy soil does not require land – it can also be done in apartments. You can fill your indoor space with pot plants and vertical gardens using kitchen scraps, cultivated microorganisms, and store-bought ground. Increased indoor vegetation positively contributes to improved mental and physical health.

Creating healthy soil not only benefits plants but benefits the environment holistically. Composting is a meaningful, easy, and effective way of reversing some negative impacts on our environment and the planet. If you have healthy soil, your plants will be healthier and more nutritious, and you will be healthier too. My motto is; take care of the soil, and it will take care of your plants.

Soil Composition and the Role of Compost

Soil is essential for life on Earth and hosts many microorganisms. These tiny organisms decompose organic matter and cycle nutrients in soil ecosystems. They also respond to and affect small changes in soil conditions. Soil microorganisms are very diverse and live in different habitats within the soil, and their diversity and abundance depend on soil properties such as carbon, pH and climate. Soil microorganisms are essential for soil health and function.

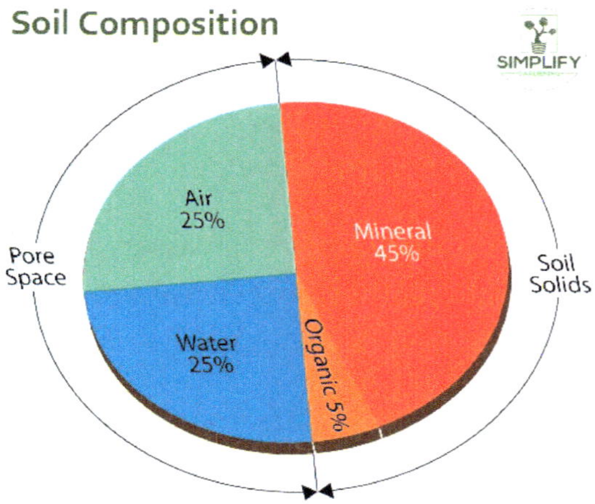

A generalized organic and inorganic mix ratio is 45% minerals, 25% air, 25% water, and 5% organic matter within the top 45 cm. We consider the above ratios because compost has an almost magical balancing effect for all of the above.

Compost aerates clay for improved soil textures, accommodating air and aerobic microorganisms; improves sand's water-holding ability and increases its organic matter; compost manages water and air content for optimal organic activity in silt. Compost is a wonder product that brings soil biology to environments that would otherwise be mostly sterile. Compost's further benefits for mineral soil are the reduction of erosion susceptibility, increased cation-exchange capacity, pH buffering capabilities, and improved soil tilth.

Reduced Erosion Susceptibility

Soil is a three-part open system with solids, liquids, and gasses with strong interaction between the parts. Primary soil particles, particularly silt and sand, would be prone to erosion if they were not cemented together in groupings called aggregates. The shape and strength of the aggregates influence pore size and distribution and water and gas holding capacities. However, the binding matter used by bacteria, fungi, and actinomycetes has built-in channels, ensuring continued porosity for air movement and moisture management.

Cation-Exchange Capacity (CEC)

Cation exchange capacity (CEC) refers to the ability of soil, sediment, or other porous material to hold positively charged ions, known as cations, and exchange them with the surrounding environment.

The CEC is determined by the number and type of negatively charged sites present in the material, which attract and hold the cations. Common cations found in soils include calcium, magnesium, potassium, and sodium.

The CEC is an important soil property because it affects the availability of nutrients to plants and the potential for contaminants to leach into groundwater. Soils with a high CEC tend to be more fertile, as they can hold more nutrients, while soils with a low CEC are more prone to leaching and nutrient depletion.

CEC is usually expressed in units of milliequivalents per 100 grams of dry soil or other material. It can be determined through laboratory analysis or estimated based on soil texture, organic matter content, and other factors.

Buffersalt Effect – pH Buffering

Compost can have a significant effect on pH buffering in soil. pH buffering refers to the ability of soil to resist changes in pH when acidic or alkaline substances are added to it.

Compost is typically slightly acidic, with a pH of around 6.0 to 7.0. When added to soil, it can help lower the pH if the soil is too alkaline and raise the pH if it is too acidic. This is because compost contains organic acids that can react with the mineral components of soil to produce neutralizing salts, which help to stabilize the pH.

In addition, compost can help to maintain a stable pH over time, even in the presence of acidic or alkaline inputs, due to its high buffering capacity. This means that it can absorb and neutralize large amounts of acidic or alkaline substances before the pH of the soil is affected.

The ability of compost to buffer pH can also improve soil fertility, as plants generally grow best in soil with a slightly acidic pH (around 6.0 to 6.5). This is because many nutrients, such as phosphorus, are most available to plants at this pH range.

Overall, adding compost to soil can positively affect pH buffering, leading to more stable soil conditions and improved plant growth.

Compost and Improved Soil Tilth

Compost can improve soil tilth, which refers to the physical condition of the soil, including its structure, texture, and porosity.

Here are some ways compost can improve soil tilth:

Improving soil structure: Compost can help bind soil particles together, creating aggregates to enhance soil structure. This improves soil aeration, water infiltration, and drainage, enhancing root growth and overall plant health.

Enhancing soil water-holding capacity: Compost can increase the soil's ability to hold water, which is vital for plant growth. Compost acts like a sponge, absorbing water and slowly releasing it as needed, which helps to prevent waterlogging and drought stress in plants.

Increasing soil nutrient availability: Compost is rich in nutrients such as nitrogen, phosphorus, and potassium, which are essential for plant growth. These nutrients are released slowly over time as the compost decomposes, giving plants a steady supply of nutrients.

Encouraging soil microbial activity: Compost is teeming with beneficial microorganisms such as bacteria and fungi, which play a crucial role in breaking down organic matter and releasing nutrients into the soil. These microorganisms also help improve soil structure and porosity and suppress harmful pathogens and pests.

Reducing soil erosion: Compost can help to reduce soil erosion by improving soil structure and water-holding capacity. This can be particularly beneficial in areas prone to heavy rainfall or runoff.

Adding compost to soil can improve soil tilth, resulting in better plant growth, higher yields, and improved soil health.

Soil Health

Listed below are the ten most essential indicators of healthy soil. You will notice that compost plays the lead role in all ten vital soil-health-building elements.

Surface Cover

Surface cover is vital in minimizing weeds, preventing soil compaction from rain, and further strengthening the soil microorganism population. Following a *See-no-Soil* policy is the productive way towards healthier soil. The surface cover can be mulch or green compost (legumes as a growing ground cover), and the role of compost is evident.

Soil Structure

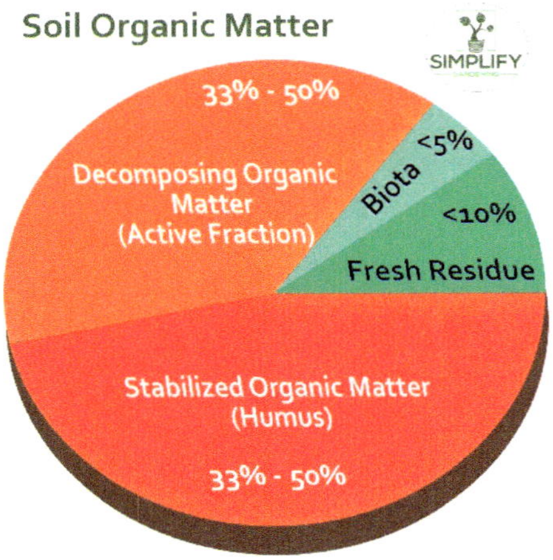

Soil structure is a factor of aggregates, tilth, and surface penetrability. The absence of hard-to-break clods indicates a healthy soil structure. Healthy soil forms a ball in your hand that readily breaks when poked. Also, consider the level of crusting on the soil surface – it should not prevent quick water absorption. Compost is essential for improving the quality and capacity of your soil. Better put, microorganisms are crucial for sustainable, healthy, nutritious gardening.

Humus

Humus is a complex, stable form of organic matter due to the decomposition of plant and animal residues, the final product of the composting process. It is an essential component of healthy soil and is crucial in maintaining soil fertility and productivity.

Here are some key characteristics of humus:

Dark colour: Humus is typically dark brown or black due to the accumulation of carbon due to the decomposition of organic matter.

Stable: Unlike fresh organic matter, which can decompose quickly, humus is relatively stable and resists further decomposition, making it a stable source of plant nutrients.

High Cation Exchange Capacity (CEC): Humus has a high CEC, which means it can hold onto nutrients and make them available to plants over time.

Improves soil structure: Humus can improve soil structure by binding soil particles together, creating soil aggregates that enhance soil porosity and aeration.

Enhances water-holding capacity: Humus can increase a soil's water-holding capacity by improving soil structure and increasing the soil's ability to absorb and retain water.

Provides nutrients: Humus is rich in nutrients such as nitrogen, phosphorus, and potassium, which are essential for plant growth. These nutrients are slowly released over time, providing a steady supply to plants.

Supports soil microorganisms: Humus provides a habitat for microorganisms such as bacteria and fungi, which play a crucial role in breaking down organic matter and releasing nutrients into the soil.

Soil Erosion

The start of soil erosion is evidenced by the formation of minor rivulets called rills. Rills form when surface runoff's shear stress exceeds the soil's shear strength, limiting the soil's ability to resist forces acting across the surface. Water breaks up soil particles and carries them down the slope, causing the erosion process to begin.

Surface cover using mulch or cover crops are good preventer of erosion. Erosion can only occur if water sufficiently accumulates on the surface to start flowing. The soil's water infiltration properties improve the rapid absorption of rain, again a product of compost addition. Roadside surface management technologies have vastly contributed to improved erosion control. Road construction often requires the travel surfaces to be lower than the surrounding landscape, leaving roadside slopes that require careful erosion management. Their research has shown that planting indigenous grass on composted surfaces is the quickest way to stabilize and strengthen soil's shear strength.

Soil Compaction

Compost is essential in alleviating soil compaction, which occurs when soil particles are pressed together, reducing the space available for air and water to move through the soil. Compacted soil can be a problem for plants, as it can limit root growth and reduce the availability of water and nutrients.

Here are some ways compost helps alleviate soil compaction:

Improving soil structure: Compost can help to improve soil structure by binding soil particles together, creating soil aggregates that improve soil porosity and aeration. This can help to break up compacted soil and create more space for air and water to move through the soil.

Enhancing soil organic matter content: Compost can increase soil's organic matter content, improving soil structure and making it more compact-resistant. Organic matter helps to hold soil particles together, creating a more stable soil structure.

Encouraging soil microbial activity: Compost is teeming with beneficial microorganisms such as bacteria and fungi, which can help to break down compacted soil and create more space for air and water to move through the soil. These microorganisms can also help to improve soil structure and porosity over time.

However, it is essential to note that for severe cases of soil compaction, additional measures may be necessary, such as deep tillage.

Water Infiltration, Drainage, and Holding Capacity

After heavy rain, water infiltrates into the soil, causing it to become saturated. The porosity of the ground is an essential factor in water infiltration. The pores' number, length, and diameter determine soil water movement and retention. Most soil flow is caused by large pores (diameter greater than 1.5mm). When it comes to water infiltration, texture and slope play a role. Sandy soils tend to be more efficient than siltier or clayey soils. Generally speaking, water drains more quickly from higher points in the landscape. Water infiltration is governed mainly by the structure of the ground. The clay particles that clog pores are caused by unstable soil aggregates disintegrate and dissolve in water. When soil is compacted, water cannot reach deeper subsoil layers, where it can be stored for use by plants.

Soil permeability refers to the ability of water or air to pass through the soil. Pore size, shape, and density determine a given soil's porousness. Soil surveys have traditionally referred to saturated hydraulic conductivity as permeability.

Available water refers to soil water accessed by plant roots and extracted from soil pores. This water resists evaporation and percolation due to suction forces within soil pores (CEC). Still, it is not so tightly held that roots cannot absorb it. The amount of water available to plants is known as the Available Water Capacity (AWC).

Soil organic matter content can be improved, but soil texture still plays a significant role in water-holding capacity. By adding compost to the soil, soil water availability can be enhanced by reducing compaction and increasing the cation-exchange capacity (CEC). Any management strategy to raise infiltration and increase soil water storage by increasing the stability and number of fine aggregates is likely to be successful – a function of compost.

Soil Biodiversity

In the next section, we delve into the different organisms in the soil biota – just an introduction. An indicator of active soil biota is the presence of earthworms.

An abundance of life can thrive in the soil's complex ecosystem. Soil contains a wide variety of organisms. Organic residue degradation and nutrient cycling in soil are made possible by various soil life forms. The ground may include a wide variety of organisms. If this is the case, plant growth will have a better chance of accessing nutrients. Pests and diseases can be suppressed by the diversity and abundance of soil organisms. Earthworms are vital as a 'keystone' participant in the soil food web.

The soil is home to a variety of earthworm species. Deep burrows are made by some species, while others make shallow holes. Large amounts of organic and mineral soil are ingested and excreted as casts on the soil surface in some burrowing forms. More plant nutrients are available in casts of earthworms than in the surrounding soil. The passageways created by the movement of earthworms through the ground improve aeration and water infiltration and lubricate soil particles. Their excrement aids in the stability of aggregates. In no-till systems, the soil mixing that earthworms provide is essential for nutrient cycling and the decomposition of organic matter.

Gardeners have a direct impact on soil microbial populations. The diversity and abundance of soil life may be improved using compost or cover crops. Conversely, soil organisms can be culled by the indiscriminate use of pesticides. Anhydrous ammonia fertilizers also negatively affect soil biota. Tillage is necessary to incorporate organic residues, but soil organisms' habitats can be disrupted due to tilling. Earthworm populations can be harmed if surface residue, which provides food and protection, is removed.

Soil biodiversity is a direct product of compost and mulching. Sometimes it's the small things that matter. In gardening, it's the creatures so small they're invisible to the naked eye – microorganisms. Composting is the fastest, cheapest, most effective microorganisms farming method. Farming and introducing microorganisms into your soil is the best possible soil health improvement measure you could take.

Plant and Root Growth

The health of individual plants in the field is a good indicator of plant vigour. Plant vigour is indicated by the uniformity of growth displayed by all crop plants in a given lot. Healthy soil increases germination rates, reduces seedling mortalities, ensures uniformity in development, and is the basis for better yields. The root system is essential to the plant's growth and development.

While photosynthesis is essential to a plant's food conversion process, building blocks are absorbed via the roots as inorganic ions. The roots of healthy plants can be as extensive as the plant's above-ground growth. For that to be possible, soil structure and vitality are essential. Root system development can be hindered by compacted subsoil layers that reduce the effective root zone. The system is paradoxically both robust and delicate. The robustness of soil is a factor in the microorganism population's diversity. Without variety, the system cannot control the proliferation of harmful bacteria, fungi, and nematodes. Good soil structure is linked to a diverse range of soil organisms.

While healthy plants indicate healthy soil, unhealthy plants can result from poor care (late planting, insufficient irrigation, rain, autumn, etc.). It's critical to determine if the disease problem is linked to soil quality, remembering that poor drainage may contribute to root-borne diseases. A healthy soil structure improves root growth, and compacted soil inhibits healthy root growth. Healthy roots are an indication of a plant's overall health and vitality.

Healthy Soil's Response to pH

Acidity and alkalinity are indicated in pH, a scale between 0 and 14. The scale is logarithmic, meaning a pH of 5.0 is ten times more acid than soil with a pH reading of 6.0. A pH of 7.0 is neutral, zero is the most acidic, and 14 is purely alkaline. pH has a significant impact on plant nutrition, directly affecting plant growth.

Plant nutrient release by weathering, soil solubility, and cation-exchange capacity (CEC) are all influenced by the pH of a soil's environment. As a result, the pH level is an excellent indicator of plant nutrient deficiencies. At pH values between 5.8 and 7.5, the availability of all plant nutrients is generally adequate. Neutral and alkaline soils have pH values between 6.66 and 7.33, while acidic soils have values below 6.66. The primary benefit of soil pH is its information about the soil's other properties. CEC values, nutrient availability, and the release of toxic aluminium are all associated with pH.

Adding lime to acidic soils is a quick and straightforward way to raise the pH – typically, dolomitic limestone is used. The pH of the top 5 cm of a field that isn't tillage-intensive needs to be closely monitored because it can change very quickly. Most crops prefer a pH of 5.8 to 6.5, and inactivation of some herbicides can occur at a pH lower than 5.8. Toxicity to plants can be caused by releasing aluminium and manganese at a pH of 5.2.

Acidity (or alkalinity) can be reduced by organic matter. Organic matter decomposes into humus, with molecules that can absorb or release hydrogen ions depending on the surrounding soil's pH. As a result, this buffering effect keeps the soil's pH stable. Organic matter also decomposes and competes for aluminium ions (Al_+) in solution, reducing its toxicity to plants.

Nutrient Holding Capacity of Healthy Soil

Cation-Exchange Capacity (CEC) is the ability to hold, retain, and exchange positively charged ionic nutrients. CEC refers to the net surface charge of soil materials that enables them to suspend charged nutrient forms against leaching. While both negative and positive charges are present, negative charges usually dominate.

Increasing the pH of the soil solution or adding compost increases the CEC. Examples of positively charged (cations) are:

- Potassium (K^{+})
- Ammonium ($NH4^{+}$)
- Calcium (Ca^{2+})
- Magnesium (Mg^{2+})
- Aluminum (Al^{3+})

Negatively charged ions (anions) are not attracted to negative surface charges and, thus, are more subject to leaching. Examples include:

- Nitrate ($N03^{-}$)
- Chloride (Cl^{-})
- Sulfate ($S04^{-}$)
- Phosphate ($H2P04^{-}$)

Phosphate and sulfate are not leached as readily as nitrate, particularly in soils with iron-coated clays. Phosphate is also less mobile in soils because it is not soluble and binds readily with clays. Factors critical to nutrient holding capacity are pH, amount and kind of organic matter, soil texture, and clay type.

Soil test results will help predict whether the soil will provide nutrients fast enough to meet the crop’s future needs. Currently, soil tests are reliable for P, K, and Mg. While soils can be tested for other nutrients, interpretations are less reliable. Soil tests can be valuable over the long run as they show which soils are building nutrient levels and which are dropping.

Applications of high levels of fertilizers can skew test results. While heavy fertilization can lead to short-term increased productivity, it can also lead to leaching and nutrient loss. This approach also does little to improve other aspects of the soil, such as tilth or infiltration. Nutrient holding capacity is best enhanced by increasing soil organic matter, which serves as a sink and a source for plant nutrients. Organic matter also extends the release of nutrients over a longer period.

Soil Amendments

Soil additives are used to improve the health and condition of the soil. Incorporating organic matter, for example, into tight clay reduces soil bulk density, generates pore spaces for air and water, and improves soil structure and tilth, allowing roots to expand. Adding organic matter to sandy soil increases water and nutrient retention, feeds soil bacteria, and improves soil structure.

Warmer temperatures accelerate decomposition, and soils may require up to twice as much organic material as colder environments. It is a good idea to mulch regions after adding organic materials. Mulch is a layer of material applied to the soil's surface around plants to provide various benefits. It can be made from organic or inorganic materials, such as leaves, straw, bark, wood chips, or plastic sheeting. Mulch can help to conserve soil moisture, suppress weed growth, regulate soil temperature, and provide nutrients to plants as it breaks down over time. It can also improve soil structure, reduce erosion, and give a decorative touch to garden beds.

Effective soil amendments include:

- Aerobic Compost
- Leaf Mould
- Vermicompost
- Organic Fertilizers

The Aerobic Composting Process

Aerobic composting is a process of breaking down organic matter using microorganisms that require oxygen. This process occurs naturally in the environment but can also be facilitated through deliberate composting.

The key to successful aerobic composting is to maintain proper temperature, moisture, and oxygen levels to support the growth of microorganisms. Specifically, aerobic composting typically involves holding a temperature range of 55-65°C for at least three days, which helps to kill off pathogens and weed seeds and break down the organic matter into stable compost.

Here's how the process of aerobic composting typically unfolds:

Start with a mix of organic materials: Combine a blend of organic materials such as yard waste, food scraps, and manure to create a compost pile. The materials should be mixed together to ensure good aeration and even moisture distribution. The starting ratio should consist of 30 parts of brown materials for every part of nitrogen-rich green garden materials.

Monitor temperature: As the microorganisms break the organic matter down, they generate heat as a byproduct of their metabolism. The compost pile's temperature should be monitored using a thermometer and kept within the optimal range of 55-65°C for at least three days to ensure that pathogens and weed seeds are killed off.

Maintain moisture levels: Composting microorganisms require moisture to thrive, so it is vital to maintain a proper balance of moisture in the compost pile. The moisture level should be around 50 to 60% by weight to ensure good microbial activity.

Turn the pile: To ensure that all parts of the compost pile are exposed to oxygen, it is essential to turn the pile periodically, usually every few weeks. This helps to ensure that the composting process is even throughout the pile and can help to speed up the process.

Test the compost: After a few weeks to several months, the compost should be tested to ensure it has reached a stable state and is ready for use. This can be done by monitoring the temperature and moisture levels.

In summary, aerobic composting is a process of breaking down organic matter using microorganisms that require oxygen and water. By maintaining proper temperature, moisture, and oxygen levels, the process can be optimized to produce stable, nutrient-rich compost that can be used to improve soil health and plant growth.

Check out my Composting Masterclass for more information on creating effective compost.

Making Leaf Mould

There are many ways to manage leaves in autumn. You could mulch them with a mulching mower, collect them with a mower, blow or rake them into heaps, or use a vac-blower to shred, collect, and store them for later use. Whatever way you choose, they're a fabulous resource.

Leaves are the tree's primary energy converters and heat regulators. Perennial trees shed their leaves annually. Shed leaves consist mainly of cellulose and lignin, and leaves with high lignin levels are slow to decompose.

Because leaves are high in cellulose and lignin, they are resistant to bacteria breakdown. Fungi do initial decomposition, with bacteria taking over later in the process. This section reviews how straightforward it is to improve your soil with leaves often discarded without a second thought.

Like with all composting processes, there are five essential ingredients:

- **Carbon** for the microorganisms.
- **Nitrogen** for the microorganisms.
- **Water** to increase the mobility of microorganisms and act as an energy supply line. Water also helps regulate temperatures and provides fungi with oxygen and hydrogen.
- **Oxygen** to help with the oxidation process of the carbon-releasing CO_2.
- **Heat** speeds up the process. Much of the heat is self-generated, and our role is merely to help prevent that generated heat from escaping. A study done by MIT showed a direct correlation between ambient temperature and decomposition rates.

Have you ever seen a fantasy ice castle – like the ones they put on ice rinks? They can do that by minimizing the exposed area of the ice. It would take ages if you took a BIG block of ice and waited for it to melt. If you take that same massive block of ice and break it down into tiny pieces, the melting process will be accelerated. The ice block's surface area has increased and is now exposed to ambient temperature, causing the ice to melt faster.

The same applies to composting – the more surface area exposed, the more area upon which microorganisms can act, the faster the decomposition. Because the construction of leaves has evolved to balance weight and efficient light exposure, leaves are generally flat. Their flat shape creates a mat of leaves stuck to each other when wet. The flat structure also makes flight possible in windy conditions – similar to a butterfly wing.

It's, therefore, a good idea to shred the leaves before adding them to your compost pile, and I shred them four times before they are fine enough. You can use various leaf-shredding methods, but here are three suggestions.

Run over them with a lawnmower with a catch-bag – you might need to repeat the process several times. You will see how fast ten bags of leaves can be reduced in volume to fit into a single bag.

Vacuum them up with a blower vac. A couple of years ago, while using this method, the static caused by the dry leaves created a conduit for a spark between the motor and my bare arm, and it wasn't fun. Lesson learned: always wear appropriate protective gear.

Put them through a shredder. Personally, I think it's worth the investment.

You'll need the following to create leaf mould:

- Lots and lots of shredded leaves – enough to create a pile of no less than a 3-foot cube. A cubic yard of shredded leaves is about 40 garbage bags of leaves.
- Some* moist soil is taken from a wooded area.
- Some* horse manure – good but not essential.
- Some urine mixed with water – urine is rich in uric acid – a rich form of nitrogen. Ideally, you'll make a 10-litre mix, which I will explain below.
- Use a bin that can hold a cubic meter of leaves. Look at my video on making leaf mould and see what I did. Alternatively, use a 1-ton bulk bag. They're great for collecting leaves and as a holding unit for leaf mould/compost production.
- A couple of sheets of wet newspaper.

*The *"some"* referred to above is about a heaped spade full – or half a 15-litre plastic shopping bag.

Making a nitrogen-rich wetting agent

To make a wetting agent loaded with nitrogen and microorganisms, you will need the following:

- A cotton bag or a commercial horticultural compost tea bag
- 5 cups of horse manure
- 5 cups of nutrient-rich soil from a wooded area
- A 10-litre bucket filled with water and topped up with 2 cups of urine

Place the horse manure and soil in the compost tea bag and soak in the water/urine mix for 48 hours. If you have an air pump (like those used in fish tanks), pumping air into the mixture will speed up the diffusion and proliferation of microorganisms in the solution.

The end product is a solution loaded with nitrogen and microorganisms that radically speed decomposition.

Making leaf mould practical

- Start with a 15 cm layer of shredded leaves.
- Drizzle the layer with the urine mixture – wetting enough that only a single drop can be squeezed out. Remember that the shredded leaves are electrostatically charged and hydrophobic, repelling water. Even though spraying the pile may seem to wet it, the layers beneath will still be dry. You must ensure all the layers are wet by agitating the pile and ensuring the WHOLE batch is moist.
- Spread a thin layer of horse manure/soil mixture.
- Cover with a wet sheet of newspaper.
- Repeat the previous steps until all the shredded leaves are used up.
- End with a layer of shredded damp leaves. Use a board or rake to compress the pile.

If you have an old rug, covering your pile will help it retain heat and considerably speed up the composting process. It could even reduce the time down to six months! That is 25% of what it usually would take (two years).

What leaves are best for composting?

Leaves with a low lignin content are ideal for making leaf compost. Plant matter such as needles, which contain a lot of lignin (a vital building block), has a narrower decay rate than leafier plants, which have less lignin and more nutrients that attract microbes. Lignin protects organic compounds from degradation by acting as a shield.

Lignon-reduced leaves (with higher calcium and nitrogen levels) include ash, cherry, elm, linden, and maple. In six months, these leaves will be completely decomposed.

Beech, birch, oak, hornbeam, magnolia, holly, and sweet chestnut are unsuitable leaves because they are high in lignin and low in nitrogen. A typical two-year breakdown period is required. Trees like oaks, beech, and sycamore with thick leaves that stick around for a long time have high lignin levels and might leach nitrogen out of the soil before giving any back.

How long does it take for leaves to compost?

Leaves vary in their decomposition times. The Long-term Intersite Decomposition Experiment Team (LIDET) study collected leaf litter from 27 North and Central America locations, from the Alaskan tundra to Panamanian rainforests. The research showed that leaves in warm and wet regions decomposed faster than those in cold and dry areas. Leaf type was also a determinant, with needles (high-lignin) deteriorating much slower than leaves with low levels of lignin.

In nature, leaves take about two years to decompose. As discussed above, decomposition can be reduced to six months in controlled environments.

Do leaves compost quicker if shredded?

Leaves are decomposed by the activities of microorganisms – mainly fungi. Because these organisms are tiny, and their action is on the material's surface, maximizing the surface area maximizes their activity.

Consider a loaf of bread. The loaf has six surface areas – two ends, a top and a bottom, and two sides. Cutting six slices increases the surface areas by 6 x 6 = 36 surface areas. The unsliced loaf will take a while to dry out (or grow mould), but the slices will dry out faster. Repeating the cutting process will increase the exposed surfaces exponentially.

Similarly, shredding your leaves increases the exposed surface area, thus increasing the fungi's activity on the leaves. Shredding and wetting your leaves can halve or even quarter the time required to make leaf mould – and it improves the quality of the end product.

Another handy way to speed up leaf composting is to create a wetting agent made from beer. Mixing a medium bottle of beer, a can of sugar-containing soda, and half a cup of ammonia with 2 gallons of water gives you an effective composting kick-starter.

What leaves should not be composted?

The general rule of thumb, a non-scientific approach, is to stick to composting thinner leaves. The following is a list of trees and shrubs that have thicker leaves and are higher in lignin content:

- Birch
- Oak
- Hornbeam
- Sweet chestnut
- Magnolia
- Holly
- Sycamore
- Eucalyptus
- Beech (to a lesser extent)
- Black walnut

These leaves have high lignin content and might leach nitrogen out of your soil before giving any back when added. Black walnut also contains juglone, a natural

fungicide that will stall your leaf-moulding efforts. While lignin is strongly associated with retarded leaf decomposition rates, the leaves' C:N ratio has also been researched and may hold a more vital link to their slow decomposition. Either way, thicker leaves, even in accelerated environments, decompose slower.

What equipment do I need to make leaf compost?

Leaf Shredder

Some ways of shredding leaves are gathering them in low piles, going over them with a mower, or vacuuming them with a blower/vac shredder. Alternatively, you can get a leaf shredder. The benefit of a leaf shredder is that it will reduce effort and the volume of leaves. An electric shredder allows you to produce one bag of shredded leaves from several bags of leaves.

An advantage is that shredded leaves compost so much faster. I shred my leaves fine; an electric shredder allows you to choose between coarse, medium, and fine shredding. Since most electric shredders come with a stand, you can fit a catchment bag to collect the shredded leaves.

You can also use the same shredder to shred paper, a handy additive to the composting processes.

Tarps

A tarp is a handy gardener's tool. You can use it to gather leaves rapidly, cover your compost pile to retain heat, and much more.

1-Ton Bulk Bag

A 1-ton bulk bag is another excellent investment I found helpful in cultivating leaf mould. The size is ideal (about a cubic meter), and the bags are well-insulated to prevent the compost from losing heat. Woven polypropylene bags are also handy for collecting leaves.

Leaf Scoops

I use scoops that fit my hands, converting them into big plastic shovels. Once you've raked your leaves into piles, use these to scoop the leaves into one of your 1-ton bags – ready for shredding.

Rake

It is easier to rake damp leaves than dry leaves, and it is much easier if you have a 75 cm broad leaf rake that is light to use. Rake in the direction of the wind to make it easier. Create multiple piles that you can gather with your hand scoops.

Watering Can

While I usually use a hose to wet my compost heaps, for my leaf compost/mould, I use one of the above wetting regimes. To spread the compost tea evenly, I like using a watering can.

Compost Tea Bags

A compost tea bag allows you to create compost tea without clogging your watering can's sprinkler. The instructions for how to do this are shared above.

How to use leaf compost

Leaf mould is a gold mine for gardeners; it has a high mineral content and can grow plants naturally without additional fertilizer. Contrary to popular belief, leaf mould is beneficial to your lawn. Leaves are the product of the tree roots extracting minerals deep underground and transporting them to the leaves, loading them with many valuable trace minerals.

Despite the negative connotations associated with mould, leaf mould is one of the best soil conditioners you'll ever use. A single leaf mould spore can hold five times its weight in water, and that's on par with peat moss, if not better. Because of this, leaf mould is an excellent mulch to use around the garden. Soil structure and texture are greatly improved when organic matter is added to sandy or clay soils.

Microbes and other beneficial organisms like earthworms thrive in leaf mould environments. As a result, your garden's soil will be vibrant and alive. There's also the fact that it's free! Don't let the lack of leaves in your yard stop you from participating. People are always willing to let you drop off bags of leaves or let you rake some for them. Find out by talking to your friends and family! If you don't like cleaning up after the leaves in the autumn, make friends with them.

It can be used as a mulch, a soil amendment, in containers and raised beds in place of peat moss, and in your compost bin as brown matter.

As a soil amendment, I turn leaf mould into the soil to a spade depth (about 20 to 24 cm). I also use between 5 and 8 cm of mulch around plants, careful not to mulch up to the plant's stem or base. Because leaf mould is so hygroscopic, the continuous moisture on the stem can provide an opportunity for diseases.

Vermicomposting

Vermicomposting is a highly effective bio-oxidative process involving earthworms and microorganisms working together to break organic matter into a potent soil amendment. While I've seen operations that produce tons of worm castings, we'll focus on residential operations. Essentially, the size of your vermicomposting process depends on available space, the amount of worm food available, and the time you want to farm worms and collect their castings.

Vermicomposting is a non-thermophilic biological oxidation process where select earthworm species, preferably *Eisenia fetida* (red wrigglers), enhance the conversion of organic waste to compost. Earthworms help influence the growth of specific microbial species that improve the soil's physical and chemical properties. The microbial population in vermicompost is essential in increasing crop productivity and maintaining the soil's structural stability.

Vermicompost highlights:

- There are approximately 9,000 earthworm species, of which seven are suitable for vermicomposting.
- Vermicomposting requires high feeders. Earthworms in your garden are unsuitable for vermicomposting; use red worms (*Eisenia fetida* and *E. Andrei*) instead.
- Worms are most active in moist environments at temperatures between 13^{0}C and 29^{0}C. Their living quarters must be dark and have enough air. Worms try to escape unsuitable environments.
- Earthworms are hermaphrodites, but two worms are required for reproduction, exchanging sperm as they lay alongside each other. Both are fertilized in the process.
- Conditions permitting, your worm population can double every two months.
- Cocoons take four to six weeks to emerge, and the two to five worms from each

cocoon take six to eight weeks to mature. Cocoons take longer to release the worms in colder conditions.

- Worms require some sand grains to strengthen their consumption capacities.
- Generally, vermicompost is equivalent to a 3:3:3 fertilizer with higher nitrate ($NO3_-$).
- It is rich in microorganisms, as worms use bacteria in their gut to process food.
- A carbon-rich diet will increase fungi populations for gardens that require better water retention.
- Worm castings are rich in enzymes.
- Worm mucus helps soil particles form aggregates.
- Improves root penetration, water usage, and nutrient availability as a product of improved soil structure.
- Desirable microorganisms thrive, increasing resilience against pests and diseases.
- Earthworms feed on decaying organic matter and microorganisms, like nematodes. Underground they eat bacteria, algae, fungi, and nematodes, releasing the minerals these microorganisms consume into the soil.
- In worm bins, they consume kitchen waste and limited yard waste.
- Avoid
  - Animal products and by-products (cheese, yoghurt, etcetera)
  - Some citrus fruits (orange peels and pineapples)
  - Glossy paper
  - Onions and garlic
  - Salt
  - Oily substances
- Advisable worm food for your worm farm
  - Fruits and vegetable scraps
  - Coffee grounds and filters (snip filters into smaller parts)
  - Grains – bread, crackers, cereals, even if they're mouldy or stale
  - Leaves

    - Eggshells
    - Paper products and shredded cardboard
    - Grass clippings if not treated with pesticides in particular, but herbicides too.
- Worms live for about one year, and because their bodies are 90% water, their dead bodies dry up and become part of the compost. The cycle of life and death is seamless and unnoticeable, with populations remaining in balance with their environment.
- Approximately 800–1,000 mature worms (or 450g) can consume about 250g of organic material daily.
- Bins can be customized depending on the volume of food scraps used to manufacture the castings.
- Useable castings take approximately three to four months to produce, depending on the bin size.

How to use worm castings in your garden

Worm castings are a slow-release nitrogen-rich fertilizer balanced with other essential minerals – generally equivalent to 3:3:3 NKP. You can safely spread it around potted plants, vegetables, and flowing plants. If you sift it finely, adding it to your lawn would replace your usual nitrogen needs. You can also incorporate it into the soil around shrubs and trees.

It's up to you whether you want to use your compost immediately, store it for the gardening season, or use it anytime. Vermicompost can be added directly to potting or garden soil as a soil amendment, making nutrients more accessible to plants. It's possible to top-dress your indoor or outdoor plants with the compost. You can also create a nutrient-loaded compost tea by straining the vermicompost in an aerated water tank for 24 hours. Don't confuse the leachate from the bottom of a poorly managed bin with composting tea. The leachate is loaded with nitrogen and should always be diluted and used with care. I advise that you test it on a single plant, review the reaction over a couple of days, and proceed if safe. Use leachate with caution, as it risks poisoning your plants.

Compost Teas

Artificial applications of the primary nutrients (nitrogen, phosphorous, and potassium) have long been promoted as the de facto route to crop yield increases. Billion-dollar marketing campaigns support synthetic fertilizers, pesticides, herbicides, and fumigants. At ground level,

though, the nutritional status of fresh produce is dropping.

Farmers face increasing input costs and diminishing yields, leading to a turn to the sciences for solutions. One solution is a new appreciation for the role of soil biology in agriculture, which is providing a strategy for sustainability. This has sparked investment in research on the role of soil biota in crop production. The benefits of composting are becoming more widely known, and gardeners are turning to water solutions of compost to boost plant health and productivity. Compost contains microorganisms, enzymes, and minerals that can significantly benefit the soil.

The use of pesticides, herbicides, and fumigants is being recognised as counterproductive, as they kill harmful and beneficial microorganisms. Without beneficial microorganisms, soil biota cannot perform essential functions such as increasing water retention, stabilising pH, fighting pathogens, and improving nutrient availability. Although compost has many benefits, it may be more effective if its composition is tailored to the specific needs of the soil and plants, taking into account the diverse range of microorganisms and pathogens present.

While most gardeners are happy with the benefits compost provides the soil, studies show that those benefits can be extended to the rest of the plant. Aerobic microorganisms, primarily bacteria, fungi, nematodes, and protozoa, can be hosted in water for short periods – if the water is well aerated and agitated. In addition, the populations of either bacteria or fungi can be boosted through feeding regimes, depending on the application need.

Healthy compost produces healthy AACT, extending the compost benefit:

- Beneficial microorganisms improve the surface protection of plant foliage. The attached microorganisms can defend the plant against disease-causing organisms.
- The representative microorganisms from the compost offer similar soil nutrition benefits – pH buffering, nutrient distribution, aggregate formation, aeration, water retention, etcetera.
- Microorganisms increase the nutrient availability where it's needed – at the roots. The soil food web's predator-prey interactions increase nutrient availability at the right time and place.
- Beneficial microorganisms can neutralize the impact of chemical-based pesticides and herbicides.
- Beneficial microorganisms reduce the loss of moisture from the leaf surface.
- Improved tilth and soil structure – an exclusive soil biota function.

Compost tea contains all the soluble nutrients extracted from the compost and representative bacteria, fungi, protozoa, and nematodes. The compost quality used in compost tea is an essential factor in the tea's efficacy. It stands to reason that if the microorganisms and nutrients are absent in the source compost, they will not be present in the tea either. However, the populations of either bacteria or fungi can be boosted by adding food to stimulate their individual growth. Humic acid boosts fungi growth, and molasses will increase the bacterial population.

Brewing an effective composting tea is dependent on several factors. Like most living organisms, including you and I, if the needs of the microorganisms are met, they thrive. Making compost tea is an evolving science, and different approaches have been developed to fully satisfy select organisms' needs. By closely monitoring the brewing environment, beneficial microorganisms can be kept alive and helped to thrive. Factors that influence the outcome are:

- the brewing temperature
- the added foods

- the levels of oxygenation during production
- the quality and microbial composition of the compost used
- the time microorganisms are immersed in water.

It's essential to remember that we're working with oxygen-dependent aerobic microorganisms. These organisms are vital to the soil, allow plants to grow unimpeded, and act as defenders of the realm. Merely soaking compost in water overnight is an excellent way to make humus-coloured water, not compost tea. Ensure the microorganisms don't perish by maintaining an oxygen level of at least 5.5 ppm.

Anything less might be counter-productive, producing microbes that could harm the plants and soil. The bacteria responsible for human diseases are almost exclusively anaerobic, and this scenario is less likely if your thermophilic process during composting is unquestionably effective.

Effective compost tea, like effective compost, is location specific. The best compost is produced by gardeners or farmers using local materials. This is because the organisms in a local system are best equipped to manage the requirements of the local pedosphere.

If buying compost tea, remember that the shelf-life is exceptionally short (about

6 hours). If buying compost tea, your best option is to buy the compost and microorganisms food and brew it at home.

Compost Tea Variations

Actively Aerated Compost Tea (AACT)

- An aerated brew of unchlorinated water and compost extract.
- It is wholly representative of the nutrients and microorganisms in the original compost.
- Added food for targeted microbial growth.

Non-Aerated Compost Extract (NCE)

- A suspended compost extract is actively aerated in solution.

- It may contain some of the compost microorganisms.
- No added food to promote microbial growth.
- Soluble nutrients and enzymes are present if used soon after making.
- Very time sensitive due to lack of aeration.
- Rich in humic acid.

Aerated compost tea is actively aerated using a bubbler, blower, or any other device to force oxygen-laden air into the liquid containing a bag of compost extract. Alternatively, compost extracts are only occasionally stirred to re-suspend solid materials that have settled to the bottom, and this process is not actively aerated.

Making Active Aerated Compost Tea (AACT)

Resources Required:

- About a 3-litre bucket with a cloth cover.
- Air pump (aquarium air pump will do).
- A length of tubing to fit the air pump – long enough to feed air into the bottom of the bucket.
- Aquarium airstones or bubblers.
- 20 litres of dechlorinated water (rainwater is suitable).
- 3 cups of finely sieved compost.
- A porous bag – compost teabags are available online. Alternatively, use a sock.

Directions:

- Start aerating the water in the bucket.
- Put mature compost in the bag or sock, attach it to a weighted object, and place the bag and weight in the bucket.
- To remove air from the compost bag, gently massage it.
- Allow the bag containing water to be aerated for 24 hours.
- If you use the AACT in a sprayer, you must filter the liquid before using it – a

cheesecloth will be adequate.

- Use the liquid within an hour after the aeration stops.

Making Non-aerated Compost Extract (NCE)

Resources Required:

- About a 30-litre bucket with a cloth cover.
- 20 litres of dechlorinated water (rainwater is suitable).
- 3 cups of finely sieved compost in a porous bag – compost teabags are available online. Alternatively, a sock or stocking will work.
- An implement to stir with.

Directions

- Place the compost-filled bag in the water.
- Help your tea draw by stirring the water and massaging the bag of compost.
- Repeat the above action twice a day for the next seven days.
- When done, filter the solution to avoid blocking your sprayer nozzles.
- Use the liquid as compost, drenching the soil around plants and spraying on foliage.

Composting Tea Review

I'm personally a fan of the AACT method. With the extended, non-aerated method, I imagine the microorganisms drowning, slowly growing weaker, until all I'm stirring are unresponsive microbodies. With the AACT method, my little divers can gulp air, have plenty of different food, and are even reproducing.

But the proof is in the pudding, as they say. There is no set recipe for compost teas; the above are guidelines. As a master gardener, you will develop what works for you, your soil, and your plants. If you want to be effective, find a lab that can analyze your soil – not for chemical content, but microbial diversity and population. That way, you can know what is abundant and what is in deficit. Diversity rules the earth – literally. The more diverse your population and balanced the predator-prey systems are, the healthier your soil and your plants happier.

Speaking of diversity, we know the thermophilic phase of composting reaches unsuitable temperatures for many fungi species. While evolution has provided them with a survival strategy, ending with a batch of compost high in bacteria remains much easier than fungi populations. Using the initial compost, AACT offers gardeners an easy way to boost the fungi populations in the soil.

Bacteria thrive on sugars, and fungi thrive on proteins. Adding a tiny amount of protein (fish hydrolysis or humic acid) can boost your fungi population in the tea and soil. The amount is approximately two teaspoons to 20 litres of water. Always use dechlorinated water when working with anything microbial. You can also fill a bucket of water from the tap and leave it in the sun for a day to neutralize the chlorine (or add some ascorbic acid).

Worthy of special mention is the manufacturing of AACT using vermicompost. Vermicompost is the most nutritious version of compost, especially if the food supply is predominantly aerobic compost and leaf mould.

Organic Fertilizers[3]

Unless otherwise specified, the items listed below are typically allowed for commercial organic growers.

Fertilizer	Primary Benefit	Average Analysis
Alfalfa meal	Organic matter	5–1–2
Algae	Organic matter	N/A
Amino acid (nonsynthetic)	Chelating agent	N/A
Ash	Liming effect, source of calcium, micronutrients	25% calcium carbonate; 9% potash

[3] https://content.ces.ncsu.edu/extension-gardener-handbook/17-organic-gardening

Basalt dust	Micronutrients	N/A
Blood meal (dried)	Nitrogen	10–0–0
Bone meal	Phosphate	3–15–0; 20% total phosphate; 24% calcium
Borax	Trace minerals	10% boron
Calcitic limestone	Calcium	65–80% calcium carbonate
Coffee grounds	Nitrogen	2–0.3–0.2
Colloidal phosphate	Phosphate	0–2–2
Compost	Organic matter	Varies with components added
Corn gluten meal	Nitrogen	9–0–0
Cottonseed meal	Nitrogen	6–4–1.5
Cotton gin trash	Nitrogen, phosphorus, potash	14–10.5–41
Dolomite	Balancer, calcium, magnesium	51% calcium carbonate; 40% magnesium carbonate
Eggshell meal	Calcium	1.2–0.4–0.1
Elemental sulfur	Balancer, nutrient	99.5% sulfur
Epsom salts	Balancer, magnesium	10% magnesium; 13% sulfur
Feather meal	Nitrogen	11–0–0
Fish emulsion	Nitrogen	5–2–2
Fish meal	Nitrogen	10–6–2
Fish powder	Nitrogen	12–0.25–1
Fur	Nitrogen	12–0–0

Granite dust	Potash	4% potash
Greensand	Potash	7% total potash
Gypsum, mined	Calcium, balancer	22% calcium; 17% sulfur
Hair	Nitrogen	12–16% nitrogen
Horse manure	Organic matter	1.7–0.7–1.8
Hoof and horn meal	Nitrogen	12–2–0
Kelp meal	Potash	1.5–0.5–2.5; trace minerals
Leaf mulch	Organic matter	0.5–0.1–0.5
Magnesium rock	Magnesium	32–35% magnesium
Oyster shells	Calcium	33.5% calcium
Peanut meal	Nitrogen	7.2–1.5–1.2
Peat moss	Organic matter	pH range 3.0–4.5
Potassium sulfate	Potassium, sulfur	22% potash; 23% sulfate
Poultry manure	Organic matter	4–4–2
Rabbit manure	Organic matter	1.5–1–1
Rock phosphate	Phosphate	0–3–0
Sawdust (untreated)	Organic matter	0.2–0–0.2
Sheep manure	Organic matter	4–1.4–3.5
Soybean meal	Nitrogen	7–0.5–2.3
Straw	Nitrogen, potash	0.2–0–0.2

Sulfur	Sulfur	50–100% sulfur
Sul-Po-Mag	Potash, magnesium	0–0–22; 11% magnesium; 22% sulfur
Wood ashes	Potash, micronutrients	0–2–6
Wood chips	Phosphorus	0–0.4–0.2
Worm castings	Organic matter	0.5–0.5–0.3

Mulches

Mulches give several advantages to plants, and the benefits vary depending on the material used, the kind of soil, the type of plant, and the cultural practices employed. Mulches can also make landscapes more appealing and useable and minimize the amount of maintenance labour required. Below are some of the benefits of mulch:

- Soil amendment
  - Improves soil granulation and aggregation
  - Increases water absorption and retention
  - It prevents soil compaction and improves aeration
- Surface insulation
  - Conserves moisture
  - Moderates extremes in temperature
  - Controls weed growth
- Beautification
  - It makes surface areas more attractive
  - Improves surface areas utility (paths, play, and sitting areas)
  - It makes maintaining areas easier

Organic Mulches

Material	Aesthetics	Resistance to wind blowing	Source of weeds and disease	Comments
Bark chunks	Excellent	Excellent	Excellent	Pricey but worth it
Cocoa shells	Excellent	Good	Excellent	High potassium content may cause problems
Coconut coir	Excellent	Excellent	Good	Sustainable alternative to peat moss
Compost	Good	Excellent	Fair	Ensure it's cured
Corn cobs	Poor	Good	Poor	Not recommended
Cottonseed hulls	Fair	Poor	Good	Better incorporated
Hay	Fair	Good	Fair	Fire risk
Lawn clippings	Poor	Good	Fair	Better composted
Leaf mould	Good	Excellent	Fair	Hygroscopic – attracts and retains moisture
Leaves	Good	Poor	Good	Compost to improve the value
Manure (well-rotted)	Fair	Excellent	Unsatisfactory	The odour may be a challenge
Pecan hulls	Excellent	Good	Excellent	A good alternative, if available
Pine needles	Good	Good	Good	Acidic
Rice hulls	Fair	Poor	Fair	Better incorporated
Sawdust (coarse)	Fair	Good	Excellent	Will extract nitrogen for the soil
Sawdust (fine)	Fair	Poor	Excellent	Will extract nitrogen for the soil
Shredded bark	Excellent	Excellent	Excellent	Good option

Straw	Poor	Poor	Poor	Not advised – will extract nitrogen from the soil
Wood chips	Good	Excellent	Excellent	Will impoverish the soil.
Wood shavings	Good	Good	Excellent	Will extract nitrogen for the soil
Wood fibres	Fair	Good	Excellent	Will extract nitrogen for the soil

Inorganic Mulches

Material	Aesthetics	Resistance to wind blowing	Source of weeds and disease	Comments
Black plastic film	Unsatisfactory	Unsatisfactory	Excellent	It needs to be anchored. Unsightly.
Crushed rock	Good	Excellent	Excellent	Avoid crushed limestone
Geotextile weed barrier	Unsatisfactory	Unsatisfactory	Excellent	It needs to be anchored
Gravel	Good	Excellent	Excellent	Use sparingly
Volcanic rock	Good	Excellent	Excellent	Small sizes are moved by water
Perlite	Good	Poor	Excellent	Rather incorporate
Vermiculite	Fair	Poor	Excellent	Rather incorporate

Mulching Vegetables

Here is a guide to mulching vegetables:

- **Prepare the soil:** Before mulching, remove any weeds or debris and loosen the top layer of soil before mulching. Make sure the soil is evenly moist.
- **Choose a mulch:** Select a mulching material appropriate for your vegetable garden. Standard options include straw, shredded leaves, grass clippings, and compost. Aim for a layer of mulch that is 5-10 centimetres thick.
- **Apply the mulch:** Spread the mulch evenly over the surface of the soil, leaving a small gap around the base of each plant to prevent moisture buildup and reduce the risk of rot. Be sure to keep the mulch away from the stems of the plants, as this can encourage disease.
- **Monitor moisture levels:** Regularly check the soil's moisture level, especially during hot or dry weather. If the ground beneath the mulch is dry, water the garden thoroughly.
- **Add more mulch**: Over time, the mulch will break down and become incorporated into the soil. Add more mulch as needed to maintain a 5-10 centimetres thick layer.
- **Consider using a reflective mulch**: Reflective mulches, such as silver or white plastic, can help to increase light reflection and reduce soil temperature, which can be beneficial for certain vegetable crops.

Mulching can provide various benefits for vegetable gardens, including conserving soil moisture, suppressing weeds, regulating soil temperature, and providing nutrients to plants as it breaks down over time.

CHAPTER 6

PROPAGATION

Plant propagation is the process of creating new plants from existing ones, and there are several different methods of plant propagation. Here are some common forms of plant propagation:

Seed propagation: This involves growing plants from seeds. Seeds can be collected from existing plants or purchased from a supplier. This method is relatively easy and can be used for most vegetable plants.

Vegetative propagation: This involves creating new plants from parts of an existing plant, such as stems, leaves, roots, or buds. Gardeners use several methods of vegetative propagation, including:

- **Potatoes** are typically propagated from "seed potatoes," small tubers allowed to sprout before planting.
- **Garlic** is propagated by planting individual cloves, which will grow into new plants.
- **Onions** are propagated by planting "sets," which are small bulbs that have been grown from seed.
- **Sweet potatoes** are propagated from "slips," which are young shoots that grow from a mature sweet potato.
- **Asparagus** is propagated by planting crowns, clumps of roots and stems.
- **Horseradish** is propagated from root cuttings, sections of the plant's roots.
- **Ginger** is propagated by planting sections of the plant's rhizomes, which are underground stems.

Tissue culture: This involves growing plants from small pieces of plant tissue, such as a single cell or a portion of a leaf or stem. This method is typically used for rare or difficult-to-propagate plants or for creating large numbers of identical plants.

Seed Propagation

Seeds

Seeds comprise three essential components: an embryo, endosperm (food storage) tissue, and a seed coat (protective tissue).

- The embryo is a tiny inactive plant – think yoke.
- The endosperm is a built-in food source found in most seeds – think albumen.
- The seed coat is a seed's protective outer coating – think shell. It protects seeds from mechanical damage as well as illnesses and insects. Furthermore, the seed coat prevents water from entering the seed until it is time to germinate. The seed coat permits seeds to be preserved for long periods.

The seed has to be of good quality for healthy plants to grow. Cultivars and hybrids are the product of cross-breeding and selection processes, often over many years, to produce a strain that offers specific size, colour, resilience, and growth habits. Hybrids are generally pricy but offer better traits, features, vigour, and region-specific resilience. Most seeds deteriorate with age, so limit purchases to immediate needs.

Store seeds in a cool, dry area if they are received long ahead of the actual sowing date (or if they are extra seeds). Laminated or foil-wrapped containers aid in dry storage. Paper packages should be stored in firmly sealed containers at 4°C and in low humidity – an *airtight* container in the refrigerator would be a nice place to keep them. Gardeners may save money while cultivating a pleasant pastime by preserving plant seeds. Open-pollinated seeds have been pollinated by an insect, an animal, the wind, or another natural pollination process. Open-pollinated plants may have distinct features from their parent plants, boosting biodiversity. This is especially true when storing hybrid seeds.

Germination

The restart of active embryo development following a latent phase is germination. For a seed to germinate, three criteria must be met:

The seed must be viable; the embryo must be alive and capable of germination.

The seed's internal conditions must be favourable for germination; any physical, chemical, or physiological barriers to germination must no longer be present.

The conditions for germination must be right – a combination of moisture, light (or the absence thereof, temperature, and oxygen.

Water absorption is the initial germination stage, and an appropriate and consistent moisture supply is required to activate germination. A dry spell may be fatal for an embryo that has started germinating.

Some species' seed germination can be stimulated or inhibited by **light**. Seed catalogues and seed packs generally provide germination and cultural information for specific plants. Light-required seeds should be sown on the soil's surface. Fluorescent lamps hung 15 to 30 cm above the soil surface can give additional light – 16 hours a day on and 8 hours off.

Dormant seeds do not respire, although they require some **oxygen**. During germination, the rate of respiration rises. The media used to plant the seeds should be loose and adequately aerated. Germination can be substantially slowed or impeded if the oxygen supply is limited or diminished during germination.

Temperature influences the percentage of germination and the speed of germination. Some seeds germinate over a wide range of temperatures, whereas others need specific temperatures. Generally, vegetable plant germination temperature advice includes minimum, maximum, and optimal temperatures. Tomato seeds, for example, have a minimum germination temperature of 10°C, a maximum germination temperature of 35°C, and an optimal germination temperature of 27°C. Suggested germination temperatures generally indicate the optimum – most seeds like soil temperatures ranging from 18 to 24°C.

Dealing with Seed Dormancy

Some seeds may not germinate due to a seed-specific inhibitory factor. There are two forms of dormancy: (a) external dormancy (seed coat) and (b) internal (endogenous) dormancy. A seed can experience both types of dormancy. In dealing with external dormancy, scarification is used, and for internal dormancy, stratification is used.

Some species' seeds have twofold dormancy. This is a hybrid of two forms of dormancy: exterior and internal. To germinate these seeds, they must be scarified and *then* stratified for the necessary time. The seeds will not grow if the treatments are given in reverse order. After you've finished these procedures, place the seeds in the right setting for germination.

Seed Scarification

Vegetable plant seed scarification is a process of breaking, scratching, or otherwise damaging the seed coat of certain vegetable seeds to facilitate germination. Some seeds have a tough, hard seed coat that can prevent water and air from reaching the embryo inside, which can delay or prevent germination. Scarification is a method that can help to overcome this barrier and improve the chances of successful germination.

Here are some methods of seed scarification that are commonly used for vegetable seeds:

Mechanical scarification: This involves physically damaging the seed coat by scratching, nicking, or rubbing it with sandpaper, a file, or a knife. This can help to create small openings in the seed coat that allow water and air to penetrate.

Chemical scarification: This involves treating the seeds with a chemical solution, such as sulfuric acid or hydrogen peroxide, that can soften or dissolve the seed coat. This method requires caution and should be used only with proper protective gear.

Hot water scarification: This involves briefly immersing the seeds in hot water (usually around 60°C), which can cause the seed coat to crack or split. This method is best suited for seeds that have a hard, impermeable seed coat.

Freeze-thaw scarification: This involves exposing the seeds to freezing temperatures, followed by thawing, which can cause the seed coat to expand and contract, creating small openings. This method is best suited for seeds that are adapted to cold climates.

It is important to note that not all vegetable seeds require scarification, and some may even be damaged by it.

Always refer to the specific seed variety's requirements and follow the recommended method of scarification if needed. Scarification should be done carefully to ensure the seeds are not damaged and the technique used is appropriate for the seed variety.

Seed Stratification

The inner seed tissues manage the second form of enforced dormancy, internal dormancy. When environmental circumstances are unsuitable for seedling survival, this dormancy inhibits many species' seeds from germinating. There are several forms of internal dormancy, each needing a specific duration of moist-chilling or moist-warming periods.

Cold stratification (wet-chilling) keeps seeds in a refrigerator after combining them with an equivalent amount of moist media (such as sand or peat). Check the medium regularly to ensure that it is moist but not wet. The time necessary to break (remove) dormancy varies depending on the species; consult reference books for recommended times. This dormancy type may be achieved organically by sowing seeds outside in the autumn. Warm stratification is identical to cold stratification, but temperatures are maintained at 21°C to 30°C.

Growing Plants From Seeds

Some seeds can be sown in situ, while others do better if first grown in seedling containers. This section will review the essential elements of growing plants from seeds:

- Media

- Containers
- Sowing Seeds
- Water and Light
- Transplanting

Growing Media

Seeds can be germinated in a variety of mediums. With practice, you'll figure out what works best for you. The germination media should be fine and homogenous while properly aerated and loose. Insects, disease organisms, nematodes, weeds, and weed seeds should not be present. It should also be low in fertility and capable of retaining moisture while being adequately drained. Purchase a commercial potting medium comprising fine-particle pine bark, coconut coir, and perlite, or mix these ingredients in equal proportions (by volume). Garden soil should not be used to start seedlings since it is not sterile, is too heavy, and generally does not drain effectively.

Containers

Plastic or polystyrene cell packs can be purchased or sanitised and reused. Each cell in this arrangement houses a single plant. When transplanting, this procedure decreases the danger of root damage. Seedlings can also be grown in peat pellets, peat pots, or inflated foam cubes. Resourceful gardeners frequently utilize cottage cheese containers, the bottoms of milk cartons, or pie pans. Just make sure there are appropriate drainage holes on the bottoms of the containers and that they are sterile. It is impossible to overstate the necessity of utilizing sterile media and containers. Before using the containers, wash them to remove any dirt, then soak them for 5 minutes in a fresh solution of one part chlorine bleach to nine parts water and allow them to drip-dry.

Sowing Seeds

Seedlings are often started inside four to 12 weeks before the final spring frost. A typical error is to sow the seeds too early and keep the seedlings in a sterile environment, resulting in tall, weak, spindly plants that fare poorly in the garden. The directions that follow are general principles for planting seeds for transplants. However, you should always follow the directions on the seed packaging for plant-specific instructions.

When sowing seeds, fill the container within 10 mm of the top with wet growth material. Use a fine, screened media for tiny seeds, such as a 6 mm layer of fine vermiculite. To create a smooth and level surface, firm the medium at the corners and edges with your fingers or a woodblock.

Make furrows 2.5 to 5 cm apart and 3 to 6 cm deep across the surface of the planting medium for medium and big seeds. Row planting promotes light and air movement; if damping-off illness develops, it is less likely to spread. At transplanting time, seedlings in rows are easier to identify and handle than those produced by disseminating seeds. Sow the seeds thinly and consistently in the rows by gently tapping the seed packet. Cover the seeds gently; a recommended planting depth is two to four times the seed's minimum diameter.

Extremely fine seeds, such as carrots and onions, should be dusted on the surface of the germination medium and watered with a thin mist rather than covered. If these seeds are spread, try to achieve a consistent stand by sowing half of the seeds in one direction and the remaining seeds in the other way.

Large seeds are typically put directly in a compact container or cell pack, obviating early transplantation requirements. Sow two or three seeds in each cell on average. Afterwards, finishing them will allow just the most robust seedlings per cell to thrive.

Indoor and outdoor seed tapes are available at most garden stores and seed merchants. Seed tapes comprise properly spaced seeds encased in an organic, water-soluble substance. When the tape is removed, the seeds germinate normally. Seed tapes are used for extremely tiny, difficult-to-handle seeds. Seed tapes provide consistent emergence, minimize overcrowding, and allow for straight-row sowing. The tapes can be cut for multiple row plantings, and thinning is rarely required – tapes are convenient, but their per-seed cost is higher.

Water and Light Requirements

Before planting, properly moisten the planting media. After sowing, spray the containers with a fine mist or set them on a pan or tray with about 25 mm of warm water. Avoid splashing or severe flooding, which may cause little seeds to be displaced. Set the container aside to drain once the planting mix has been soaked. The soil should be damp but not soggy.

During the germination stage, the seed flats should be kept wet. On the other hand, excessive moisture might cause damping-off or other disease or pest issues. Place the entire flat or pot in a transparent plastic bag to keep the moisture in. The plastic should be placed at least 25 mm above the dirt. Keep the container away from direct sunshine; otherwise, the temperature will rise and harm the seeds. Instead of using a plastic bag, many home gardeners cover their flats with glass panes. When the first seedlings appear, remove the plastic bag or glass cover.

After the seeds have germinated, transfer the flats to a well-lit area, maintaining temperatures between 18 to 21°C during the day and 13 to 16°C at night. This inhibits weak, leggy growth and reduces disease issues. Certain crops, of course, may require specific temperatures.

After germination, seedlings require intense light. Place them in a south-facing window or beneath fluorescent lights if a large, bright site is unavailable. Two 40-watt cool-white fluorescent bulbs or special plant development lights are recommended. Place the plants 15 cm below the light source and give them 16 hours of light daily. The lights should be increased as the seedlings develop.

Transplanting Seedlings

Plants that have not been sown separately must ultimately be moved into their pots as seedlings to allow them to grow properly. A typical blunder is leaving the seedlings on the flat for too long. When the first genuine leaves develop, it is time to transfer young seedlings.

With a knife or plastic plant label, carefully remove the little plants. Allow the seedlings to autumn apart and pluck out individual plants. Allow them to separate gently to minimize root harm. Small seedlings should be handled by their leaves rather than their delicate stems. Punch a hole in the medium with a tiny instrument or your finger. Plant a seedling at the same depth that it grew in the seed flat, i.e. level to the growing medium. Firm the dirt with your hands and water carefully. Keep newly transplanted seedlings in the shade or under fluorescent lights for a few days. Place them away from direct heat sources. Continue to water and fertilize as you did with the seed flats.

Hardening Plants

The process of preparing a plant for outdoor development is known as hardening. If plants grown indoors are put outside without a hardening phase, their growth may be significantly hampered. When harsh weather circumstances are likely, early crops require the most hardening.

Hardening is performed by progressively lowering the temperature and relative humidity and reducing the amount of water. This method causes glucose buildup and cell wall thickening, transitioning the plant from soft, succulent growth to stiffer, tougher development.

Start hardening plants off at least two weeks before planting. On warm days, place seedlings outside in a sheltered area and gradually increase the length of exposure. Tender seedlings should not be planted outside on windy days or when temperatures autumn below 7°C. Even cold-hardy plants will be harmed if exposed to freezing temperatures before hardening.

The purpose of hardening is to slow plant development. Hardening, when taken to the extreme, can inflict substantial harm. Cauliflower, for example, generates thumb-sized heads and fails to develop further if too tough; cucumbers and melons cease developing totally.

CHAPTER 7

GROWING VEGETABLES

And now, we get to the fun part – growing your vegetables. This chapter includes all the vegetables alphabetically and references the different plant families. The grouping is vital in managing soil nutrients and soil-borne diseases common to a given group of plants. Planting alternate families sequentially in a location interrupts diseases and pests common to one group, increasing your chance of a successful crop. The eight vegetable families are:

Chenopodiaceae – The Leafy-Roots Family

The Amaranth family includes beets, chard, spinach, sugar beets – and quinoa.

Brassicaceae – The Mustard Family

The Brassica family – also known as the mustards, the crucifers, or the cabbage family includes broccoli, Brussels sprouts, cabbage, cauliflower, collards, kale, kohlrabi, mustard, radishes, rutabaga, and turnip.

Asteraceae – The most highly evolved plants

The Composite family includes artichokes, endive, lettuce, and sunflowers.

Cucurbitaceae – The Gourd Family

The Cucurbits family includes cucumbers, melons, squashes, pumpkins, and gourds.

Fabaceae – The Pea Family

The Pea family consists of all the legumes – beans, peas, lentils, chickpeas, fava beans, lima beans, and soybeans.

Liliaceae – The Lilly Family that includes the Allium Vegetables

The Lily family includes asparagus, chives, garlic, leeks, onions, scallions, and shallots.

Solanaceae – The Nightshade Family

The Solanaceae family (nightshades) consists of eggplant, pepper, potato, and tomato.

Apiaceae – Fragrant plants with small flowers borne in umbels

The Umbellifers family consists of angelica, anise, caraway, carrot, celery, coriander, cumin, dill, fennel, lovage, parsley, and parsnip.

Of course, there has to be one that doesn't fit in any of the families – rhubarb – which belongs to the **Polygonaceae** family. Planting your first vegetable garden should be fun. I like planting my perennials in the ground and other veggies in raised beds, hills, or containers, which help soils heat faster and provide better drainage and air circulation.

Container Planting

If you're planting in containers, great options include:

- Herbs
- Potatoes
- Tomatoes
- Swiss chard (and spinach)
- Eggplants
- Peppers
- Cucumbers
- Summer squash (zucchinis)
- Carrots
- Lettuce

Companion Planting

Several combo-garden options provide the ingredients you need for various dishes. You may want to create a pizza planter – a tomato plant surrounded by basil and onions. Another traditional favourite is the three sisters: a sweetcorn plant, a pole bean and summer squash. Other great combos include:

- Lettuce and herbs
- Adding the carrots to the three sisters – corn, beans, squash, *and* carrots
- Spinach, chard, onions, and turnips
- Beans and eggplants (aubergine)
- Beans with cucumber, peas, and lettuce
- Broccoli with onion
- Cauliflower with celery
- Eggplant and spinach
- Leeks with carrots
- Lettuce with strawberries or radishes
- Onions with bell pepper
- Squash with sweetcorn
- Swiss chard with onion
- Root crops (like radish) with other vegetables – kale and radish especially
- Marigolds repel Mexican bean beetles, squash bugs, thrips, tomato hornworms, whiteflies, and nematodes, so include them in any garden

If friends grow well together, there must be some that shouldn't be grown together. Below is a list of interplanting options that should be *avoided*:

- Beans and peas shouldn't be interplanted with allium plants (onions, garlic, etc.)
- Carrots shouldn't be planted with fennel or dill (family members)
- Asparagus and garlic
- Beets and beans
- Broccoli and beans
- Cabbage and strawberries
- Carrots and celery
- Corn and tomatoes
- Potatoes should always be a singular crop

Interplanting can maximize limited space, but whatever you choose to do – plan it, map it, and keep a log to learn what works in your unique environment. I have created a reference with the vital information in easy-to-reference tables for each plant – colour-coded for warm-season and cool-season vegetables.

Have fun.

Artichokes (Cynara scolymus)

Family	Season	Sun	Soil		pH
Asteraceae	Perennial	Full Sun	Organic, deep, well-drained		6.5-8.0
Height	Spread	Tolerance	Ease-of-Care	Germination	Emergence
90 – 180 cm	60 – 120 cm	Frost & Salt	Challenging	21 - 24°C	8–12 days

The **Asteraceae family** includes artichokes, endive, lettuce, and sunflowers.

Perennial vegetables, such as asparagus and rhubarb, are picked in the spring but permitted to grow all year. Others, such as Jerusalem artichoke and horseradish, are picked fully at the end of the season, but a root or stem piece is kept for planting the following year. This latter group may be moved about the garden yearly, although asparagus and rhubarb remain in the same position for years.

Planting Artichokes

Artichokes thrive in temperate climates. There are two main types of artichokes: Globe artichokes (Cynara scolymus) and Jerusalem artichokes (Helianthus tuberosus). Globe artichokes are more commonly grown in the UK and are known for their large, edible flower buds. On the other hand, Jerusalem artichokes are grown for their edible tubers.

Choose the right variety: For the UK climate, it's best to choose hardy and early maturing varieties like 'Green Globe', 'Violetto', or 'Imperial Star'. These varieties are better suited to the UK's weather conditions and shorter growing seasons.

Planting time: Globe artichokes can be started from seeds or root divisions. Sow seeds indoors from January to March, and transplant the seedlings outdoors in late spring (April to May) after the risk of frost has passed. Plant root divisions in early spring (March to April) if you're using root divisions.

Soil and site: Choose a well-draining, fertile soil with a pH of 6.5 to 8.0. Artichokes prefer full sun but can tolerate light shade. Ensure the planting site is sheltered from strong winds, as artichoke plants can be top-heavy and may break in strong gusts.

Planting: Space the plants about 1 meter apart to give them enough room to grow. Dig a hole large enough for the root system, and plant the seedlings or root divisions at the same depth they were in their original container. Water well after planting.

Watering and feeding: Keep the soil consistently moist but not waterlogged. Artichokes have deep roots and need regular watering, especially during dry spells. Apply a balanced, all-purpose fertilizer or well-rotted compost/manure during the growing season to encourage strong growth.

Mulching: Apply a layer of organic mulch, like well-rotted compost, straw, or bark chippings, around the base of the plants. This will help retain moisture, suppress weeds, and regulate soil temperature.

Pest and disease control: Slugs and snails can be problematic, so use organic or chemical control methods. Aphids and artichoke plume moths can also affect plants; remove them by hand or use insecticidal soap. To prevent fungal diseases, ensure good air circulation and avoid overwatering.

Harvesting: You can start harvesting Globe artichokes when the flower buds are still tight and have not begun to open. Cut the stem about 5-8 cm below the bud. The main bud matures first, followed by smaller side buds.

Overwintering: In colder areas, protect the plants by cutting back the stems to around 30 cm and covering the crowns with a thick layer of straw, compost, or leaves. Alternatively, you can lift the plants, pot them, and store them in a frost-free environment, such as a greenhouse or cold frame.

Asparagus (Asparagus officianalis)

Family	Season	Sun	Soil		pH
Liliceae	Perennial	Full Sun	Organic, deep, well-drained		6.8 to 7.2
Height	Spread	Tolerance	Ease-of-Care	Germination	Emergence
1.5 – 2.7 m	60 – 75 cm	Frost & Salt	Easy	21 -25°C	10–12 days

The **Lily family** includes asparagus, chives, garlic, leeks, onions, scallions, and shallots.

Asparagus is a perennial vegetable that can produce tender shoots for up to 20 years if well cared for. You need a sunny site with well-drained soil rich in organic matter to grow asparagus. You can plant asparagus crowns in March or April. Asparagus takes a few years to establish, so you should not harvest spears until the third year. After that, you can enjoy a delicious harvest for about eight weeks in spring and early summer. Asparagus is prone to asparagus beetle and fungal diseases, so keep an eye on your plants and remove any affected parts. Cut back the ferny foliage in autumn and mulch with compost to protect the crowns over winter.

Planting Asparagus

Choose the right variety: For the UK climate, choose hardy and disease-resistant varieties like 'Gijnlim', 'Mondeo', 'Pacific Purple', or 'Stewart's Purple'. These varieties are better suited to the UK's weather conditions.

Planting time: Asparagus can be grown from seeds or one-year-old crowns. If starting from seeds, sow them indoors in late winter (February to March) and transplant the seedlings outdoors in late spring (April to May). If using crowns, plant them in early spring (March to April) after the risk of frost has passed.

Soil and site: Asparagus prefers well-draining, fertile, sandy loam soil with a pH of 6.5 to 7.5. It requires full sun and a sheltered location. Since asparagus is a long-term crop, prepare the soil by digging in plenty of well-rotted manure or compost to improve fertility and drainage.

Planting: Dig a trench about 30 cm (12 inches) wide and 20 cm (8 inches) deep. Create a small ridge in the bottom of the trench, and place the crowns on top, spreading the roots out evenly. Space crowns about 30-45 cm (12-18 inches) apart and cover with 5-8 cm (2-3 inches) of soil. As shoots emerge, gradually fill the trench with soil until it is level with the surrounding ground.

Watering and feeding: Keep the soil consistently moist but not soggy, especially during the first two growing seasons. Water deeply to encourage deep root growth. Apply a balanced, all-purpose fertilizer or well-rotted compost/manure in spring as the shoots emerge to promote strong growth.

Weed control: Keep the asparagus bed weed-free by hand weeding or using a hoe, taking care not to damage the shallow roots of the asparagus plants.

Pest and disease control: Asparagus beetles, slugs, and snails can be problematic. Remove pests by hand or use organic or chemical control methods as needed. To prevent fungal diseases like asparagus rust, ensure good air circulation and avoid overwatering.

Harvesting: Do not harvest asparagus in the first two years after planting, as the plants need time to establish a strong root system. In the third year, harvest spears for about 4-6 weeks. You can extend the harvest period to 6-8 weeks in subsequent years. Harvest spears when about 15-20 cm (6-8 inches) tall and before the tips open. Snap or cut the spears at the soil level.

Overwintering: Cut the stems down to ground level after the foliage turns yellow and dies back in autumn. Apply a layer of well-rotted compost or manure to the asparagus bed to provide nutrients for the following growing season.

Aubergines (Solanum melongena)

Family	Season	Sun	Soil		pH
Solanaceae	Warm	Full Sun	Well-drained, composted, fertile		6.0 to 6.8
Height	Spread	Tolerance	Ease-of-Care	Germination	Emergence
90 cm	90 cm		Moderately Challenging	18 – 24°C	7–10 days

The aubergine plant, known as eggplant in some countries, is a warm-season perennial

vegetable belonging to the Solanaceae family, closely related to tomatoes, peppers, and potatoes. Aubergines are prized for their glossy, deep purple fruit with a tender, creamy texture and mild, earthy flavour, making them a versatile ingredient in various dishes, such as ratatouille, moussaka, and baba ganoush. The plant features large, velvety leaves and delicate, violet-coloured flowers that give way to the oval or elongated fruit.

Growing Aubergines

Choose the right variety: Select aubergine varieties suitable for the UK climate, such as 'Bonica', 'Black Beauty', or 'Ophelia'. These varieties are more likely to produce a good crop in cooler weather.

Planting time: Sow aubergine seeds indoors from February to April. This will give the plants ample time to grow and mature before the cooler autumn weather sets in.

Soil and site: Aubergines prefer well-draining, fertile soil with a pH of 6.0 to 6.8. Choose a sunny and sheltered location in your garden, or plant in a greenhouse or polytunnel for extra warmth and protection.

Planting: Sow seeds 6 mm deep in seed trays or pots filled with seed compost. Keep the compost moist and maintain a temperature of 18 to 24°C for germination. Transplant seedlings into 15 cm pots when they have at least two true leaves. Move them to their final growing position, either in large pots or directly in the ground, when they are about 30 cm tall, and the risk of frost has passed. Space plants 60 to 90 cm apart.

Support: Support the plants using stakes or cages to prevent the heavy fruit from causing the stems to bend or break.

Watering and feeding: Keep the soil consistently moist but not waterlogged. Aubergines are heavy feeders, so apply a balanced, all-purpose fertilizer or well-rotted compost/manure during the growing season to promote healthy growth.

Weed control: Keep the planting area weed-free by hand weeding or using a hoe, not damaging the aubergine's shallow roots.

Pest and disease control: Common pests affecting aubergines include aphids, red spider mites, and whiteflies. Use organic or chemical control methods as needed. To prevent diseases like verticillium wilt and mosaic virus, ensure good air circulation, avoid overwatering, and practice crop rotation.

Harvesting: Harvest aubergines when the fruit is glossy and firm, typically 16 to 24 weeks after sowing, depending on the variety. Use a sharp knife or pruning shears to cut the fruit from the plant, leaving a short stalk attached.

Beans (Phaseolus vulgaris)

Family Fabaceae	Season Warm	Sun Full Sun	Soil Consistently moist		pH 6.0 to 6.8
Height 30–90cm	Spread 30-60cm	Tolerance Average Fertility	Ease-of-Care Easy	Germination 21 - 24°C	Emergence 8–10 days

Green beans, or French or runner beans, are a popular and easy-to-grow vegetable. There are two main types: climbing beans (which require support) and bush beans (which grow more compactly).

Growing Beans

Choose the right variety: Opt for varieties well-suited to the UK climate, such as 'Blue Lake', 'Tendergreen', 'Cobra', or 'Safari'. These varieties are known for their reliability and good performance in the UK's weather conditions.

Planting time: Green beans are tender plants and should be sown after the risk of frost has passed. You can sow seeds directly outdoors from mid-May to July or start them indoors in April and transplant them outside in late May or early June.

Soil and site: Green beans thrive in well-draining, fertile soil with a pH of 6.0 to 6.8. They prefer a sunny, sheltered location. Before planting, work in some well-rotted compost or manure to improve soil fertility and structure.

Planting: For bush beans, sow seeds about 2.5 cm (1 inch) deep and 10 cm (4 inches) apart in rows that are 45 cm (18 inches) apart. For climbing beans, sow seeds 2.5 cm (1 inch) deep and 15 cm (6 inches) apart at the base of a support structure, such as a trellis or bamboo cane wigwam. If starting seeds indoors, use biodegradable pots to avoid disturbing the roots when transplanting.

Support: Climbing beans will need support to grow upwards. Install a trellis, netting, or bamboo cane wigwam when planting, so the plants can climb as they grow.

Watering and feeding: Keep the soil consistently moist, especially during flowering and pod development. Water deeply to encourage strong root growth. Apply a balanced, all-purpose fertilizer or well-rotted compost/manure during the growing season to promote healthy growth.

Weed control: Keep the planting area weed-free by hand weeding or using a hoe, taking care not to damage the shallow roots of the bean plants.

Pest and disease control: Common pests include aphids, slugs, and snails. Remove them by hand or use organic or chemical control methods as needed. To prevent diseases like bean rust and mosaic virus, ensure good air circulation, avoid overwatering, and practice crop rotation.

Harvesting: Harvest green beans when young and tender and before the seeds inside the pods have fully developed. This is usually around 60 days after planting for bush beans and

70 days for climbing beans, and regularly picking beans encourages more pod production.

Beetroot (Beta vulgaris subsp. vulgaris)

Family	Season	Sun	Soil		pH
Chenopodiaceae	Cool	Full Sun Part Shade	Well-drained sandy loam		6.0 to 7.0
Height	Spread	Tolerance	Ease-of-Care	Germination	Emergence
30 cm	15 cm	Low Fertility	Easy	10 - 29°C	5–8 days

The **Goosefoot family** includes beetroots, Swiss chard, spinach, sugar beets – and quinoa.

Beetroot is an easy-to-grow, versatile vegetable well-suited to the UK's temperate climate. To grow beetroot, select a suitable variety like 'Boltardy' or 'Detroit 2' and sow seeds directly outdoors between mid-April and July.

Planting Beetroot

Growing beetroot is relatively easy, as this versatile vegetable thrives in temperate climates.

Choose the right variety: There are several beetroot varieties suitable for the UK climate, including 'Boltardy', 'Detroit 2', 'Golden', and 'Chioggia'. These varieties are known for their good performance and resistance to bolting in the UK's weather conditions.

Planting time: Beetroot seeds can be sown in situ outdoors from mid-April to July. You can also start seeds indoors or under a cloche in late March or early April for transplanting outdoors later.

Soil and site: Beetroot prefers well-draining, fertile soil with a pH of 6.0 to 7.0. Choose a sunny or partially shaded location. Before planting, incorporate well-rotted compost or manure to improve soil fertility and structure.

Planting: Sow seeds about 2.5 cm (1 inch) deep and 10 cm (4 inches) apart in rows that are 30 cm (12 inches) apart. Thin seedlings to 5-10 cm (2-4 inches) apart when they reach around 2.5 cm (1 inch) tall. If starting seeds indoors, use biodegradable pots to avoid disturbing the roots when transplanting.

Watering and feeding: Keep the soil consistently moist but not waterlogged. Water deeply to encourage strong root growth. Consistent watering can help prevent woody roots and promote uniform growth. A balanced, all-purpose fertilizer or well-rotted compost/manure during the growing season can promote healthy growth.

Weed control: Keep the planting area weed-free by hand weeding or using a hoe, not damaging the beetroot's shallow roots.

Pest and disease control: Common beetroot pests include aphids and flea beetles. Remove them by hand or use organic or chemical control methods as needed. To prevent diseases like powdery mildew and leaf spot, ensure good air circulation, avoid overwatering, and practice crop rotation.

Harvesting: Beetroots can be harvested when they reach the desired size, usually between golf and tennis ball sizes. Depending on the variety, this typically occurs around 8-12 weeks after sowing. Smaller beets tend to be more tender and flavorful. To harvest, gently twist and pull the beetroot from the ground, not damaging the roots.

Storing: Freshly harvested beetroot can be stored in a cool, dark place for several weeks. Cut off the leaves and store them separately, as they can also be eaten when cooked.

Bok/Pak Choi (Brassica rapa var. chinensis)

Family	Season	Sun	Soil		pH
Brassicaceae	Cool	Full Sun Part Shade	Well-drained composted, moist		6.0 to 7.5
Height	Spread	Tolerance	Ease-of-Care	Germination	Emergence
30 - 60cm	4 cm	Slight Alkalinity, Frost	Moderately Challenging	10 – 27°C	4–7 days

Bok choy (Brassica rapa var. chinensis), pak choi or Chinese cabbage, is a leafy green vegetable native to Asia and a popular ingredient in many Asian cuisines. This cool-season crop and broccoli, kale, and cabbage belong to the Brassica family. Bok choy is characterized by its dark green leaves and crisp, white or pale green stalks, forming a compact rosette. The plant is highly nutritious, rich in vitamins A, C, and K and minerals like calcium and potassium.

Growing Pak Choi

Bok choy is a cool-season crop that can adapt to the temperate climate.

Choose the right variety: Opt for varieties that are well-suited to the UK climate, such as 'Joi Choi', 'Violetta', or 'Green Fortune'. These varieties are known for their good performance and resistance to bolting in cooler climates.

Planting time: Bok choy can be sown directly outdoors from March to August or started indoors from February to July. This will allow for multiple harvests. Plant in early spring or late summer to avoid bolting during hot summer months.

Soil and site: Bok choy prefers well-draining, fertile soil with a pH of 6.0 to 7.0. Choose a sunny or partially shaded location. Before planting, incorporate well-rotted compost or manure to improve soil fertility and structure.

Planting: Sow seeds about 1 cm (0.5 inch) deep and 2.5 cm (1 inch) apart in rows that are 30 cm (12 inches) apart. Thin seedlings to 15-20 cm (6-8 inches) apart when they reach around 5 cm (2 inches) tall. If starting seeds indoors, use biodegradable pots to avoid disturbing the roots when transplanting.

Watering and feeding: Keep the soil consistently moist but not waterlogged. Water deeply to encourage strong root growth. Consistent watering can help prevent bolting and promote uniform growth. Apply a balanced, all-purpose fertilizer or well-rotted compost/manure during the growing season to promote healthy growth.

Weed control: Keep the planting area weed-free by hand weeding or using a hoe, not damaging the bok choy's shallow roots.

Pest and disease control: Common pests affecting bok choy include aphids, cabbage loopers, and flea beetles. Remove them by hand or use organic or chemical control methods as needed. To prevent diseases like clubroot and downy mildew, ensure good air circulation, avoid overwatering, and practice crop rotation.

Harvesting: Depending on the variety, Bok choy can be harvested when the leaves have reached the desired size, typically between 45 to 60 days after sowing. Cut the entire plant at the base or harvest individual leaves as needed, allowing the plant to continue producing new leaves.

Broccoli (Brassica oleracea var. italica)

Family	Season	Sun	Soil		pH
Brassicaceae	Cool	Full Sun Min. Shade	Well-drained composted, moist		6.0 to 7.5
Height	Spread	Tolerance	Ease-of-Care	Germination	Emergence
60 - 90cm	60 - 90cm	Slight Alkalinity, Frost	Moderately Challenging	7 - 29°C	4–7 days

Broccoli thrives in the United Kingdom's cool and temperate climate. To successfully grow broccoli, sow seeds indoors from February to May or directly outdoors from April to June. Plant in fertile, well-draining soil with a pH of 6.0 to 7.5 in a sunny or partially shaded location. Keep the soil consistently moist and weed-free, and watch for pests like aphids, caterpillars, and flea beetles. Harvest the main head when it reaches the desired size, usually between 12 to 16 weeks after sowing, and continue harvesting side shoots as they develop.

Planting Broccoli

Choose the right variety: Opt for varieties such as 'Calabrese', 'Purple Sprouting', 'Early Purple Sprouting', or 'Green Goliath'. These varieties perform well in cooler climates.

Planting time: Sow seeds indoors from February to May or directly outdoors from April to June. This will allow for multiple harvests throughout the growing season.

Soil and site: Broccoli prefers well-draining, fertile soil with a pH of 6.0 to 7.5. Choose a sunny or partially shaded location. Before planting, incorporate compost to improve soil fertility and structure.

Planting: Sow seeds about 12 mm (0.5 inch) deep and 7.5 cm (3 inches) apart in trays or pots if starting indoors. Transplant seedlings outdoors when they have at least two true leaves and are about 10 to 15 cm (4-6 inches) tall, spacing them 45 to 60 cm (18-24 inches) apart in rows that are 60 to 90 cm (24-36 inches) apart. If sowing seeds directly outdoors, sow them 12 mm (0.5 inch) deep and 30 cm (12 inches) apart in rows that are 45 cm (18 inches) apart. Thin seedlings to 45 to 60 cm (18-24 inches) apart as they grow.

Watering and feeding: Keep the soil consistently moist but not waterlogged. Water deeply to encourage strong root growth. Apply a balanced, all-purpose fertilizer or well-rotted manure during the growing season to promote healthy growth.

Weed control: Keep the planting area weed-free by hand weeding or using a hoe, taking care not to damage the broccoli's shallow roots.

Pest and disease control: Common pests affecting broccoli include aphids, caterpillars, and flea beetles. Remove them by hand or use organic or chemical control methods as needed. To prevent diseases like clubroot and downy mildew, ensure good air circulation, avoid overwatering, and practice crop rotation.

Harvesting: Harvest the main head when it reaches the desired size, usually between 12-16 weeks after sowing, depending on the variety. Cut the main head with a sharp knife, leaving some of the stem attached. After harvesting the main head, side shoots will continue to develop, which can also be harvested as they grow.

Brussels sprouts (Brassica oleracea var. gemmifera)

Family	Season	Sun	Soil		pH
Brassicaceae	Cool	Full Sun Min. Shade	Well-drained composted, moist		6.0 to 7.5
Height	Spread	Tolerance	Ease-of-Care	Germination	Emergence
60 - 90cm	45 - 60cm	Slight Alkalinity, Frost	Moderately Challenging	7 - 29°C	5–8 days

Brussels sprouts are well-suited to the cool and temperate climates. To successfully grow

Brussels sprouts, select a suitable variety like 'Trafalgar' or 'Montgomery' and sow seeds indoors from February to April or directly outdoors from March to April. Plant in fertile, well-draining soil with a pH of 6.0-7.0 in a sunny or partially shaded location. Keep the soil consistently moist and weed-free, and monitor for pests like aphids, caterpillars, and whiteflies. Harvest sprouts from the bottom of the stalk upwards when they reach the size of a walnut, typically between September and December.

Growing Brussels Sprouts

Choose the right variety: Opt for varieties such as 'Trafalgar', 'Montgomery', 'Jade Cross', or 'Wellington'. These varieties perform well in cooler climates.

Planting time: Sow seeds indoors from February to April or directly outdoors from March to April. This will allow for harvests between September and December.

Soil and site: Brussels sprouts prefer well-draining, fertile soil with a pH of 6.0 to 7.5. Choose a sunny or partially shaded location. Before planting, incorporate well-rotted compost or manure to improve soil fertility and structure.

Planting: Sow seeds about 12 mm deep and 7.5 cm apart in trays or pots if starting indoors. Transplant seedlings outdoors when they have at least two true leaves and are about 10 to 15 cm tall, spacing them 60 to 75 cm apart in rows 75 to 90 cm apart. If sowing seeds directly outdoors, sow them 12 mm deep and 30 cm apart in rows 60 to 75 cm apart. Thin seedlings to 60 to 75 cm apart as they grow.

Watering and feeding: Keep the soil consistently moist but not waterlogged. Water deeply to encourage strong root growth. Apply a balanced, all-purpose fertilizer or well-rotted compost/manure during the growing season to promote healthy growth.

Weed control: Keep the planting area weed-free by hand weeding or using a hoe, taking care not to damage the Brussels sprouts' shallow roots.

Pest and disease control: Common pests affecting Brussels sprouts include aphids, caterpillars, and whiteflies. Remove them by hand or use organic or chemical control methods as needed. To prevent diseases like clubroot and downy mildew, ensure good air circulation, avoid overwatering, and practice crop rotation.

Harvesting: Harvest sprouts from the bottom of the stalk upwards when they reach the size of a walnut, typically between September and December. Use a sharp knife to remove the sprouts, ensuring not to damage the stalk or neighbouring sprouts.

Butter Beans (Phaseolus lunatus)

Family	Season	Sun	Soil		pH
Fabaceae	Warm	Full Sun	Consistently moist		6.0 to 6.8
Height	Spread	Tolerance	Ease-of-Care	Germination	Emergence
1–90 cm	30-60cm	Average Fertility	Easy	21 - 24°C	8–10 days

Butter beans, or lima beans, are a delightful legume, appreciated for their creamy texture and mild, buttery flavour. While not as commonly grown in the UK as other beans, butter bean plants can still be cultivated in warmer, sunnier parts of the country. These climbing plants produce flat, slightly curved pods containing plump, kidney-shaped beans that vary in colour from pale green to white. As a tasty and nutritious addition to soups, stews, and salads, butter beans are a welcome and versatile addition to the British garden and kitchen, given the right growing conditions.

How to Grow Butter Beans

Choose the right variety: Select butter bean varieties more suited to the UK climate, such as 'Fordhook 242' or 'King of the Garden'.

Planting time: Start butter bean seeds indoors in April or May, as they are sensitive to cold temperatures and frost. Alternatively, you can sow them directly outdoors in late May or early June when the soil has warmed up.

Soil and site: Butter beans prefer well-draining, fertile soil with a pH of 6.0 to 6.8. Choose a sunny location in your garden that is sheltered from strong winds.

Sowing seeds: Sow seeds 5 cm deep and 10 cm apart in pots or seed trays if starting indoors. If sowing directly outdoors, plant seeds 5 cm deep and 15 cm apart, with 60 cm between rows.

Transplanting: If you started seeds indoors, transplant seedlings outdoors once the risk of frost has passed and nighttime temperatures consistently stay above 10°C (50°F). Harden off the seedlings before transplanting by gradually exposing them to outdoor conditions for 7 to 10 days.

Supporting the plants: Support your butter bean plants using trellises, canes, or netting to encourage healthy growth and make harvesting easier.

Watering and feeding: Keep the soil consistently moist, especially during flowering and pod development. Water at the base of the plant to prevent excess moisture on leaves, which can lead to disease. Apply a balanced, all-purpose fertilizer or well-rotted compost/manure during the growing season to promote healthy growth.

Weed control: Keep the planting area weed-free by hand weeding or using a hoe, not damaging the butter bean's roots.

Pest and disease control: Butter beans can be affected by common pests like aphids and bean weevils and diseases such as bean rust and mosaic virus. Monitor your plants closely and employ appropriate organic control methods.

Harvesting: Harvest butter beans when the pods are plump, firm, and still green, typically around 60-80 days after planting. Pick pods regularly to encourage further production.

Cabbage (Brassica oleracea var. capitata)

Family	Season	Sun	Soil		pH
Brassicaceae	Cool	Full Sun Min. Shade	Well-drained composted, moist		6.0 to 7.5
Height	Spread	Tolerance	Ease-of-Care	Germination	Emergence
30 - 60cm	45 - 90cm	Frost (limited)	Moderately Challenging	7 - 29°C	4–7 days

The **Brassica family** – also known as the mustards, the crucifers, or the cabbage family includes broccoli, Brussels sprouts, cabbage, cauliflower, collards, kale, kohlrabi, mustard, radishes, rutabaga, and turnip.

Cabbage is a robust vegetable that thrives in well-drained soil. Greens in various colours, as well as red and purple varieties, are available. The most common head form is round, but it can also be flattened or pointed. The leaves of most cultivars are smooth, but the Savoy variety has crinkly textured leaves.

Cabbage is simple to cultivate if you choose the right kinds and follow proper culture and insect management practices. Cabbage has long been acknowledged as a rich source of vitamins and is becoming increasingly popular for its disease-prevention characteristics.

How to Grow Cabbages

Choose the right variety: Select varieties suitable for the UK climate, such as 'Savoy King', 'Greyhound', 'Golden Acre', or 'January King'. Consider the different types of cabbages, including green, red, and Savoy.

Planting time: Sow seeds indoors from January to April or directly outdoors from April to August, depending on the specific variety. This will allow for harvests from summer through winter.

Soil and site: Cabbages prefer well-draining, fertile soil with a pH of 6.0 to 7.5. Choose a sunny or partially shaded location. Before planting, incorporate well-rotted compost or manure to improve soil fertility and structure.

Planting: Sow seeds about 12 mm deep and 7.5 cm apart in trays or pots if starting indoors. Transplant seedlings outdoors when they have at least two true leaves and are about 10-15 cm tall, spacing them 30-45 cm apart for smaller varieties and 45-60 cm apart for larger varieties. Rows should be 60-90 cm apart. If sowing seeds directly outdoors, sow them 12 mm deep and 30 cm apart in rows that are 45 cm apart. Thin seedlings as they grow.

Watering and feeding: Keep the soil consistently moist but not waterlogged. Water deeply to encourage strong root growth. Apply a balanced, all-purpose fertilizer or well-rotted compost/manure during the growing season to promote healthy growth.

Weed control: Keep the planting area weed-free by hand weeding or using a hoe, not damaging the cabbage's shallow roots.

Pest and disease control: Common pests affecting cabbages include aphids, caterpillars, and cabbage root flies. Remove them by hand or use organic or chemical control methods as needed. To prevent diseases like clubroot and downy mildew, ensure good air circulation, avoid overwatering, and practice crop rotation.

Harvesting: Harvest cabbages when the heads reach the desired size and are firm to the touch, typically between 10-20 weeks after sowing, depending on the variety. Cut the cabbage head with a sharp knife, leaving some of the lower leaves attached to the stem.

Storing Cabbages

Storing cabbages properly can help prolong their freshness and maintain their quality.

In the refrigerator:

- Remove any loose or damaged outer leaves.
- Wrap the whole cabbage head in a slightly damp paper towel or clean cloth.
- Place the wrapped cabbage in a perforated plastic bag or an open container to allow air circulation.
- Store the cabbage in the crisper drawer of your refrigerator.
- Green and red cabbages can last up to 2 weeks, while Savoy cabbages typically last about 1 week when stored this way.

In a cool, dark place:

- If you have a basement, cellar, or garage with a consistent temperature between 0-

4°C and high humidity, you can store cabbages there.

- Do not remove the outer leaves; they help protect the inner leaves.
- Place the cabbages on a raised surface or hang them in mesh bags to allow air circulation.
- Ensure the cabbages do not touch each other to prevent the spread of any potential rot.
- Check regularly for signs of spoilage and remove any affected cabbages immediately.
- When stored this way, cabbages can last for 3 to 4 months.

Freezing

- Remove any damaged or wilted outer leaves.
- Cut the cabbage into wedges or shred it, depending on your preference.
- Blanch the cabbage pieces in boiling water for 1.5 to 3 minutes, depending on the size, and then quickly transfer them to an ice bath to stop the cooking process.
- Drain the cabbage well and pat dry with paper towels.
- Place the cabbage in airtight freezer bags or containers, removing as much air as possible.
- Label and date the bags or containers.
- Frozen cabbage can last up to 9 to 12 months, but it's best to use it within 6 months for optimal taste and texture.

Remember that the freezing method alters the texture of the cabbage, making it more suitable for cooked dishes such as soups, stews, or casseroles after thawing.

Carrots (Daucus carota var. sativus)

Family	Season	Sun	Soil	pH
Apiaceae	Cool	Full Sun Shade	Well-drained, deep, composted, moist	6.0 to 6.8

Height	Spread	Tolerance	Ease-of-Care	Germination	Emergence
30 - 60cm	30 cm	Shade, Acidity	Easy	10 - 29°C	7–21 days

Carrots are a cool-season root vegetable available in various colours and are packed with beta carotene, a substance converted to vitamin A in the body. A half-cup serving of cooked carrots contains four times the recommended daily vitamin A. Beta carotene is also a potent antioxidant effective in fighting against different cancers.

Carrots need soil free of rocks up to 20 cm – sandy loam is ideal. Raised beds with sieved soil work well. The easier the root can penetrate the soil, the better the root quality. Plant shorter variants if your soil is heavier. Avoid excessive nitrogen, as your roots will have fingers.

Growing Carrots

Choose the right variety: Select varieties suitable for the UK climate, such as 'Nantes', 'Chantenay', 'Autumn King', or 'Flyaway'. Consider size, shape, and colour when choosing your carrot variety.

Planting time: Sow carrot seeds directly outdoors from March to July, allowing for harvests from late spring through autumn.

Soil and site: Carrots prefer light, well-draining, and stone-free soil with a pH of 6.0 to 6.8. Choose a sunny location. Before planting, ensure the soil is loose and free of large clumps or rocks, as these can cause the carrots to fork or become misshapen.

Planting: Create shallow drills about 12 mm deep and 15 to 20 cm apart. Sow the seeds thinly along the drill and cover them lightly with soil. Water the area gently to settle the soil. As seedlings emerge, thin them to about 5 cm apart for smaller varieties and 7.5 cm apart for larger varieties.

Watering and feeding: Keep the soil consistently moist but not waterlogged. Water deeply to encourage strong root growth. Carrots do not require much feeding, but adding a balanced, all-purpose fertilizer or well-rotted compost/manure before planting can promote healthy growth.

Weed control: Keep the planting area weed-free by hand weeding or using a hoe, taking care not to damage the carrot's shallow roots.

Pest control: The most common pest affecting carrots is the carrot fly. Use fine mesh netting or insect-proof barriers to protect your carrots from carrot flies. Companion planting with onions, leeks, or chives can also help deter carrot flies.

Harvesting: Carrots can be harvested when they reach the desired size, usually 10 to 16 weeks after sowing, depending on the variety. Gently loosen the soil around the carrot with a hand fork or trowel and pull it out by its foliage. Carrots can be left in the ground until needed, but it's best to harvest them before the first heavy frost.

Cauliflower (Brassica oleracea var. botrytis)

Family	Season	Sun	Soil		pH
Brassicaceae	Cool	Full Sun Min. Shade	Well-drained composted, moist		6.0 to 7.5
Height	**Spread**	**Tolerance**	**Ease-of-Care**	**Germination**	**Emergence**
30 - 60cm	60 - 90cm	Frost (limited)	Moderately Challenging	7 - 29°C	5–21 days

Cauliflower is a cool-season cruciferous vegetable belonging to the Brassicaceae family, closely related to broccoli, cabbage, and kale. It is known for its dense, creamy-white head, called the "curd," formed by clusters of immature flower buds, which is the edible part of the plant. Cauliflower is highly nutritious, rich in vitamins, minerals, and antioxidants, and can be enjoyed in various dishes, such as steamed, roasted, or even as a substitute for rice or potatoes. This versatile vegetable can be grown in cool climates, and different cultivars offer a range of colours, including purple, green, and orange, adding visual interest to both the garden and the plate.

Growing Cauliflower

Choose the right variety: Select varieties suitable for the UK climate, such as 'All the Year Round', 'Snowball', 'Graffiti' (purple), or 'Romanesco' (green). Consider size, colour, and maturity time when choosing your cauliflower variety.

Planting time: Sow cauliflower seeds indoors from December to April or directly outdoors from April to June, depending on the specific variety. This will allow for harvests from late spring through autumn.

Soil and site: Cauliflower prefers well-draining, fertile soil with a pH of 6.0 to 7.5. Choose a sunny or partially shaded location. Before planting, incorporate well-rotted compost or manure to improve soil fertility and structure.

Planting: Sow seeds about 12 mm deep and 7.5 cm apart in trays or pots if starting indoors. Transplant seedlings outdoors when they have at least two true leaves and are about 10-15 cm tall, spacing them 60 cm apart in rows that are 75 cm apart. If sowing seeds directly outdoors, sow them 12 mm deep and 15 cm apart in rows that are 60 cm apart. Thin seedlings as they grow.

Watering and feeding: Keep the soil consistently moist but not waterlogged. Water deeply to encourage strong root growth. Apply a balanced, all-purpose fertilizer or well-rotted compost/manure during the growing season to promote healthy growth.

Weed control: Keep the planting area weed-free by hand weeding or using a hoe, taking care not to damage the cauliflower's shallow roots.

Pest and disease control: Pests like cabbage root flies, caterpillars, and aphids can infest and damage brassicas, affecting their growth and quality. The cabbage root fly lays eggs at the base of plants, and the larvae feed on the roots, leading to wilting and stunted growth. Caterpillars, such as the cabbage white butterfly and the cabbage moth, can cause extensive damage by feeding on leaves and heads. Aphids can cause distortion and discolouration of leaves, and they can also transmit viral diseases. Clubroot, a soil-borne disease caused by the fungus Plasmodiophora brassicae, can lead to swollen, distorted roots and reduced plant growth. Downy mildew and other fungal diseases can cause leaf spotting, yellowing, and decay. Managing these pests and diseases requires a combination of good gardening practices, such as crop rotation, proper spacing, regular monitoring, and chemical or organic control methods when necessary.

Blanching: To maintain the white colour of the curd, you may need to blanch it. When the curd reaches the size of a golf ball, fold the outer leaves over it and secure them with a rubber band, twine, or a clothespin. This will protect the curd from sunlight and maintain its white colour.

Harvesting: Harvest cauliflower when the curd reaches the desired size and is still compact, typically between 12 to 24 weeks after sowing, depending on the variety. Cut the cauliflower head with a sharp knife, leaving a few leaves attached to protect it during transport and storage.

Celery (Apium graviolens var. dulce)

Family	Season	Sun	Soil		pH
Apiaceae	Cool	Full Sun Part Shade	Composted, moist, fertile soil		6.0 to 7.0
Height	Spread	Tolerance	Ease-of-Care	Germination	Emergence
75 cm	36 cm	Wet Feet	Challenging	21 - 24°C	14–21 days

The celery plant, scientifically known as Apium graveolens, is a biennial herb belonging to the Apiaceae family, closely related to parsley and carrots. Celery is cultivated primarily for its crisp, crunchy stalks, rich in vitamins and minerals, such as vitamin K, potassium, and folate. The stalks are commonly consumed raw in salads, as a healthy snack, or cooked in various dishes, such as soups, stews, and stir-fries. Celery plants prefer a cool, moist environment and can be grown in temperate climates. In addition to the familiar green celery, there are also varieties with golden or red stalks, offering a range of flavours and colours for the garden and kitchen.

Growing Celery

Choose the right variety: Select varieties such as 'Victoria', 'Giant Red', or 'Tall Utah'. Consider factors like size, colour, and resistance to bolting when choosing your celery variety.

Planting time: Sow celery seeds indoors from February to April or directly outdoors from April to May, depending on the specific variety. This will allow for harvests from late summer through autumn.

Soil and site: Celery prefers rich, well-draining soil with a pH of 6.0 to 7.0. Choose a sunny or partially shaded location. Before planting, incorporate well-rotted compost or manure to improve soil fertility and structure.

Planting: Sow seeds about 6 to 12 mm apart in trays or pots if starting indoors. Transplant seedlings outdoors when they have at least three true leaves and are about 10 to 15 cm tall, spacing them 20 to 25 cm apart in rows that are 30 cm apart. If sowing seeds directly outdoors, sow them 10 mm deep and 20 cm apart in rows that are 30 cm apart. Thin seedlings as they grow.

Watering and feeding: Keep the soil consistently moist but not waterlogged. Celery is a heavy feeder, so apply a balanced, all-purpose fertilizer or cured compost during the growing season to promote healthy growth.

Weed control: Keep the planting area weed-free by hand weeding or using a hoe, taking care not to damage the celery's shallow roots.

Pest and disease control: Common celery pests include aphids, slugs, and snails. Remove them by hand or use organic or chemical control methods as needed. To prevent diseases like celery leaf spot and fusarium wilt, ensure good air circulation, avoid overwatering, and practice crop rotation.

Blanching (optional): To produce tender, less bitter celery stalks, blanch the plants by wrapping them with cardboard, paper, or a light fabric when they are about 30 cm (12 inches) tall. This should be done about 2-3 weeks before harvesting.

Harvesting: Harvest celery when the stalks reach the desired size, typically between 14 to 16 weeks after sowing, depending on the variety. Cut the whole plant at soil level with a sharp knife, or pick individual stalks as needed.

Chives (Allium schoenoprasum)

Family Lialiaceae	Season Cool Perennial	Sun Full Sun Part Shade	Soil Not fussy, slight acidity		pH 6.0 to 7.0
Height 15 – 30 cm	Spread 30 cm	Tolerance General	Ease-of-Care Easy	Germination 7 – 29°C	Emergence 7–21 days

The chive plant, scientifically known as Allium schoenoprasum, is a perennial herb belonging to

the Allium family, closely related to onions, garlic, and leeks. Chives are valued for their slender, hollow, green leaves with a mild onion-like flavour, making them a popular addition to various dishes such as salads, omelettes, soups, and baked potatoes. They also produce attractive, edible purple flowers, which can be used as a garnish or added to dishes for a subtle onion flavour and a pop of colour. Chives are easy to grow, adaptable to various conditions, and can be cultivated in containers, garden beds, or even as part of an ornamental border. As a low-maintenance plant, chives are a great addition to any herb garden, providing fresh, flavorful leaves throughout the growing season.

Growing Chives

Planting time: Sow chive seeds indoors in early spring or directly outdoors from March to April.

Soil and site: Chives prefer well-draining soil with a pH of 6.0 to 7.0. Choose a sunny or partially shaded location in your garden or a container with good-quality potting soil for planting.

Planting: If starting chives from seeds, sow them 6 mm deep in seed trays or pots, and cover them lightly with soil. Transplant seedlings outdoors when they reach about 7.5 to 10 cm high, spacing them 15 to 20 cm in rows 20-30 cm apart. If you're dividing established clumps, separate the roots gently and replant them in the prepared location, maintaining the same spacing.

Watering and feeding: Keep the soil consistently moist but not waterlogged. Add a balanced, all-purpose fertilizer or well-rotted compost to the soil at the beginning of the growing season to promote healthy growth.

Weed control: Remove any weeds surrounding the chives to prevent competition for nutrients and water.

Pest and disease control: Chives are relatively resistant to pests and diseases. However, they can occasionally be affected by aphids, thrips, or mildew. Remove affected foliage and apply organic or chemical control methods if necessary.

Harvesting: Chives can be harvested as soon as the leaves are large enough to use, typically 6-8 weeks after sowing. Snip the leaves with scissors, cutting them about 25 mm above the base of the plant. Regular harvesting promotes bushy growth and prevents the plants from becoming too tall and floppy.

Collard Greens (Brassica oleracea var. acephala)

Family Brassicaceae	Season Cool	Sun Full Sun Min. Shade	Soil Well-drained composted, moist		pH 6.0 to 7.5
Height 45 – 90 cm	Spread 30 – 60 cm	Tolerance Frost improves crop	Ease-of-Care Easy	Germination 7 - 29°C	Emergence 4–7 days

These nutritious plants are known for their large, dark green, slightly bitter leaves, rich in

vitamins A, C, and K, and minerals like calcium and iron. Collard greens are commonly used in Southern American and African dishes, often cooked slowly with meats or other vegetables to create flavorful, tender dishes. They are a cool-season crop that can be grown in spring and fall, making them a versatile addition to any vegetable garden. With their attractive foliage and nutritional benefits, collard greens offer a delicious and healthy option for gardeners and cooks alike.

Growing Collards

Planting time: Sow collard green seeds indoors in late winter or early spring or directly outdoors from April to July. Depending on the specific variety, this will allow for harvests from late summer through late autumn or even early winter.

Soil and site: Collard greens prefer well-draining, fertile soil with a pH of 6.0 to 7.5. Choose a sunny or partially shaded location in your garden. Incorporate well-rotted compost or manure to improve soil fertility and structure before planting.

Planting: Sow seeds about 1 cm deep and 5 cm apart in seed trays or pots if starting indoors. Transplant seedlings outdoors when they have at least three true leaves and are about 10 to 15 cm tall, spacing them 45 to 60 cm apart in rows 60 to 90 cm apart. Thin seedlings to the proper spacing as they grow.

Watering and feeding: Keep the soil consistently moist, especially during dry periods. Collard greens are heavy feeders, so apply a balanced, all-purpose fertilizer or well-rotted compost/manure during the growing season to promote healthy growth.

Weed control: Keep the planting area weed-free by hand weeding or using a hoe, taking care not to damage the collard green's shallow roots.

Pest and disease control: Common pests affecting collard greens include aphids, cabbage loopers, and root maggots. Remove them by hand or use organic or chemical control methods as needed. To prevent diseases like clubroot and black rot, ensure good air circulation, avoid overwatering, and practice crop rotation.

Harvesting: Harvest collard greens when the leaves reach the desired size, typically about 60 to 75 days after sowing, depending on the variety. Pick the outer leaves first, allowing the plant to continue producing new leaves from the centre.

Sweetcorn (*Zea mays*)

Family	Season	Sun	Soil		pH
Poaceae	Warm	Full Sun	Deep, well-drained, composted, fertile		6.0 to 6.8
Height	**Spread**	**Tolerance**	**Ease-of-Care**	**Germination**	**Emergence**
1.2 – 1.8m	30 - 45cm	Frost (limited)	Moderately Challenging	18 – 29°C	4–7 days

The UK sweetcorn plant, scientifically known as *Zea mays var. saccharata*, is a warm-season crop belonging to the Poaceae family, closely related to field corn. Sweetcorn is valued for its delicious, juicy kernels rich in natural sugars, making them a popular and versatile ingredient in various dishes, such as salads, soups, and side dishes. The plant features tall, sturdy stalks with long, ribbon-like leaves and a tassel at the top, which releases pollen to fertilize the silky strands of the developing corn ears. Sweetcorn varieties suitable for the UK's climate have been developed to ensure successful cultivation, as the plant requires a relatively long and warm growing season. UK gardeners can enjoy homegrown sweetcorn's unique flavour and texture with proper care and timing.

Growing Sweetcorn

Choose the right variety: Select early-maturing or cold-tolerant varieties suitable for the UK climate, such as 'Swift', 'Lark', or 'Earlibird'. These varieties have a shorter growing season and are more likely to produce a good crop.

Planting time: Sow sweetcorn seeds indoors in April or directly outdoors from mid-May to early June, depending on the specific variety and local weather conditions. Sweetcorn requires warm soil temperatures to germinate and grow well.

Soil and site: Sweetcorn prefers well-draining, fertile soil with a pH of 6.0 to 6.8. Choose a sunny and sheltered location to ensure the plants receive adequate warmth and sunlight.

Planting: If starting sweetcorn from seeds indoors, sow them 25 mm deep in seed trays or pots. Transplant seedlings outdoors when they have at least two true leaves and are about 10 to 15 cm tall after the risk of frost has passed. Plant seedlings or direct-sown seeds in blocks rather than rows to facilitate wind pollination. Space plants 45 cm apart, with 60 cm between rows.

Watering and feeding: Keep the soil consistently moist, especially during the crucial pollination and ear-filling stages. Sweetcorn is a heavy feeder, so apply a balanced, all-purpose fertilizer or well-rotted compost/manure during the growing season to promote healthy growth.

Weed control: Keep the planting area weed-free by hand weeding or using a hoe, taking care not to damage the sweetcorn's shallow roots.

Pest and disease control: Common pests affecting sweetcorn include aphids, corn earworms, and birds. Use organic or chemical control methods as needed, and consider netting to protect the plants from birds. To prevent diseases like smut and rust, ensure good air circulation, avoid overwatering, and practice crop rotation.

Harvesting: Harvest sweetcorn when the tassels turn brown, and the kernels are plump, tender, and filled with a milky liquid, usually around 70 to 100 days after sowing, depending on the variety. To test for ripeness, pierce a kernel with your thumbnail; if a milky liquid squirts out, the sweetcorn is ready to harvest

Cucumber (Cucumis sativus)

Family	Season	Sun	Soil		pH
Cucurbiteae	Warm	Full Sun	Well-drained, composted, fertile		6.8 to 7.2
Height	Spread	Tolerance	Ease-of-Care	Germination	Emergence
30 - 180cm	30 - 180cm		Easy	15 – 30 °C	7–21 days

Cucumbers are valued for their crisp, refreshing, and slightly sweet flesh, making them a popular ingredient in salads, sandwiches, and various dishes. The plant features long, trailing vines with large, lobed leaves and delicate yellow flowers that give way to cylindrical, green fruit. Cucumbers come in various shapes, sizes, and colours, with two main types: slicing and pickling. They require a relatively long, warm growing season and benefit from trellising to keep the fruit off the ground and promote healthy growth. Cucumber plants can be a productive and rewarding addition to any vegetable garden with proper care and attention.

Growing and Caring for Cucumbers

Choose the right variety: Opt for cucumber varieties such as 'Carmen', 'Marketmore', or 'Telegraph Improved'. These varieties are more likely to produce a good crop in the cooler UK weather.

Planting time: Sow cucumber seeds indoors from late March to April or directly outdoors from mid-May to early June, depending on the specific variety and local weather conditions. Cucumbers require warm soil temperatures to germinate and grow well.

Soil and site: Cucumbers prefer well-draining, fertile soil with a pH of 6.8 to 7.2. Choose a sunny and sheltered location in your garden, or consider planting in a greenhouse or polytunnel to provide additional warmth.

Planting: If starting cucumbers from seeds indoors, sow them 12 mm deep in seed trays or pots. Transplant seedlings outdoors when they have at least two true leaves and are about 10 cm tall after the risk of frost has passed. Plant seedlings or direct-sown seeds 90 cm apart in 120 cm rows.

Trellising: Provide a trellis, stake, or other support for the cucumber vines to climb, which will help keep the fruit off the ground, promote air circulation, and reduce the risk of disease.

Watering and feeding: Keep the soil consistently moist but not waterlogged, as cucumbers have shallow roots and need regular water to produce well-formed fruit. Apply a balanced, all-purpose fertilizer or well-rotted compost/manure during the growing season to promote healthy growth.

Weed control: Keep the planting area weed-free by hand weeding or using a hoe, not damaging the cucumber's shallow roots.

Pest and disease control: Common pests affecting cucumbers include aphids, spider mites, and slugs. Use organic or chemical control methods as needed. To prevent diseases like powdery mildew and mosaic virus, ensure good air circulation, avoid overwatering, and practice crop rotation.

Harvesting: Harvest cucumbers when they reach the desired size, typically 50 to 70 days after planting, depending on the variety. Regular harvesting encourages the plant to produce more fruit.

Edamame (Glycine max)

Family	Season	Sun	Soil		pH
Fabaceae	Warm	Full Sun Partial Shade	Well-drained, composted, consistently moist		6.0 to 6.8
Height	Spread	Tolerance	Ease-of-Care	Germination	Emergence

30 - 240 cm	15–30 cm	Average Fertility	Easy	15.6 – 29°C	9–13 days

Edamame, the young, green soybeans prized for their rich flavour and nutritional value, are an increasingly popular addition to British gardens. Traditionally grown in East Asian countries, edamame has gained widespread recognition for its versatility in the culinary world and its health benefits. Edamame allows gardeners to diversify and grow a unique and delicious crop. With their attractive foliage and easy-to-grow nature, edamame plants will provide you with a nutritious and tasty harvest and add an interesting element to your garden landscape.

Growing Edamame

Choose the right variety: Select edamame varieties suited to the UK's climate and have a shorter growing season, such as 'Envy', 'Beer Friend', 'Green Legend', or 'Summer Shell'. These varieties can better cope with the UK's cooler and shorter growing season.

Start seeds indoors: Edamame plants require a long growing season of around 90 to 100 days with warm temperatures. It is best to start seeds indoors in the UK in late April to early May. Sow seeds 25 mm deep in individual pots or seed trays filled with well-draining compost. Keep the compost moist and maintain a temperature of 15 to 20°C.

Harden off seedlings: Once the risk of frost has passed and seedlings have developed two sets of true leaves, harden them off by gradually exposing them to outdoor conditions over 7 to 10 days. This will help them acclimate to the outdoor environment.

Soil preparation: Edamame plants prefer well-drained, fertile soil with a pH of 6.0 to 6.5. Incorporate plenty of well-rotted organic matter or compost into the soil to improve its structure and fertility.

Planting out: After hardening off, transplant seedlings into well-prepared soil in a sunny, sheltered location. Space the plants 45 to 60 cm apart in rows spaced 60 to 75 cm apart.

Watering: Water the plants consistently throughout the growing season, ensuring the soil remains moist but not waterlogged. Adequate water is especially important during the flowering and pod development stages.

Weed control: Regularly weed around the plants to reduce competition for nutrients and water. Be careful not to disturb the shallow roots of the edamame plants while weeding.

Pest management: Keep an eye out for pests such as aphids, slugs, and snails, and use organic methods to control them if necessary.

Harvesting: Edamame is usually ready to harvest 80 to 100 days after sowing when the pods have filled out but are still bright green and firm. Harvest the entire plant by cutting it at the base, or pick individual pods as needed. Edamame is best eaten fresh but can be blanched and frozen later.

Endive (Cichorium endiva)

Family	Season	Sun	Soil		pH
Asteraceae	Cool	Full Sun Part Shade	Well-drained, composted, fertile		6.8 to 7.2
Height	Spread	Tolerance	Ease-of-Care	Germination	Emergence
15 – 60 cm	20 – 60 cm	Frost improves flavour	Moderately Challenging	2 – 29°C	5–7 days

The endive plant is a leafy, cool-season vegetable belonging to the Asteraceae family, related to chicory and lettuce. Endives are valued for their slightly bitter, crunchy leaves, which add a unique flavour and texture to salads, soups, and various dishes. The plant is available in two main types: curly endive, also known as frisée, with its finely cut and frilly leaves; and broad-leaved endive, or escarole, featuring broader, less serrated leaves. Endives thrive in the UK's

cooler climate, making them an excellent choice for British vegetable gardens. They prefer well-draining soil and a sunny to partially shaded location. With proper care and attention, endive plants can be a productive and flavoursome addition to your culinary repertoire.

Growing Endive

Choose the right variety: Opt for endive varieties such as 'Batavian', 'Frisee', or 'Romaine'. These varieties are more likely to produce a good crop in cooler weather.

Planting time: Sow endive seeds indoors from late February to March or directly outdoors from April to August, depending on the specific variety and local weather conditions. Stagger your sowings every two weeks for a continuous harvest throughout the growing season.

Soil and site: Endives prefer well-draining, fertile soil with a pH of 6.0 to 7.0. Choose a sunny or partially shaded location in your garden, as endives can tolerate some shade.

Planting: Sow seeds 0.5 cm (0.25 inch) deep in seed trays or pots if starting indoors. Transplant seedlings outdoors when they have at least two true leaves and are about 7.5 cm (3 inches) tall, after the risk of frost has passed. For direct sowing, plant seeds 0.5 cm (0.25 inch) deep and 15 cm (6 inches) apart, with 30 cm (12 inches) between rows.

Watering and feeding: Keep the soil consistently moist but not waterlogged, as endives require regular water for healthy growth. Apply a balanced, all-purpose fertilizer or well-rotted compost/manure during the growing season to promote healthy growth.

Weed control: Keep the planting area weed-free by hand weeding or using a hoe, taking care not to damage the endive's shallow roots.

Pest and disease control: Common pests affecting endives include aphids, slugs, and snails. Use organic or chemical control methods as needed. To prevent diseases like downy mildew and root rot, ensure good air circulation, avoid overwatering, and practice crop rotation.

Harvesting: Harvest endive leaves when they are young and tender, typically 70-90 days after planting, depending on the variety. You can either harvest individual leaves or cut the entire plant at the base, leaving a small stump for possible regrowth.

Garlic (Allium sativum)

Family	Season	Sun	Soil		pH
Liliaceae	Warm	Full Sun	Well-drained, composted, fertile		6.2 to 6.8
Height	Spread	Tolerance	Ease-of-Care	Germination	Emergence
30 – 60 cm	15 - 30cm	Light Frost	Easy	15 – 30°C	7–10 days

Garlic, a popular and flavourful allium, is grown widely in the UK and comes in two main types: hardneck and softneck. Hardneck garlic varieties, such as 'Rocambole' and 'Purple Stripe', are characterised by their stiff, central stalk and produce fewer but larger cloves with a complex, spicy flavour. They also produce edible flower stalks called "scapes," which can be harvested and used in various dishes. Softneck garlic varieties, like 'Artichoke' and 'Silverskin', are more common in supermarkets and have a flexible stalk suitable for braiding. They produce many smaller cloves and have a milder, longer-lasting flavour. Both hardneck and softneck garlic plants thrive in the UK climate, given well-draining soil, ample sunlight, and appropriate care.

Growing Garlic

Choose the right variety: Consider garlic varieties such as 'Solent Wight' (softneck) or 'Lautrec

Wight' (hardneck). These varieties are more likely to produce a good crop in cooler weather.

Planting time: Plant garlic cloves in the autumn, typically between October and December, allowing them to experience a period of cold weather that promotes proper bulb development.

Soil and site: Garlic prefers well-draining, fertile soil with a pH of 6.0 to 7.0. Choose a sunny location in your garden, as garlic needs plenty of sunlight for optimal growth.

Planting: Break apart garlic bulbs into individual cloves just before planting. Plant cloves with the pointed end facing up, 25 mm deep, and 10 to 15 cm apart, with 30 cm between rows.

Watering and feeding: Keep the soil consistently moist but not soggy, especially during bulb formation. Garlic has relatively low nutrient requirements, but you can apply a balanced, all-purpose fertilizer or well-rotted compost/manure at planting time to encourage healthy growth.

Weed control: Keep the planting area weed-free by hand weeding or using a hoe, taking care not to damage the garlic's shallow roots.

Pest and disease control: Common garlic pests include onion thrips, white rot, and rust. Practice crop rotation and maintain proper garden hygiene to prevent these issues.

Harvesting: Harvest garlic when the lower leaves have yellowed, and the upper leaves are still green, typically between June and August, depending on the variety. Gently loosen the soil with a fork before lifting the bulbs. Avoid pulling the plant by the stalk to prevent damage to the bulb.

Curing and storage: Allow the harvested garlic bulbs to cure in a dry, well-ventilated area for 2 to 4 weeks. Once the outer skins are dry, you can trim the roots, remove any excess dirt, and store them in a cool, dry place.

Gourd (lagenaria siceraria)

Family	Season	Sun	Soil	pH
Cucurbitaceae	Warm	Full Sun	Well-drained, composted, fertile	5.8 to 6.8

Height	Spread	Tolerance	Ease-of-Care	Germination	Emergence
45-90cm	3-9 m		Easy	15 - 30°C	5–10 days

Gourd plants, encompassing a diverse range of species within the Cucurbitaceae family, are grown for their ornamental, edible, or practical value. In the UK, gourds such as ornamental, bottle, and luffa are cultivated for their distinct shapes, vibrant colours, and versatile applications. Gourds require a long, warm growing season, which can be challenging in the UK's cooler climate.

However, they can thrive in British gardens with proper care and attention, adding visual interest and providing a unique talking point. Gardeners can grow gourds from seed, planting them in well-draining soil and providing ample sunlight, water, and nutrients. Gourd plants are a fascinating and rewarding addition to the garden, offering opportunities for creative uses in crafts, decoration, and even culinary dishes for some edible varieties.

Growing Grounds

Choose the right variety: Opt for gourd varieties with a shorter growing season, as they are more likely to mature before the cool weather sets in. Examples of such varieties include 'Small Warted', 'Crown of Thorns', and 'Spoon'.

Start seeds indoors: Sow gourd seeds indoors 3 to 4 weeks before the last expected frost date, typically around late April to early May. This head start allows the plants to grow in a warm environment before being transplanted outside.

Soil and site: Gourds prefer well-draining, fertile soil with a pH of 5.8 to 6.8. Choose a sunny location in your garden, as gourds need plenty of sunlight for optimal growth.

Harden off seedlings: Gradually expose the seedlings to outdoor conditions over a week to acclimate them to cooler temperatures and sunlight.

Planting: Transplant seedlings outdoors when the risk of frost has passed, and the soil has warmed, usually around late May to early June. Plant seedlings 60 to 120 cm apart, depending on the variety, with 90 to 150 cm between rows.

Watering and feeding: Gourds require consistent moisture, especially during flowering and fruit development. Apply a balanced, all-purpose fertilizer or well-rotted compost/manure during the growing season to promote healthy growth.

Support and training: Provide trellises, arbours, or fences to support the vining growth of gourd plants, helping to manage their spread, improve air circulation, and reduce the risk of diseases.

Pest and disease control: Gourds can be affected by common pests like aphids, squash bugs, and cucumber beetles, as well as diseases such as powdery mildew and mosaic virus. Monitor your plants closely and employ appropriate organic control methods.

Harvesting: Harvest gourds when their skin hardens and their colour fully develops. This is typically late summer or early autumn, before the first frost for ornamental gourds. Cut the stem with a sharp knife or pruners, leaving a few centimetres of stem attached to the fruit.

Curing and Storage: Cure ornamental gourds in a well-ventilated, dry area for several weeks to remove any remaining moisture, which helps prolong their shelf life. Store them in a cool, dry place away from direct sunlight.

Horseradish (Armoracia rusticana)

Family	Season	Sun	Soil		pH
Brassicaceae	Cool	Full Sun	Deep, rich, moist, loam		6.1 to 8.4
Height	Spread	Tolerance	Ease-of-Care	Germination	Emergence
60-90cm	15-30cm	Slight Alkalinity, Frost	Easy	Vegetative	4–7 days

Horseradish, a robust perennial plant known as Armoracia rusticana, is highly valued for its pungent, spicy roots, commonly used as a condiment in a variety of cuisines. The plant thrives in the UK's temperate climate, preferring well-draining, fertile soil and a sunny or partially shaded location. Horseradish plants can grow up to 1.5 meters tall, with large, coarse leaves and small white flowers appearing in the summer. In the UK, horseradish roots are traditionally harvested in the autumn or spring, when the flavour is at its peak.

Given its vigorous growth habit and tendency to spread, horseradish is best grown in a designated area or a large container to prevent it from overtaking the garden. With proper care, horseradish plants can be a long-lasting and flavoursome addition to the British garden, providing a zesty kick to a variety of dishes.

Growing Horseradish

Choose the right variety: Select horseradish varieties suitable for the UK climate, such as 'Maliner Kren' or 'Big Top'.

Planting time: Plant horseradish roots or root cuttings (also called "sets") in early spring, usually between March and April.

Soil and site: Horseradish prefers well-draining, fertile soil with a pH of 6.0 to 7.0. Choose a sunny or partially shaded location in your garden, as horseradish can tolerate some shade. If you're concerned about the plant spreading, consider planting it in a large container or a designated garden area.

Planting: Plant horseradish sets 30 to 45 cm apart and 10 to 15 cm deep, with the slanted end pointing downward. If planting in rows, maintain a 60 to 90 distance cm between rows.

Watering and feeding: Keep the soil consistently moist but not waterlogged. Apply a balanced, all-purpose fertilizer or well-rotted compost/manure during the growing season to promote healthy growth.

Weed control: Keep the planting area weed-free by hand weeding or using a hoe, not damaging the horseradish's roots.

Pest and disease control: Horseradish is relatively pest and disease-resistant. However, practice crop rotation and proper garden hygiene to prevent potential issues.

Harvesting: Horseradish roots can be harvested in the autumn or spring, depending on your preference. The flavour is often more potent after the first frost. Gently loosen the soil with a garden fork and carefully lift the roots, not breaking them.

Storage: Clean and dry the harvested roots before storing them in a cool, dark, and well-ventilated area. You can also grate and mix the roots with vinegar, creating a prepared horseradish condiment that can be stored in the refrigerator.

Kale (Brassica oleracea var. acephala)

Family	Season	Sun	Soil		pH
Brassicaceae	Cool	Full Sun Light Shade	Well-drained, composted, fertile		6.0 to 7.5
Height	Spread	Tolerance	Ease-of-Care	Germination	Emergence
45 – 90cm	45 cm	Frost for taste	Easy	7 – 29°C	4–7 days

Kale, a nutrient-dense member of the Brassica family, is a popular leafy green vegetable due to its hardiness and versatility in the kitchen. This resilient plant can withstand frosty conditions, with its flavour often improving after a touch of frost. Kale prefers well-draining, fertile soil and a sunny or partially shaded location in the garden. The plant produces robust, frilly leaves and, depending on the variety, can exhibit stunning colours ranging from deep green to vibrant purple. Kale is a rewarding addition to the garden, providing a bountiful supply of delicious, nutritious leaves that can be used in a wide array of dishes, from smoothies and salads to stir-fries and soups.

Growing Kale

Choose a variety: Select kale varieties that are well-suited to the UK climate, such as 'Dwarf Green Curled', 'Lacinato', 'Redbor', or 'Red Russian'.

Planting time: You can sow kale seeds directly outdoors from late March to early June. Alternatively, start seeds indoors 6 to 8 weeks before the last expected frost date and transplant seedlings later.

Soil and site: Kale prefers well-draining, fertile soil with a pH of 6.0 to 7.5. Choose a sunny or partially shaded location in your garden.

Sowing seeds: Sow seeds 1 cm deep and 7.5 cm apart, with 45 cm between rows.

Thinning and transplanting: Thin seedlings to 30-45 cm apart once they reach a height of 7.5 to 10 cm. If you started seeds indoors, transplant seedlings outdoors when they have 4 to 5 true leaves, spacing them 30-45 cm apart.

Watering and feeding: Keep the soil consistently moist, especially during dry spells. Apply a balanced, all-purpose fertilizer or well-rotted compost/manure during the growing season to promote healthy growth.

Weed control: Keep the planting area weed-free by hand weeding or using a hoe, taking care not to damage the kale's roots.

Pest and disease control: Kale can be affected by common pests like cabbage worms, aphids, and flea beetles, as well as diseases such as clubroot and downy mildew. Monitor your plants closely and employ appropriate organic control methods.

Harvesting: Begin harvesting kale leaves when they are around 15 cm long, starting with the lower leaves and working your way up. This encourages the plant to produce more leaves throughout the season. Kale can be harvested throughout the winter months, as it is frost-tolerant.

Kohlrabi (Brassica oleracea var. gongylodes)

Family	Season	Sun	Soil	pH
Brassicaceae	Cool	Full Sun Min. Shade	Well-drained composted, moist	6.0 to 7.5

Height	Spread	Tolerance	Ease-of-Care	Germination	Emergence
30-45cm	30-45cm	Slight Alkalinity	Easy	7 - 29°C	4–7 days

Kohlrabi, a member of the Brassica family, is an intriguing and lesser-known vegetable in the UK, appreciated for its unique, bulbous stem and mildly sweet, crunchy texture. Resembling a cross between a turnip and a cabbage, kohlrabi is available in various colours, including green, white, and purple. It thrives in the UK's temperate climate, preferring well-draining, fertile soil and a sunny or partially shaded location. Kohlrabi plants produce beautiful blue-green leaves that sprout from the edible stem, which can be harvested when it reaches the size of a tennis ball. The stem and leaves can be consumed raw in salads, slaws, or cooked in soups and stews. With its distinctive appearance and delectable flavour, kohlrabi is an interesting and nutritious

addition to British gardens and kitchens.

Growing Kohlrabi

Choose a suitable variety: Select kohlrabi varieties that are well-adapted to the UK climate, such as 'Kolibri', 'Gigante', or 'Early White Vienna'.

Planting time: Sow kohlrabi seeds directly outdoors from late March to early July, or start seeds indoors 4 to 6 weeks before the last expected frost date and transplant seedlings later.

Soil and site: Kohlrabi prefers well-draining, fertile soil with a pH of 6.0 to 7.5. Choose a sunny or partially shaded location in your garden.

Sowing seeds: Sow seeds 12 mm deep and 25 mm apart, with 30 to 45 cm between rows.

Thinning and transplanting: Thin seedlings to 15 to 20 cm apart once they reach a height of 5 cm. If you started seeds indoors, transplant seedlings outdoors when they have 3 to 4 true leaves, spacing them 15 to 20 cm apart.

Watering and feeding: Keep the soil consistently moist, especially during dry spells. Apply a balanced, all-purpose fertilizer or well-rotted compost/manure during the growing season to promote healthy growth.

Weed control: Keep the planting area weed-free by hand weeding or using a hoe, not damaging the kohlrabi's roots.

Pest and disease control: Kohlrabi can be affected by common brassica pests like cabbage worms, aphids, and flea beetles, as well as clubroot and black rot. Monitor your plants closely and employ appropriate organic control methods.

Harvesting: Harvest kohlrabi when the swollen stem reaches the size of a tennis ball, usually around 8-10 weeks after planting. The leaves can also be harvested and used like kale or collard greens.

Leeks (Allium ampeloprasum var. porrum)

Family	Season	Sun	Soil		pH
Liliaceae	Cool	Full Sun Part Shade	Well-drained, fertile, composted		6.2 to 6.8
Height	Spread	Tolerance	Ease-of-Care	Germination	Emergence
60-90cm	30 cm	Frost	Moderately Challenging	7 - 30°C	5–7 days

Leeks, an Allium family member, are a quintessential British vegetable celebrated for their mild, onion-like flavour and versatility in the kitchen. Often used in traditional dishes such as leek and potato soup, leeks are a staple in the UK's cool, temperate climate. The leek plant produces long, cylindrical stems with layered, flat leaves that are dark green at the top and transition to white towards the base. These hardy plants prefer well-draining, fertile soil and a sunny or partially shaded location in the garden. Leeks are typically sown as seeds and then transplanted as seedlings, requiring a unique technique called "dibbing" to encourage the development of a long, blanched stem. Leeks are a classic and cherished addition to the British garden and kitchen, offering a delightful, subtle flavour and culinary possibilities.

Growing Leeks

Choose the right variety: Select leek varieties such as 'Musselburgh', 'King Richard', or 'Apollo'.

Planting time: Sow leek seeds indoors from January to February or directly outdoors from March to April.

Soil and site: Leeks prefer well-draining, fertile soil with a pH of 6.0 to 7.0. Choose a sunny or partially shaded location in your garden.

Sowing seeds: Sow seeds 12 mm deep and 25 mm apart in seed trays or pots if starting indoors or in a seedbed outdoors.

Transplanting: When seedlings are around 20 cm tall and as thick as a pencil, transplant them to their final growing position. Space them 15 cm apart, with 30 cm between rows.

Dibbing: Create holes 15-20 cm deep using a dibber or a broom handle. Place one seedling per hole, then water the seedling, allowing the soil to wash in and fill the hole. This technique encourages the development of a long, blanched stem.

Watering and feeding: Keep the soil consistently moist, especially during dry spells. Apply a balanced, all-purpose fertilizer or well-rotted compost/manure during the growing season to promote healthy growth.

Weed control: Keep the planting area weed-free by hand weeding or using a hoe, not damaging the leek's roots.

Pest and disease control: Leeks can be affected by common pests like leek moth, onion thrips, and allium leaf miner, as well as diseases such as rust and white tip. Monitor your plants closely and employ appropriate organic or chemical control methods.

Harvesting: Depending on the variety, leeks can be harvested from autumn until late winter. Gently loosen the soil with a garden fork and carefully lift the leeks without damaging them.

Lettuce (Lactuca sativa)

Family	Season	Sun	Soil		pH
Asteraceae	Cool	Full Sun	Organic, deep, well-drained		6.2 - 6.8
Height	Spread	Tolerance	Ease-of-Care	Germination	Emergence
15 to 60 cm	15 to 60 cm	Light Frost	Easy	4.4 to 29°C	2–15 days

Lettuce, a classic salad staple, is a versatile and popular leafy green, cherished for its wide array of textures, flavours, and colours. Lettuce plants prefer well-draining, fertile soil and a sunny or partially shaded location in the garden.

They can be grown from seeds or seedlings and often have a relatively quick growth cycle, which allows for successive plantings throughout the season. With their delicate, tender leaves, lettuces add a refreshing, crisp element to salads, sandwiches, and even wraps. Given their adaptability and ease of cultivation, lettuce plants are a delightful and indispensable addition to gardens and kitchens.

Growing Lettuce

Choose the right variety: You have hundreds of variety choices between 'Butterhead', 'Cos', 'Crisphead', or 'Loose-leaf' types.

Planting time: Sow lettuce seeds directly outdoors from March to September, or start seeds indoors and transplant seedlings later.

Soil and site: Lettuce prefers well-draining, fertile soil with a pH of 6.0 to 6.8. Choose a sunny or partially shaded location in your garden.

Sowing seeds: Sow seeds 12 mm deep and 25 mm apart, with 30 cm between rows.

Thinning and transplanting: Thin seedlings to 20 to 30 cm apart once they reach a height of 5 cm. If you started seeds indoors, transplant seedlings outdoors when they have 3 to 4 true leaves, spacing them 20 to 30 cm apart.

Watering and feeding: Keep the soil consistently moist, especially during dry spells. Apply a balanced, all-purpose fertilizer or well-rotted compost/manure during the growing season to promote healthy growth.

Weed control: Keep the planting area weed-free by hand weeding or using a hoe, not damaging the lettuce's roots.

Pest and disease control: Lettuce can be affected by common pests like aphids, slugs, and snails, as well as diseases such as downy mildew and bottom rot. Monitor your plants closely and employ appropriate organic control methods.

Harvesting: Harvest lettuce leaves as needed once they reach a suitable size. You can pick individual leaves for loose-leaf varieties, while for head-forming varieties, harvest the entire head when it is firm.

Melon (Cucumis melo)

Family	Season	Sun	Soil		pH
Cucurbiteaee	Warm	Full Sun	Well-drained composted, moist		6.5 to 7.5
Height	Spread		Ease-of-Care	Germination	Emergence
30 – 45 cm	3 m		Easy	15 – 35°C	3–10 days

Melon plants, known for their juicy, sweet, and aromatic fruits, are a more challenging crop to grow in the UK due to the country's cooler and often unpredictable climate. However, cultivating melons can still be rewarding with the right care and suitable growing conditions. Melons, including popular varieties like cantaloupe, honeydew, and watermelon, require a long, warm growing season and plenty of sunlight. These vining plants develop large leaves and tendrils and produce both male and female flowers. In the UK, melons are best grown in a greenhouse or polytunnel, which provides the necessary warmth and protection from the elements. With careful attention to temperature, watering, and pollination, melon plants can be a delightful, if somewhat challenging, addition to the British garden, offering a delicious and exotic treat for those willing to invest the effort.

Growing Melons

Choose the right variety: Select melon varieties that are more suited to the UK climate and have a shorter growing season, such as 'Emir', 'Sweetheart', or 'Minnesota Midget'.

Planting time: Start melon seeds indoors in late March or April, as they require a long, warm growing season and need to be protected from cold temperatures and frost.

Soil and site: Melons prefer well-draining, fertile soil with a pH of 6.5 to 7.5. Choose a sunny location in your garden or greenhouse, as they need plenty of sunlight to thrive.

Sowing seeds: Sow seeds 2 cm (0.8 inch) deep in pots or seed trays filled with seed compost. Place pots in a propagator or cover with a plastic bag and maintain a temperature of around 20-25°C.

Transplanting: Once seedlings have developed two true leaves and the risk of frost has passed, transplant them into a greenhouse, polytunnel, or outdoors if you live in a warmer region. Space them 90 cm apart, with 120 cm between rows. Harden off seedlings before transplanting by gradually exposing them to outdoor conditions for 7 to 10 days.

Supporting the plants: Support your melon plants with a trellis if you want to grow them vertically. Alternatively, you can allow the vines to sprawl on the ground.

Watering and feeding: Keep the soil consistently moist but avoid overwatering, which can lead to root rot. Water at the base of the plant to prevent excess moisture on leaves, which can lead to disease. Apply a balanced, all-purpose fertilizer or well-rotted compost/manure during the growing season to promote healthy growth.

Pollination: Hand-pollination may be necessary, especially in greenhouse conditions. Use a small paintbrush or cotton swab to transfer pollen from male to female flowers to ensure successful fruit development.

Pruning and thinning: Prune the plants to encourage larger fruit production. Remove all but 3-4 fruits per plant, and trim excess foliage and lateral branches to improve air circulation and sunlight penetration.

Harvesting: Harvest melons when fully ripe, which can be determined by a change in colour, a pleasant aroma, and a slight softening of the fruit. Gently twist the fruit off the vine or cut it with a sharp knife.

Mustard (Brassica juncea)

Family	Season	Sun	Soil		pH
Brassicaceae	Cool	Full Sun Minimum Shade	Well-drained composted, moist		6.0 to 7.5
Height	**Spread**	**Tolerance**	**Ease-of-Care**	**Germination**	**Emergence**
15 to 60cm	30-60cm	Slight Alkalinity, Light Frost	Easy	7 - 29°C	4–7 days

Mustard plants, belonging to the Brassica family, are a versatile and zesty addition to the British garden. Valued for their spicy seeds and peppery leaves, they offer a range of culinary uses, from condiments to salad greens. Mustard varieties such as white, brown, and black are grown for their seeds, while others, like 'Green in Snow' and 'Red Giant', are cultivated for their edible leaves. These fast-growing, cool-season crops thrive in the UK's temperate climate and can be sown directly outdoors from early spring to late summer. Mustard plants favour well-draining, fertile soil and a sunny or partially shaded location. As a popular companion plant, they can deter pests and improve soil quality in the garden. Mustard plants are an easy-to-grow, flavoursome, and multipurpose addition to any garden, providing seeds and leaves that add a delightful kick to various dishes.

Growing Mustard Greens

Choose the right variety: Select mustard green varieties well-suited for the UK climate, such as 'Green in Snow', 'Red Giant', or 'Mizuna'.

Planting time: Sow mustard green seeds directly outdoors from early spring to late summer. For a continuous supply, sow seeds every two to three weeks.

Soil and site: Mustard greens prefer well-draining, fertile soil with a pH of 6.0 to 7.0. Choose a sunny or partially shaded location in your garden.

Sowing seeds: Sow seeds 12 mm deep and 25 mm apart, with 30 cm between rows. Mustard greens can also be grown in containers.

Thinning and transplanting: Thin seedlings to 15 cm apart once they reach a height of 5 cm. If you started seeds indoors, transplant seedlings outdoors when they have 3 to 4 true leaves, spacing them 15 cm apart.

Watering and feeding: Keep the soil consistently moist, especially during dry spells. Apply a balanced, all-purpose fertilizer or well-rotted compost/manure during the growing season to promote healthy growth.

Pest and disease control: Mustard greens can be affected by common pests like aphids, caterpillars, and slugs, as well as diseases such as downy mildew and clubroot. Monitor your plants closely and employ appropriate organic control methods.

Harvesting: Harvest mustard greens when leaves are young and tender, around 4-6 weeks after sowing. Pick individual leaves or cut the entire plant at the base, leaving the roots to encourage regrowth. For varieties grown for their seeds, harvest the seed pods when they turn brown and start to dry.

Onions (Allium cepa)

Family	Season	Sun	Soil	pH
Liliaceae	Cool	Full Sun Part Shade	Well-drained, fertile, composted, moist	6.2 to 6.8

Height	Spread	Tolerance	Ease-of-Care	Germination	Emergence
30 – 90 cm	15–30 cm	Frost	Moderately Challenging	7 – 29°C	4–5 days

Onion plants, an essential ingredient in countless dishes, are a staple in British gardens. Known for their distinct flavour, onions can be grown in various colours and sizes, including the popular red, white, and brown varieties. Onions can be cultivated from seeds or sets, with sets being the more popular choice for their ease and reliability. These hardy, cool-season crops prefer well-draining, fertile soil and a sunny location in the garden. Sowing onion seeds in late winter or early spring, or planting sets in early spring, allows for a summer harvest. Proper care, including regular watering and weed control, onions can be successfully grown and stored for year-round use. Onions add flavour to countless recipes and provide essential nutrients, making them a valuable and versatile addition to any garden.

Growing Onions

Choose a suitable variety: Select onion varieties that meet your needs, such as 'Sturon', 'Centurion', or 'Red Baron'.

Planting time: Sow onion seeds indoors from late winter to early spring (February to March) or plant onion sets outdoors in early spring (March to April).

Soil and site: Onions prefer well-draining, fertile soil with a pH of 6.2 to 6.8. Choose a sunny location in your garden that has not recently grown onions or other alliums.

Preparing the soil: Dig well, remove weeds or large stones, and incorporate organic matter such as well-rotted compost or manure.

Sowing seeds: If starting onions from seeds, sow them 12 mm deep in seed trays or pots filled with seed compost. Transplant seedlings outdoors when they reach pencil thickness, usually around mid-April to May.

Planting sets: If planting onion sets, place them in the soil with the pointed end facing up, about 5 cm deep, and space them 10-15 cm apart in rows 30 cm apart.

Watering: Keep the soil consistently moist, especially during dry spells, but avoid overwatering as this can lead to rot.

Weed control: Keep the planting area weed-free by hand weeding or using a hoe, not damaging the onion's shallow root system.

Pest and disease control: Onions can be affected by pests such as onion flies and diseases like white rot. Monitor your plants closely and employ appropriate organic control methods.

Harvesting: Harvest onions when the foliage starts to yellow and topple over, usually from late summer to early autumn. Gently loosen the soil with a fork, then lift the onions to dry before storing.

Storing: Storing onions properly is essential for preserving their quality and extending their shelf life. After harvesting and allowing the onions to dry and cure for several days in a well-ventilated area, remove any remaining dirt and loose outer layers. Ensure that the onions are fully dry, with their outer skins papery and their necks tightly closed. Store them in a cool, dry, dark place, such as a garage, shed, or pantry, with temperatures between 0-4°C and relative humidity around 65 to 70%.

Place the onions in mesh bags, slatted crates, or hanging in a mesh or net, ensuring good air circulation. Keep them away from potatoes, as the gases released by each can cause the other to spoil more quickly. Inspect the stored onions regularly and remove any that show signs of rot or sprouting. When stored correctly, onions can last several months, providing a continuous supply for your culinary needs.

Parsnips (Pastinaca sativa)

Family	Season	Sun	Soil		pH
Apiaceae	Cool	Full Sun Part Shade	Well-drained, deep, composted, moist		6.0 to 7.0
Height	**Spread**	**Tolerance**	**Ease-of-Care**	**Germination**	**Emergence**
60 – 90 cm	15–30 cm	Frost	Moderately Challenging	10 - 29°C	10–28 days

Parsnips, a classic root vegetable in British cuisine, are well-adapted to the UK's cool climate. Revered for their sweet, earthy flavour, which intensifies after exposure to frost, parsnips are commonly used in soups, stews, and as a roasted side dish. Parsnips are a hardy, cool-season crop that thrives in well-draining, fertile soil with a pH of 6.0 to 7.0. Sowing parsnip seeds directly outdoors from late winter to early spring in a sunny or partially shaded location will result in a bountiful harvest from autumn to winter. Patience is required when germinating parsnip seeds, as they can take up to three weeks to sprout. With diligent care, including consistent watering and weed control, parsnips can be grown successfully and stored for winter use. As a nutritious and flavoursome root vegetable, parsnips are a rewarding addition to any garden.

Some people are sensitive to parsnip leaves, so exercise caution (skin rash, blisters). Wear long trousers and a shirt with long sleeves when working with parsnips.

Growing Parsnips

Choose the right variety: Select parsnip varieties well-suited for the UK climate, such as 'Tender and True', 'Gladiator', or 'White Gem'.

Planting time: Sow parsnip seeds directly outdoors from late winter to early spring (February to April).

Soil and site: Parsnips prefer well-draining, fertile soil with a pH of 6.0 to 7.0. Choose a sunny or partially shaded location in your garden. Avoid planting where previous root crops were grown, and ensure the soil is free from rocks and large stones, which can cause forking.

Preparing the soil: Dig deeply, remove weeds or stones, and incorporate organic matter such as well-rotted compost or manure.

Sowing seeds: Sow seeds 12 mm deep and 25 mm apart in rows spaced 30 cm apart.

Thinning and transplanting: Thin seedlings to 10 15 cm apart once they reach a height of 5 cm. Thin them by snipping them off.

Watering: Keep the soil consistently moist, especially during dry spells, but avoid overwatering, which can lead to root rot.

Pest and disease control: Parsnips can be affected by pests such as carrot flies and diseases like canker. Monitor your plants closely and employ appropriate organic control methods.

Harvesting: Harvest parsnips from autumn to winter after the first frost to enhance their sweetness. Gently loosen the soil with a fork and then lift the parsnips out. Leave some in the ground for a continuous winter harvest, as their taste improves in cold temperatures.

Peas (Pisum sativum)

Family	Season	Sun	Soil		pH
Fabaceae	Warm	Full Sun Partial Shade	Well-Drained, Composted		6.0 to 7.0
Height	Spread	Tolerance	Ease-of-Care	Germination	Emergence
30cm to 1.8m	15–30 cm	Average Fertility	Easy	16 – 30°C	9–13 days

Pea plants are a popular and versatile garden crop, valued for their sweet, tender pods and nutritious peas. As with all legume plants, peas are nitrogen-fixing, improving soil fertility and making them an excellent companion plant in gardens. They are cool-season crops that thrive in well-draining, fertile soil and prefer a sunny or partially shaded location. Pea plants are typically sown in early spring, with dwarf varieties requiring little support and climbing varieties needing trellises or netting for proper growth. With proper care, including regular watering and pest control, pea plants can provide an abundant harvest for fresh consumption, freezing, or drying, making them a delightful and practical addition to any garden.

Choose the right variety: Select pea varieties well-suited for the UK climate, such as 'Kelvedon Wonder', 'Hurst Green Shaft', or 'Sugar Snap'.

Planting time: Sow pea seeds directly outdoors in early spring (March to April) for a summer harvest or in late autumn (October to November) for an early summer harvest the following year.

Soil and site: Peas prefer well-draining, fertile soil with a pH of 6.0 to 7.0. Choose a sunny or partially shaded location in your garden.

Preparing the soil: Dig well, remove weeds and incorporate organic matter such as cured compost or well-rotted manure.

Sowing seeds: Sow seeds 5 cm deep and 5 cm apart in rows spaced 60 to 90 cm apart. To save space, you can also sow peas in double rows or wide rows.

Support: Provide support for climbing pea varieties using trellises, netting, or twiggy sticks. Dwarf varieties may need minimal support or none at all.

Watering: Keep the soil consistently moist, especially during flowering and pod formation, but avoid overwatering, which can lead to root rot.

Weed control: Keep the planting area weed-free by hand weeding or using a hoe, not damaging the pea plants' shallow root system.

Pest and disease control: Peas can be affected by pests such as pea aphids and pea moths and diseases like powdery mildew. Monitor your plants closely and employ appropriate organic or chemical control methods as needed.

Harvesting: Harvest peas when the pods are plump and filled with peas but still tender. Regular picking encourages the plants to produce more pods. Harvest snap peas and snow peas when the pods are still tender.

Peppers (Capsicum annuum)

Family	Season	Sun	Soil		pH
Solanaceae	Warm	Full Sun	Well-drained, composted, fertile		5.8 to 7.0
Height	Spread	Tolerance	Ease-of-Care	Germination	Emergence
30–90 cm	30–90 cm		Moderately Challenging	18 – 21°C	7–10 days

Pepper plants, part of the Capsicum genus, are a diverse and popular group of vegetables cherished for their vibrant colours and varying heat levels and flavours. These varieties offer unique culinary uses and health benefits, ranging from mild and sweet bell peppers to fiery hot chilli peppers. As warm-season crops, peppers thrive in well-draining, fertile soil, requiring plenty of sunlight and consistent temperatures to flourish. In the UK, pepper plants are typically started indoors and transplanted outside or into a greenhouse once the weather has warmed up. With regular watering, feeding, and staking to support their fruit production, pepper plants can yield a bountiful harvest, adding colour, flavour, and nutritional value to various dishes in British cuisine.

Growing Peppers

Growing peppers in the UK can be a bit more challenging due to the cooler climate, but it is possible with careful planning and the right conditions.

Choose the right variety: Select pepper varieties suitable for the UK climate, such as 'Gypsy', 'Bell Boy', or 'King of the North' for sweet peppers, and 'Apache', 'Hungarian Hot Wax', or 'Jalapeno' for chilli peppers.

Planting time: Start pepper seeds indoors from late winter to early spring (February to March) to give them a head start, as they require a long growing season.

Soil and site: Peppers prefer well-draining, fertile soil with a pH of 5.8 to 7.0. Choose a sunny and sheltered location in your garden or greenhouse, as peppers need warmth and consistent temperatures to thrive.

Preparing the soil: Incorporate organic matter, such as cured compost or well-rotted manure, into the soil to improve its fertility and structure.

Sowing seeds: Sow seeds 6mm deep in seed trays or pots filled with seed compost, and cover lightly with vermiculite or sieved compost. Keep the compost moist and maintain a temperature of 18-21°C for germination.

Transplanting: Once seedlings have at least two sets of true leaves and outdoor temperatures have warmed up (night-time temperatures consistently above 10°C / 50°F), transplant them into their final growing location. Space the plants 45-60 cm (18-24 inches) apart, depending on the variety.

Watering: Keep the soil consistently moist but not waterlogged. Erratic watering can cause issues such as blossom-end rot.

Feeding: Feed pepper plants with a high-potassium liquid fertiliser, such as tomato feed, once the first fruits begin to form.

Support: Stake pepper plants or use small cages to support the weight of the fruit, especially for larger varieties.

Pest and disease control: Monitor your plants for common pests like aphids or diseases like blight, and employ appropriate organic or chemical control methods as needed.

Harvesting: Harvest peppers when they reach the desired size and maturity, typically from mid-summer to early autumn. Picking peppers regularly encourages the production of more fruit.

Potatoes (Solanum tuberosum)

Family	Season	Sun	Soil		pH
Solanaceae	Warm	Full Sun	Well-drained, deep, composted, acidic		5.5 to 6.5
Height	Spread	Tolerance	Ease-of-Care	Germination	Emergence
45-90cm	45-90cm		Easy	10 – 21°C	14–28 days

The potato plant, a member of the Solanaceae family, is one of the most popular and widely consumed vegetables in the UK. Originally from South America, potatoes are cool-season crops

that thrive in cool and moist growing conditions. They are relatively easy to grow in the UK, with seed potatoes planted in the ground or containers in early spring. Potatoes grow best in loose, well-draining soil enriched with organic matter. Indeterminate potato varieties (late-season) should be hilled as they grow to promote more tuber production. Potatoes need regular watering and adequate fertilisation to maximise yield. In the UK, wide potato varieties, including early, second, and maincrop varieties, offer unique texture, taste, and culinary uses.

Growing Potatoes

Choosing the right variety: Choose potato varieties suitable for your soil type, location, and desired use. Popular UK varieties include 'Maris Piper', 'Charlotte', 'Desiree', and 'King Edward'.

Planting time: Plant seed potatoes in mid to late March or April, depending on the variety and location. Early potatoes can be planted in late February or early March.

Soil and site: Potatoes prefer fertile, well-draining soil with a pH of 5.5 to 6.5. Choose a sunny or partially shaded location with good air circulation.

Preparing the soil: Loosen the soil to a depth of at least 30 cm and remove any rocks, weeds, or other debris. Incorporate well-rotted compost or manure to improve the soil's fertility.

Chitting the seed potatoes: Place seed potatoes in a cool, dry, and light place for 4-6 weeks before planting to encourage sprouting.

Planting the seed potatoes: Plant seed potatoes 10 to 15 cm deep and 30-40 cm apart in rows spaced 60 to 90 cm apart. Ensure that the sprouts are facing upwards.

Hilling: As the plants grow, gradually mound soil around the stems to prevent sunlight from reaching the tubers and turning them green. This process also encourages the production of more tubers in indeterminate varieties.

Watering: Keep the soil consistently moist, especially during the tuber formation stage, but avoid overwatering, which can cause rotting. Ensure the buckets or grow bags have adequate drainage if growing in containers.

Pest and disease control: Monitor your plants for common pests like potato beetles or diseases like blight, and employ appropriate organic or chemical control methods as needed.

Harvesting: Harvest potatoes when the leaves start to yellow and die back, typically 10-12 weeks after planting for early varieties and 15 to 20 weeks for maincrop varieties. Carefully dig up the tubers with a fork, taking care not to damage them.

Pumpkin (Cucurbita pepo)

Family	Season	Sun	Soil		pH
Cucurbitaceae	Warm	Full Sun	Well-drained, composted, fertile		5.8 to 6.8
Height	Spread	Tolerance	Ease-of-Care	Germination	Emergence
45-90cm	1.5-4.5m		Easy	15 – 40°C	5–10 days

The pumpkin plant, part of the Cucurbitaceae family, is a popular and versatile vegetable in the UK. With its bright orange colour and sweet flavour, pumpkin is commonly used in soups, stews, pies, and other baked goods. In the UK, pumpkins are typically grown as an autumn crop, planted in late May or early June and harvested in September or October. They require well-draining, fertile soil and plenty of sunlight to thrive. Pumpkin plants are heavy feeders, so it's important to incorporate plenty of organic matter into the soil and fertilise regularly throughout the growing season. They also need consistent watering and protection from pests and diseases like powdery mildew and vine borers. With the right care and attention, pumpkin plants can produce a bountiful harvest, providing a tasty and nutritious addition to any meal.

Growing Pumpkins

Choosing the right variety: Choose pumpkin varieties suitable for your location and desired use. Popular UK varieties include 'Atlantic Giant', 'Jack O'Lantern', 'Crown Prince', and 'Cinderella'.

Planting time: Plant pumpkin seeds in late May or early June, when the soil has warmed up to above 15°C, and there's no more risk of frost.

Soil and site: Pumpkins prefer well-draining, fertile soil with a pH of 6.0 to 7.0. Choose a sunny location with plenty of space, as pumpkin plants can spread up to 3 metres in diameter.

Preparing the soil: Loosen the soil to a depth of at least 30 cm and incorporate cured compost or well-rotted manure to improve its fertility.

Sowing seeds: Sow pumpkin seeds 25 mm deep in hills or mounds of soil spaced 1.8 to 2.4 metres apart. Plant 4 to 6 seeds per hill and thin to the two strongest plants after germination.

Watering: Keep the soil consistently moist, but avoid overwatering, which can cause the fruit to split.

Fertilising: Feed pumpkin plants with a balanced fertiliser every two weeks until the fruit starts to form, then switch to a high-potassium fertiliser to encourage fruit development.

Support: Place a bed of straw or a board underneath the developing fruit to prevent rot and keep them off the damp soil. You can also stake the vine to keep it off the ground.

Pest and disease control: Monitor your plants for common pests like aphids or diseases like powdery mildew, and employ appropriate organic or chemical control methods as needed.

Harvesting: Harvest pumpkins when the fruit fully matures, typically from September to November. Cut the fruit off the vine with a sharp knife, leaving at least 5 cm (2 inches) of stem attached.

Radish (Raphanus sativus)

Family	Season	Sun	Soil		pH
Brassicaceae	Cool	Full Sun Part Shade	Well-drained composted, loose		5.8 to 6.8
Height	Spread	Tolerance	Ease-of-Care	Germination	Emergence
15 – 45 cm	13 – 50 cm	Frost	Easy	13 – 29°C	3 – 4 days

Radish plants, a member of the Brassicaceae family, are a fast-growing and popular vegetable in the UK. Known for their crisp texture and spicy flavour, radishes are often enjoyed raw in salads or pickled in sandwiches. Radishes are cool-season crops that are easy to grow, making them an ideal choice for novice gardeners. In the UK, radishes can be grown throughout the year, but they perform best in early spring and autumn when the temperatures are mild. Radishes are a versatile and healthy addition to any meal, providing a burst of flavour and nutrition in British cuisine.

Growing Radish

Choosing the right variety: Choose a radish variety that suits your taste and the season. Some popular UK varieties include 'French Breakfast', 'Cherry Belle', and 'Easter Egg'.

Soil and site: Radishes grow best in fertile, well-draining soil with a pH of 6.0 to 7.0. They prefer cooler temperatures between 10-18°C and thrive in a sunny or partially shaded location.

Planting time: Radishes are cool-season crops and can be sown throughout the year in the UK. For a spring crop, sow the seeds in early March. For an autumn crop, sow the seeds in early August.

Sowing seeds: Sow radish seeds directly into the ground or containers, spacing them 2.5 to 5 cm apart and planting them 32 mm deep. Cover the seeds with soil and water well.

Watering: Keep the soil consistently moist, but avoid overwatering, which can cause the radishes to split.

Thinning: Once the radishes have germinated and grown a few leaves, thin them out to provide enough space for the remaining plants to grow. Leave the strongest seedlings, spacing them 5 to 7.5 cm apart.

Harvesting: Radishes can be harvested in 3-4 weeks after sowing when they reach the desired size. Simply grasp the radish and pull it out of the soil. Radishes can be enjoyed raw, pickled or cooked in various dishes.

Use the fast-germinating radish to remind you where slower germinating seeds have been planted.

Rhubarb (Rheum rhabarbarum)

Family	Season	Sun	Soil	pH
Pologonaceae	Perennial	Full Sun	Well-drained composted, acidic	5.2 to 6.8
Height	**Spread**	**Tolerance**	**Ease-of-Care**	**Germination**
60-90cm	90-120cm	Drought	Easy	Vegetative

		Frost		

Rhubarb, a member of the Polygonaceae family, is a popular perennial vegetable in the UK, grown for its tart stalks used in pies, jams, and other desserts. Rhubarb is a hardy crop that can thrive in cooler climates, making it ideal for growing in the UK. It prefers well-draining, fertile soil with a pH of 5.2 to 6.8 and can be grown in a sunny or partially shaded location. Rhubarb is a nutritious and versatile vegetable that uniquely flavours many British dishes.

Growing Rhubarb

Choose a sunny spot: Rhubarb prefers a sunny spot but can also tolerate some shade. Choose a spot in your garden with at least 6 hours of sunlight daily.

Prepare the soil: Rhubarb likes a well-draining, fertile soil rich in organic matter. Dig in plenty of well-rotted manure or compost before planting.

Plant the crowns: Rhubarb is usually grown from crowns, which are small sections of the plant's root system. Plant the crowns in early spring, spacing them about 90cm apart. Make sure the crowns are planted with the buds just below the soil surface.

Water and feed regularly: Rhubarb needs plenty of water, especially during dry spells. Water the plants regularly and mulch around them to help retain moisture. Feed the plants with a balanced fertilizer in early spring and again in mid-summer.

Harvest carefully: You can start harvesting rhubarb in the second year after planting. Only take a few stems at a time; don't harvest all the stems from a plant at once. Cut the stems off at the base, rather than pulling them, to avoid damaging the plant.

Divide the plants: Rhubarb plants can become overcrowded over time, so dividing them every 4 to 5 years is a good idea. Dig up the plant and divide it into smaller sections, each with at least one healthy bud. Replant the sections in fresh soil.

Spring Onions (Allium fistulosum)

Family Liliaceae	Season Cool	Sun Full Sun Part Shade	Soil Well-drained, fertile, composted, moist		pH 6.0 to 7.0
Height 30-90 cm	Spread 15–30 cm	Tolerance Frost	Ease-of-Care Moderately Challenging	Germination 7 – 40°C	Emergence 4–5 days

Spring onions, also known as scallions or green onions, are a popular and versatile vegetable that can be easily grown in the UK. They are a staple ingredient in many dishes, adding a mild, fresh flavour and a delightful crunch. These hardy, cool-season plants are simple to cultivate, making them an excellent choice for novice and experienced gardeners. As they require only a small amount of space and have a relatively short growing season, spring onions are perfect for gardens of all sizes and container gardening. Embraced by chefs and home cooks alike, spring onions are a must-have addition to any British kitchen garden.

Growing Spring Onions

Choose the right variety: Select spring onion varieties well-suited to the UK climate, such as 'White Lisbon', 'Ishikura', 'Guardsman', or 'Performer'. These varieties are known for their cold tolerance and excellent flavour.

Prepare the soil: Spring onions prefer well-drained, fertile soil with a pH of 6.0 to 7.0. Work in plenty of well-rotted organic matter or compost to improve soil structure and fertility.

Sow seeds: You can sow spring onion seeds directly outdoors from March to August or earlier if you're using a cold frame or greenhouse. Sow seeds thinly, around 10 mm, and 10 mm apart in rows spaced 15 to 20 cm apart.

Watering: Keep the soil consistently moist but not waterlogged. Consistent moisture is essential for the steady growth of spring onions and helps prevent bolting (when the plant starts producing flowers and seeds).

Weed control: Regularly weed around the plants to reduce competition for nutrients and water. Be careful not to disturb the shallow roots of the spring onions while weeding.

Thinning and harvesting: As spring onions grow, thin them out to a spacing of 2.5 to 5 cm apart. This will give the remaining plants room to grow and provide you with a harvest of small, tender spring onions. You can harvest spring onions once they have reached pencil thickness, usually 8 to 12 weeks after sowing.

Successional sowing: To ensure a continuous supply of spring onions throughout the growing season, sow seeds every 2 to 4 weeks.

Pest management: Keep an eye out for pests such as onion flies and thrips, and use organic methods to control them if necessary.

Shallots (Allium cepa var. aggregatum)

Family	Season	Sun	Soil		pH
Liliaceae	Cool	Full Sun Part Shade	Well-drained, fertile, composted, moist		6.0 to 7.0
Height	Spread	Tolerance	Ease-of-Care	Germination	Emergence
30-90 cm	15–30 cm	Frost	Moderately Challenging	Moderately Challenging	4–5 days

Shallots, cherished for their delicate, sweet flavour, are a favourite among British gardeners and a delightful addition to any kitchen garden. Closely related to onions and garlic, these versatile bulbs bring a subtle complexity to several dishes. Growing shallots in the UK is a rewarding and manageable endeavour, as they are well-adapted to the country's climate and require minimal maintenance. By cultivating shallots in your garden, you'll have access to a gourmet ingredient that enhances your culinary creations and adds a touch of sophistication to your homegrown produce.

Growing Shallots

Choose the right variety: Select shallot varieties well-suited to the UK climate, such as 'Golden Gourmet', 'Jermor', 'Red Sun', or 'Echalote Grise'. These varieties are known for their hardiness, good storage potential, and excellent taste.

Prepare the soil: Shallots prefer well-drained, fertile soil with a pH of 6.0 to 7.0. Incorporate plenty of well-rotted organic matter or compost to improve soil structure and fertility. Avoid planting shallots in areas where you have recently grown onions or other alliums to reduce the disease risk.

Planting: Plant shallot sets (small, immature bulbs) in the autumn or spring. Autumn planting (October-November) will give you an earlier harvest, while spring planting (February-March) may produce slightly larger bulbs. Space the sets 15-20 cm apart, with 30 cm between rows. Plant each set with the tip just visible above the soil surface.

Watering: Water shallots consistently during dry spells, but avoid overwatering, which can lead to bulb rot. Shallots have a shallow root system, so keeping the soil consistently moist and not soggy is essential.

Weed control: Regularly weed around the plants to reduce competition for nutrients and water. Be careful not to disturb the shallow roots of the shallots while weeding.

Pest and disease management: Keep an eye out for pests such as onion fly and allium leaf miner, as well as diseases like white rot and downy mildew. Implement good garden hygiene and use organic methods to control pests and diseases.

Harvesting: Shallots are ready to harvest when the foliage has turned yellow and started to fall over, typically around mid-summer for spring-planted sets and early summer for autumn-planted sets. Gently lift the bulbs with a garden fork, being careful not to damage them.

Curing and storage: Allow the harvested shallots to dry and cure in a warm, well-ventilated area for 2 to 3 weeks. Once the foliage is completely dry and the outer skins are papery, trim the roots and tops and store the shallots in a cool, dark, and well-ventilated place. Properly cured shallots can be stored for several months.

Spinach (Spinacia oleracea)

Family	Season	Sun	Soil		pH
Chenoppodiaceae	Cool	Full Sun Part Shade	Well-drained, fertile, composted		6.5 to 7.5
Height	**Spread**	**Tolerance**	**Ease-of-Care**	**Germination**	**Emergence**
15–30 cm	15 cm	Frost	Moderately Challenging	4 – 21°C	6–10 days

Spinach is a leafy green vegetable that belongs to the family of *Chenopodiaceae*. It is native to central and western Asia but has been cultivated and consumed in many parts of the world for centuries. Spinach is rich in iron, vitamin A, vitamin C, and antioxidants and can be eaten raw in salads, cooked in soups, stir-fries, pies, and casseroles, or blended in smoothies and juices.

Growing Spinach

Choose the right variety: Select spinach varieties well-suited to the UK climate, such as 'Medania', 'Apollo', 'Perpetual Spinach', or 'F1 Amazon'. These varieties are known for their cold tolerance, disease resistance, and excellent flavour.

Prepare the soil: Spinach prefers well-drained, fertile soil with a pH of 6.0 to 7.0. Work in plenty of well-rotted organic matter or compost to improve soil structure and fertility.

Sow seeds: Spinach seeds can be sown directly outdoors from March to September. Sow seeds thinly, around 10 mm deep and 5 cm apart in rows spaced 30 cm apart. For an earlier crop, sow seeds indoors in February and transplant seedlings outdoors in March.

Watering: Keep the soil consistently moist but not waterlogged. Consistent moisture is essential for the steady growth of spinach and helps prevent bolting (when the plant starts producing flowers and seeds).

Weed control: Regularly weed around the plants to reduce competition for nutrients and water.

Be careful not to disturb the shallow roots of the spinach while weeding.

Thinning and harvesting: As spinach plants grow, thin them out to a spacing of 15 cm apart. This will give the remaining plants room to grow and provide you with a harvest of tender baby spinach leaves. Begin harvesting spinach when leaves have reached an adequate size, usually 4 to 6 weeks after sowing. Harvest by cutting the outer leaves, allowing the inner leaves to continue growing.

Successional sowing: To ensure a continuous supply of spinach throughout the growing season, sow seeds every 3 to 4 weeks.

Pest management: Keep an eye out for pests such as aphids, slugs, and snails, and use organic methods to control them if necessary.

Disease prevention: Practice crop rotation and avoid planting spinach in the same spot as other goosefoot family plants for at least three years to prevent the buildup of soil-borne diseases.

Squash – Summer (*Cucurbita pepo*)

Family	Season	Sun	Soil		pH
Cucurbiteae	Warm	Full Sun	Well-drained, composted, fertile		6.8 to 7.2
Height and Spread		Tolerance	Ease-of-Care	Germination	Emergence
30 to 180 cm			Easy	18 – 40°C	7–21 days

Summer squash, encompassing a variety of tender and flavoursome vegetables such as courgettes, zucchini, and pattypan squash, is a delightful addition to any garden. These warm-season plants provide a bountiful harvest of colourful and versatile produce, perfect for grilling, sautéing, or adding to salads and stir-fries. With a relatively short growing season and a generous yield, summer squash plants allow gardeners to cultivate a prolific and delicious crop that adds diversity and culinary inspiration to their homegrown vegetable selection.

Select summer squash varieties well-suited to the UK climate, such as 'Harrier', 'Sunbeam', 'Gold Rush', 'Soleil', or 'Scallopini'. These varieties are known for their disease resistance, high yields, and excellent flavour.

Growing Summer Squash

Start seeds indoors: Summer squash requires a warm growing season, so it's best to start seeds indoors in late April to early May. Sow seeds 25 mm deep in individual pots or seed trays filled with well-draining compost. Keep the compost moist and maintain a temperature of 20-25°C.

Harden off seedlings: Once the risk of frost has passed and seedlings have developed two sets of true leaves, harden them off by gradually exposing them to outdoor conditions over 7 to 10 days. This will help them acclimate to the outdoor environment.

Soil preparation: Summer squash prefers well-drained, fertile soil with a pH of 6.0 to 6.8. Incorporate plenty of well-rotted organic matter or compost into the soil to improve its structure and fertility.

Planting out: After hardening off, transplant seedlings into well-prepared soil in a sunny, sheltered location. Space the plants 60 to 90 cm apart in rows spaced 90 to 120 cm apart.

Watering: Water the plants consistently throughout the growing season, ensuring the soil remains moist but not waterlogged. Adequate water is especially important during the flowering and fruit development stages.

Weed control: Regularly weed around the plants to reduce competition for nutrients and water. Be careful not to disturb the shallow roots of the summer squash plants while weeding.

Pest management: Keep an eye out for pests such as aphids, squash bugs, and slugs, and use organic methods to control them if necessary.

Harvesting: Summer squash is usually ready to harvest 50-65 days after sowing when the fruits are still young and tender. Regularly picking the fruits will encourage the plants to produce more. Use a sharp knife or secateurs to cut the fruits from the plants, leaving a short stem attached.

Squash – Winter (Cucurbita maxima, C. pepo, C. moschata)

Family	Season	Sun	Soil		pH
Cucurbiteae	Warm	Full Sun	Well-drained, composted, fertile		6.0 to 6.8
Height and Spread		Tolerance	Ease-of-Care	Germination	Emergence
30 to 180 cm			Easy	15 – 40°C	7–21 days

Winter squash, a diverse group of hardy and flavourful vegetables such as butternut, acorn, and spaghetti squash, offers a delightful addition to any garden. These versatile plants produce a bountiful harvest of nutrient-rich, long-lasting fruits, ideal for hearty autumn and winter dishes. Cultivating winter squash presents a unique opportunity for gardeners to enjoy a seasonal crop that enhances their homegrown vegetable repertoire and adds a touch of warmth and comfort to their culinary creations during the cooler months.

Growing Winter Squash

Choose the right variety: Select winter squash varieties that are well-suited to the UK climate, such as 'Waltham Butternut', 'Sweet Dumpling', 'Crown Prince', or 'Autumn Crown'. These varieties are known for their cold tolerance, disease resistance, and excellent flavour.

Soil preparation: Winter squash prefers well-drained, fertile soil with a pH of 6.0 to 6.8. Incorporate plenty of well-rotted organic matter or compost into the soil to improve its structure and fertility.

Start seeds indoors: Winter squash requires a long growing season, so it's best to start seeds indoors in late April to early May. Sow seeds 25 mm deep in individual pots or seed trays filled with well-draining compost. Keep the compost moist and maintain a temperature of 20 to 25°C.

Harden off seedlings: Once the risk of frost has passed and seedlings have developed two sets of true leaves, harden them off by gradually exposing them to outdoor conditions over 7 to 10 days. This will help them acclimate to the outdoor environment.

Planting out: After hardening off, transplant seedlings into well-prepared soil in a sunny, sheltered location. Space the plants 90 to 120 cm apart in rows spaced 120 to 150 cm apart.

Watering: Water the plants consistently throughout the growing season, ensuring the soil remains moist but not waterlogged. Adequate water is especially important during the flowering and fruit development stages.

Weed control: Regularly weed around the plants to reduce competition for nutrients and water. Be careful not to disturb the shallow roots of the winter squash plants while weeding.

Pest management: Keep an eye out for pests such as aphids, squash bugs, and slugs, and use organic methods to control them if necessary.

Harvesting: Winter squash is usually ready to harvest when the fruits have a hard rind and deep colour, typically 100 to 120 days after sowing. Cut the fruits from the plants using a sharp knife or secateurs, leaving a few inches of stem attached. Allow the harvested squash to cure in a warm, dry place for 10 to 14 days to improve storage life.

Storage: Store cured winter squash in a cool, dry, well-ventilated area with a temperature of 10-15°C. Most varieties will keep for several months when stored correctly.

Swede (Brassica napus var. napobrassica)

Family	Season	Sun	Soil		pH
Brassicaceae	Cool	Full sun, minimal shade	Well-drained composted, moist		6.0 to 7.5
Height	**Spread**	**Tolerance**	**Ease-of-Care**	**Germination**	**Emergence**
60-90cm	60-90cm	Slight Alkalinity, Frost	Moderately Challenging	7 - 29°C	4–7 days

Swede, or rutabaga or yellow turnip, is a root vegetable popular in British cuisine. It is a hardy plant that can withstand cool temperatures and is commonly grown in the UK. The swede has a distinctive yellow flesh and a slightly sweet, earthy flavour. It can be harvested from autumn through to winter and cooked in various ways, including roasted, mashed, or used in soups and stews. Swede is a nutritious vegetable with vitamin C, dietary fibre, and a versatile ingredient in many British dishes..

Growing Rutabaga

Choose the right variety: Select swede varieties suitable for the UK climate, such as 'Marian', 'Invitation', 'Ruby' or 'Brora'. These varieties are known for their resistance to clubroot, a common disease affecting brassicas.

Prepare the soil: Swede prefers well-drained, fertile soil with a pH of 6.0 to 7.5. Dig in plenty of quality aerobic compost to improve soil structure and fertility.

Sow seeds: Sow seeds directly in the ground from late April to mid-June, spacing them about 1.5 to 2 cm apart and 12 mm deep. Thin seedlings to a final spacing of 20 to 25 cm apart once they have developed two true leaves.

Watering: Keep the soil consistently moist but not waterlogged. Watering is especially important during dry spells, as inconsistent moisture levels can lead to woody or split roots.

Weed control: Regularly weed around the plants to reduce competition for nutrients and water. Take care not to damage the shallow root system while weeding.

Pest and disease management: Regularly check for signs of pests, such as flea beetles, aphids, or cabbage root flies, and use organic methods to control them if necessary. To prevent clubroot, practice crop rotation and avoid planting swede in the same spot for at least four years.

Harvesting: Swedes are usually ready to harvest from October to February, depending on when they were sown. The flavour of swede improves after the first frost, as the cold temperatures help to convert the starches into sugars. To harvest, simply lift the roots with a garden fork, taking care not to damage them.

Storage: Swede can be stored for several months in a cool, dark, and well-ventilated place, such as a garage or shed. Alternatively, you can leave them in the ground and cover them with a thick layer of straw or mulch to protect them from frost, then harvest as needed throughout winter.

Swiss Chard (Beta vulgaris var. cicla)

Family	Season	Sun	Soil		pH
Chenopodiaceae	Cool	Full Sun Part Shade	Well-drained sandy loam		6.5 to 7.0
Height	Spread	Tolerance	Ease-of-Care	Germination	Emergence
30 cm	15 cm	Low Fertility	Easy	10 - 29°C	5–8 days

Swiss chard, a vibrant and versatile leafy green, is a delightful addition to any garden. Swiss chard is valued for its nutritional benefits and distinctive, colourful stalks, offering gardeners an attractive and delicious crop that can be harvested throughout the growing season. Easy to cultivate Swiss chard thrive in various conditions, making it an excellent choice for experienced and novice gardeners seeking to diversify their homegrown vegetable selection and enhance their culinary creations with fresh, healthy ingredients.

Growing Swiss Chard

Choose the right variety: Select Swiss chard varieties well-suited to the UK climate, such as 'Bright Lights', 'Fordhook Giant', 'Rhubarb Chard', or 'Perpetual Spinach'. These varieties are known for their cold tolerance, disease resistance, and excellent flavour.

Prepare the soil: Swiss chard prefers well-drained, fertile soil with a pH of 6.0 to 7.0. Work in plenty of well-rotted organic matter or compost to improve soil structure and fertility.

Sow seeds: Swiss chard seeds can be sown directly outdoors from March to August. Sow seeds thinly, around 1.5 cm deep, and 30 cm apart in rows spaced 30 cm apart. For an earlier crop, sow seeds indoors in February and transplant seedlings outdoors in March.

Watering: Keep the soil consistently moist but not waterlogged. Consistent moisture is essential for the steady growth of Swiss chard and helps prevent the leaves from becoming tough.

Weed control: Regularly weed around the plants to reduce competition for nutrients and water. Be careful not to disturb the shallow roots of the Swiss chard while weeding.

Thinning and harvesting: As Swiss chard plants grow, thin them out to a spacing of 15 to 20 cm apart. This will give the remaining plants room to grow and provide you with a harvest of tender baby chard leaves. Begin harvesting Swiss chard when leaves have reached an adequate size, usually 4 to 6 weeks after sowing. Harvest by cutting the outer leaves, allowing the inner leaves to continue growing.

Successional sowing: To ensure a continuous supply of Swiss chard throughout the growing season, sow seeds every 4-6 weeks.

Pest management: Keep an eye out for pests such as aphids, slugs, and snails, and use organic methods to control them if necessary.

Disease prevention: Practice crop rotation and avoid planting Swiss chard in the same spot for at least three years to prevent the buildup of soil-borne diseases.

Tomatoes (Solanum Lycopersicum)

Family	Season	Sun	Soil		pH
Solanaceae	Warm	Full Sun	Well-drained, composted, fertile		6.0 to 6.8
Height and Spread		Ease-of-Care		Germination	Emergence
60 – 180 cm		Moderately challenging		16 – 35°C	6–12 days

Tomato plants, with their vast array of shapes, sizes, and flavours, are a must-have for any British gardener looking to enhance their homegrown produce repertoire. From bite-sized cherry tomatoes to meaty beefsteak varieties, these versatile fruits cater to a wide range of culinary applications and can be grown successfully in the UK's climate. Cultivating tomatoes in the British garden offers gardeners the satisfaction of harvesting their own delicious and fresh produce. It allows them to explore the remarkable diversity of tomato plants, adding colour, flavour, and a touch of Mediterranean charm to their vegetable gardens.

Growing Tomatoes

There is such a wide variety of tomato cultivars that knowledge of the basic categories is important before considering adding tomatoes to your first vegetable garden. Two main categories are important – determinate and indeterminate tomatoes.

Determinate Varieties

Determined tomatoes have a genetically programmed growth restriction, reaching a specific height before flowering and producing fruit all at once. They are great for container plants or in garden settings with limited space since they are compact with bushier growth rather than vining.

- Containers are ideal for growing determinate varieties.
- The plant is smaller and grows at a slower rate.
- Fruit ripens early in the season, producing a large quantity of fruit at once, perfect for processing and storage.
- Little staking or caging is required.
- It's possible to include it in flower gardens.

Indeterminate Varieties

Throughout the growing season, indeterminate tomatoes continue to develop and produce. Indeterminate tomatoes may become fairly substantial bushes if allowed to grow. Throughout the season, they will also require extra staking or caging. The growth pattern on certain indeterminate kinds is so strong that regular wire cages are frequently insufficient.

- Ideal for big, devoted vegetable gardens.
- Plants have a wide spread of growth.
- The fruit matures from early to late in the season, and production continues until frost.
- Large pots may work, but in-ground planting is preferable.
- Ideal for big, devoted vegetable gardens.

Planting Type	Depth	Spacing	Row
Determinate	Sow and lightly cover	12 to 24 inches	5 feet
Indeterminate (Staked)	Sow and lightly cover	14 to 20 inches	5 feet
Indeterminate (Unstaked)	Sow and lightly cover	24 to 36 inches	12 feet

Choose the right variety. There are hundreds of tomato varieties to choose from, but not all of them are suitable for the British climate. Some varieties need a long and warm growing season, which is not guaranteed in Britain. Others are more tolerant of cold and wet conditions and can produce a good crop even in a poor summer. Some examples of cold-tolerant varieties are 'Sungold', 'Gardener's Delight', 'Tumbling Tom' and 'Moneymaker'.

Start your seeds early. Tomatoes need a long growing season to ripen their fruits, so starting your seeds indoors in late winter or early spring is advisable. You can sow your seeds in small pots or trays filled with seed compost and place them in a warm and sunny spot, such as a windowsill or a heated propagator. Keep the compost moist but not soggy, and transplant the seedlings into larger pots when they have two sets of true leaves.

Harden off your plants. Before planting your tomatoes outdoors, you must acclimate them to the outside conditions. This process is called hardening off, and it involves gradually exposing your plants to lower temperatures and more sunlight for one to two weeks. You can start by placing your plants outside during the day and bringing them back indoors at night. Then, you can leave them outside for longer periods until they are ready to be planted out.

Plant your tomatoes in a sunny and sheltered spot. Tomatoes need at least six hours of direct sunlight daily to produce a good crop. They also need protection from strong winds and heavy rain, which can damage their stems and fruits. Choose a sunny and sheltered spot in your garden, or use a greenhouse, polytunnel or cloche if you have one. You can also grow tomatoes in pots or containers on a sunny patio or balcony, if you water them regularly and feed them with a high-potash fertiliser every week.

Support your plants. Tomatoes are either determinate or indeterminate, depending on how they grow. Determinate tomatoes grow to a certain height and stop, producing all their fruits simultaneously. Indeterminate tomatoes keep growing and producing fruits until they are killed by frost or disease. Determinate tomatoes do not need much support, but indeterminate tomatoes need to be staked or tied to a trellis or cage to prevent them from collapsing under their own weight. It would be best if you also pinched out the side shoots that grow between the main stem and the branches, as they will divert energy from the fruits.

Harvest your tomatoes. Tomatoes are ready to harvest when fully coloured and firm to the touch. You can pick them individually as they ripen or cut off the whole truss if you want to ripen them indoors. You can store your tomatoes at room temperature for up to a week or freeze them for longer storage. You can also make tomato sauce, salsa, chutney or ketchup with your surplus tomatoes.

Excessive nitrogen treatment might result in excessive foliage and a poor fruit set. Also, avoid applying fresh manure or fertilizers with a high nitrogen content (three times more nitrogen than phosphorus or potassium). Heavy rain or temperatures that are either too warm (above 32°C) or too low (below 4°C) can also induce a poor fruit set (below 13°F).

When the fruits are approximately 1 inch in diameter and harvest begins, side-dress about half a cup of 5-10-5 per plant worked shallowly into the top inch of soil.

Potential Challenges to Growing Tomatoes

A typical tomato challenge to avoid is blossom end rot – keep the soil equally wet. This can also help avoid cracking when fruit absorbs too much water after a hard rain after a drought. Leaves that shade the fruit and prevent sunscald should not be removed. Due to cold weather, incomplete pollination causes catfacing (misshaped, malformed fruit). Wait until the weather has settled and the soil is warm before transplanting.

Turnip (Brassica rapa)

Family		Season	Sun	Soil		pH
Brassicaceae		Cool	Full Sun Min. Shade	Well-drained composted, moist		6.0 to 7.5
Height and Spread			Tolerance	Ease-of-Care	Germination	Emergence
60-90cm			Slight Alkalinity, Frost	Easy	7 - 29°C	4–7 days

With their versatile and nutritious roots and leafy greens, turnip plants are a fantastic addition to any garden. These cool-season crops are well-suited to the UK's climate and can be grown for their tender roots and vitamin-rich leaves. Cultivating turnips offers gardeners a reliable and rewarding experience, allowing them to enjoy the benefits of homegrown produce that can be used in various culinary applications, from hearty stews to delicious side dishes. Turnips provide a valuable opportunity for gardeners to grow a versatile, cold-tolerant vegetable that can be harvested throughout the year, enriching their garden and kitchen.

Growing Turnips

Choose the right variety: Select turnip varieties well-suited to the UK climate, such as 'Milan Purple Top', 'Snowball', 'Golden Ball', or 'Tokyo Cross'. These varieties are known for their cold tolerance, disease resistance, and excellent flavour.

Prepare the soil: Turnips prefer well-drained, fertile soil with a pH of 6.0 to 7.5. Work in plenty of well-rotted manure or cured compost to improve soil structure and fertility.

Sow seeds: Turnip seeds can be sown directly outdoors from March to August. Sow seeds thinly, around 1 cm deep, and 15 cm apart in rows spaced 30 cm apart. For an earlier crop, sow seeds indoors in February and transplant seedlings outdoors in March.

Watering: Keep the soil consistently moist but not waterlogged. Consistent moisture is essential for the steady growth of turnips and helps prevent the roots from becoming tough or woody.

Weed control: Regularly weed around the plants to reduce competition for nutrients and water. Be careful not to disturb the shallow roots of the turnips while weeding.

Thinning and harvesting: As turnip plants grow, thin them out to a spacing of 10 to 15 cm apart. This will give the remaining plants room to grow and provide you with a harvest of tender baby turnip leaves. Begin harvesting turnip roots when they have reached an adequate size, usually 5 to 7 cm in diameter, around 8 to 10 weeks after sowing. Harvest turnip leaves as needed, cutting the outer leaves and allowing the inner leaves to continue growing.

Successional sowing: To ensure a continuous supply of turnips throughout the growing season, sow seeds every 2 to 3 weeks.

Pest management: Keep an eye out for pests such as aphids, flea beetles, cutworms, and root maggots, and use organic methods to control them if necessary.

Disease prevention: Practice crop rotation and avoid planting turnips in the same spot as other brassica crops for at least three years to prevent the buildup of soil-borne diseases.

Watermelon (Citrullus lanatus)

Family	Season	Sun	Soil	pH

Cucurbiteae	Warm	Full Sun	Well-drained, composted, fertile		6.5 to 7.5
Height 30 – 90 cm	Spread 1 – 6m	Tolerance	Ease-of-Care Challenging	Germination 21 – 35°C	Emergence 3–5 days

Although traditionally associated with warmer climates, watermelon plants can be a delightful and adventurous addition to any British gardener's repertoire. With the right variety and care, these luscious, juicy fruits can be cultivated in the UK, allowing gardeners to enjoy the refreshing taste of homegrown watermelons throughout the summer months. Embracing the challenge of growing watermelons in the British climate not only adds a touch of the exotic to a gardener's collection but also provides a rewarding and satisfying experience, resulting in an impressive and tasty harvest that can be shared with friends and family.

Growing Watermelon

Choose the right variety: Select watermelon varieties well-suited to the UK climate, such as 'Sugar Baby', 'Quetzali', 'Crimson Sweet', or 'Blacktail Mountain'. These varieties are known for their early maturation, cold tolerance, and excellent flavour.

Start seeds indoors: Watermelon seeds should be sown indoors in late April to early May, about 4-6 weeks before the last expected frost. Sow seeds 1 to 2 cm deep in seed trays or individual pots filled with well-draining compost. Keep the compost moist and maintain a temperature of 21 to 27°C.

Harden off seedlings: Once the risk of frost has passed and seedlings have developed two sets of true leaves, harden them off by gradually exposing them to outdoor conditions over 7-10 days. This will help them acclimate to the outdoor environment.

Soil preparation: Watermelons prefer well-drained, fertile soil with a pH of 6.5 to 7.5. Incorporate plenty of well-rotted organic matter or compost into the soil to improve its structure and fertility.

Planting out: After hardening off, transplant seedlings into well-prepared soil in a sunny, sheltered location. Space the plants at least 90 cm apart in rows spaced 1.5 m apart.

Mulching: Use a layer of black plastic mulch or a thick layer of organic mulch to help retain soil moisture, suppress weeds, and keep the developing fruits clean.

Watering: Water the plants consistently throughout the growing season, ensuring the soil remains moist but not waterlogged. Consistent watering is crucial for preventing fruit cracking and blossom end rot.

Feeding: Apply a balanced liquid fertilizer every 2 to 3 weeks once the first fruits form, switching to a high-potassium fertilizer as the fruits ripen.

Support: As the vines grow, you may need to provide support to keep the developing fruits off the ground. This can be done with slings made of soft cloth or netting.

Pest management: Keep an eye out for pests such as aphids, whiteflies, and cucumber beetles, and use organic methods to control them if necessary.

Disease prevention: Practice crop rotation and avoid planting watermelons in the same spot for at least three years to prevent the buildup of soil-borne diseases. Keep the foliage dry by watering at the base of the plant, and ensure proper spacing for good air circulation.

Harvesting: Watermelons are usually ready to harvest when the tendril nearest the fruit turns brown and dries up. The fruit has a dull surface, and the bottom, where the fruit touches the ground, changes from white to cream or yellow. Gently tap the fruit and listen for a deep, hollow sound, another indication of ripeness.

CHAPTER 8

GROWING HERBS

Herbs are plant leaves, whereas spices are non-leafy portions such as seeds, berries, roots, and bark. Some plants are classified as both herbs and spices. Cilantro and dill leaves, for example, are herbs, whereas their seeds are spices (e.g. coriander and dill seed).

Basil (Ocimum spp.)

Basil is a fragrant, spicy-tasting warm-season plant. Basil comes in a variety of sizes, colours, and flavours. While sweet basil is the most prevalent, there are also Thai, purple, cinnamon, lemon, and other types. African blue basil has a lot of blossoms that attract pollinators, but the flavour isn't very good. From early spring through late autumn, plant basil transplants or seeds, pinch off, and utilize the delicious stem tips as they develop. This will promote branching and leaf growth. Remove any flower spikes that appear, or the leaves will lose their taste. The fragile leaves can be utilized fresh or dried at any time. Basil loves damp (but not soggy) soil and modest fertilizer treatments periodically. Cuttings are simple to root. In the South, Basil Downy Mildew is a severe fungal disease. Choose disease-resistant cultivars like Amazel Basil, Pesto Besto, and others.

Fresh basil should be stored in a cool but not cold environment since the leaves brown below 4°C. Basil keeps best in vinegar or other liquids since it neither freezes nor dries well. Purple basil will colour white wine vinegar maroon. In salsa and pesto, use vinegar instead of fresh basil. Drying basil between layers of coarse salt produces flavorful salt (after the basil is dried and brown, remove it).

Bay Leaf (Laurus nobilis)

To successfully grow bay leaves in the UK, select a sheltered location that receives partial to full sunlight. Bay laurel prefers well-draining soil with a pH between 6.0 and 7.0, so amend the soil with compost or organic matter if necessary to improve its fertility and structure. Plant bay laurel either in the ground or in a container, allowing adequate space for the plant to grow, as it can reach heights of up to 7.5 metres when grown outdoors, though it can be pruned to maintain a smaller size.

Water bay laurel plants moderately, ensuring the soil remains consistently moist but not soggy. As the plants establish themselves, reduce the watering frequency, as bay laurel can tolerate some drought once established. During winter, protect your bay laurel plants from harsh frosts by wrapping them in horticultural fleece or moving potted plants into a greenhouse or conservatory.

Borage (Borago officinalis)

To successfully grow borage, choose a location with well-draining soil that receives full sun to partial shade. Borage tolerates various soil types but prefers a slightly alkaline pH between 6.0 and 7.0. Sow borage seeds directly outdoors in spring or early summer after the risk of frost has passed, spacing them about 30 cm apart. Borage seeds can also be sown in autumn for an early spring display. The seeds should germinate within 7 to 14 days, depending on soil temperature and moisture.

Borage requires minimal maintenance once established, as it is relatively drought-tolerant and self-seeding. Water the plants consistently during dry spells, ensuring the soil remains moist but not soggy. Borage has few pest issues, although aphids can occasionally be a problem, which can be controlled using organic methods.

As borage can grow up to 60 to 90 cm tall, it may require support in windy locations. Borage flowers are a magnet for pollinators, such as bees and butterflies, which can benefit your garden's overall health and productivity. Harvest borage leaves and flowers as needed throughout the growing season, using them fresh in salads, soups, or as a garnish for drinks, and enjoy the unique flavour and visual appeal that this herb brings to your garden and kitchen.

Cardamom (Elettaria cardamomum)

Cardamom is native to the humid forests of southern India and requires specific growing conditions that differ from the UK's temperate climate. However, with a bit of dedication and the right care, it is possible to cultivate cardamom in the UK, allowing gardeners to enjoy the unique and aromatic flavour of homegrown cardamom pods in their culinary creations.

To successfully grow cardamom in the UK, it is crucial to recreate the plant's natural environment as closely as possible. Cardamom thrives in warm, humid conditions with filtered sunlight, making it an ideal candidate for greenhouse or conservatory cultivation. Plant cardamom rhizomes in pots filled with a well-draining, fertile potting mix and maintain a consistent temperature of 15-25°C (59-77°F) with high humidity. A humidifier can be used to increase the humidity levels if necessary. Ensure the potting mix remains consistently moist but not waterlogged, as cardamom plants are sensitive to both drought and overwatering.

Cardamom plants can grow up to 2-3 metres (6-10 feet) tall, so ensure they have adequate space to develop. During the growing season, feed cardamom plants with a balanced liquid fertilizer every 4-6 weeks to support their growth. Cardamom plants are relatively pest-free, but monitoring them for signs of aphids, spider mites, or fungal diseases is essential, and using organic methods for control is necessary.

It can take two to three years for cardamom plants to mature and produce flowers, eventually developing into the prized cardamom pods. Harvest the pods when they turn a pale green or begin to split, then dry them in a well-ventilated area for several days before storing them in airtight containers.

Chervil (Anthriscus cerefolium)

Growing chervil can be a delightful and easy endeavour for UK gardeners, as this delicate and aromatic herb thrives in the country's temperate climate. Chervil, a parsley family member, is often used in French cuisine and provides a subtle aniseed flavour to various dishes. With its finely divided, fern-like leaves and small white flowers, chervil adds a lovely touch to any garden. Its culinary versatility makes it valuable to a gardener's herb collection.

To successfully grow chervil, select a location with well-draining soil that receives partial shade, as chervil prefers cooler conditions and may bolt (produce flowers and seeds prematurely) if exposed to too much sunlight or heat. Chervil grows best in slightly alkaline soil with a pH between 6.5 and 7.5, so amend the soil with compost or organic matter if necessary to improve its fertility and structure.

Sow chervil seeds directly outdoors in spring or autumn, spacing them about 15 cm (6 inches) apart. Chervil can also be sown in succession every 2-3 weeks during the growing season to ensure a continuous supply of fresh leaves. Depending on soil temperature and moisture, the seeds should germinate within 10-14 days.

Chervil requires minimal maintenance once established, as it is relatively drought-tolerant and self-seeding. Water the plants consistently during dry spells, ensuring the soil remains moist but not soggy. Chervil has few pest issues, although aphids and slugs can occasionally be a problem, in which case they can be controlled using organic methods.

Harvest chervil leaves as needed throughout the growing season, preferably in the morning when the plant's aromatic oils are most concentrated. Use chervil leaves fresh, as their delicate flavour does not hold up well to drying or prolonged cooking. Enjoy this herb's unique flavour and visual appeal to your garden and kitchen.

Coriander (Coriandrum sativum)

Growing coriander, also known as Coriandrum sativum or cilantro, can be an enjoyable and rewarding experience for gardeners, as this versatile and aromatic herb offers culinary and medicinal benefits. Widely used in various global cuisines, coriander provides a distinct and vibrant flavour to dishes, with its leaves, seeds, and roots all edible. Its delicate, feathery leaves and small white or pale pink flowers also add a touch of visual appeal to any garden, making coriander an attractive and useful addition to a gardener's herb collection.

To successfully grow coriander in the UK, choose a location with well-draining soil that receives full sun to light shade. Coriander prefers neutral to slightly alkaline soil with a pH between 6.0 and 7.5, so amend the soil with compost or organic matter if necessary to improve its fertility and structure. Coriander can be grown either in the ground or in containers, which can be especially useful for controlling its growth and preventing it from becoming invasive.

Sow coriander seeds directly outdoors in spring or early summer once the risk of frost has passed, spacing them about 20 cm (8 inches) apart. Coriander can also be sown in succession every 3-4 weeks during the growing season to ensure a continuous supply of fresh leaves. The seeds should germinate within 7-10 days, depending on soil temperature and moisture.

Coriander requires moderate maintenance, as it is sensitive to both overwatering and drought. Water the plants consistently, ensuring the soil remains moist but not soggy. Coriander can be prone to bolting, especially in hot weather, so regular watering and shade during the hottest part of the day can help delay this process. Coriander has few pest issues, although aphids can occasionally be a problem, which can be controlled using organic methods.

Harvest coriander leaves as needed throughout the growing season, preferably in the morning when the plant's aromatic oils are most concentrated. Coriander seeds can be harvested when they turn brown and become fragrant, usually a few weeks after blooming. Enjoy this herb's unique flavour and visual appeal to your garden and kitchen.

Culantro (Eryngium foetidum)

Growing culantro, also known as long coriander, can be a fascinating and rewarding experience for UK gardeners, as this lesser-known aromatic herb offers unique culinary benefits. Culantro, native to the Caribbean and Central America, has a similar flavour profile to coriander (cilantro) but with a more intense and robust taste. Its elongated, serrated leaves and small white flowers make culantro an interesting addition to the garden. Its distinctive taste lends a bold flavour to various dishes, especially Caribbean, Latin American, and Asian cuisine.

To successfully grow culantro in the UK, choose a location with well-draining soil that receives partial to full sunlight, as culantro prefers warmth and humidity. However, it can tolerate light shade and still produce a respectable harvest. Culantro grows best in fertile, slightly acidic soil with a pH between 5.5 and 6.5, so amend the soil with compost or organic matter if necessary to improve its fertility and structure.

Sow culantro seeds indoors in late winter or early spring, and transplant the seedlings outdoors after the risk of frost has passed, spacing them about 20 cm (8 inches) apart. Culantro can also be sown directly outdoors in the UK, but germination may take longer, especially if the soil temperatures are cool. Depending on soil temperature and moisture, the seeds should germinate within 14-21 days.

Culantro requires moderate maintenance once established. Water the plants consistently, ensuring the soil remains moist but not soggy. Culantro can be prone to bolting, especially in hot weather, so regular watering and shade during the hottest part of the day can help delay this process. Culantro has few pest issues, although aphids and slugs can occasionally be a problem, in which case they can be controlled using organic methods.

Harvest culantro leaves as needed throughout the growing season, preferably in the morning when the plant's aromatic oils are most concentrated. Use culantro leaves fresh or frozen, as their intense flavour does not hold up well to drying. Enjoy this herb's unique taste and visual appeal to your garden and kitchen.

Dill (Anethum graveolens)

Growing dill, also known as Anethum graveolens, can be a delightful and easy experience for UK gardeners, as this aromatic and versatile herb thrives in the country's temperate climate. Dill is widely used in various global cuisines, particularly in European and Asian dishes, offering recipes a fresh and slightly tangy flavour. With its feathery green leaves, slender stems, and yellow umbrella-like flowers, dill adds an attractive touch to any garden, making it a valuable addition to a gardener's herb collection.

To successfully grow dill in the UK, choose a location with well-draining soil that receives full sun, as dill prefers a minimum of six hours of sunlight per day. Dill grows best in fertile, loamy soil with a slightly acidic to neutral pH between 6.0 and 7.5, so amend the soil with compost or organic matter if necessary to improve its fertility and structure.

Sow dill seeds directly outdoors in spring or early summer once the risk of frost has passed, spacing them about 30 cm (12 inches) apart. Dill can also be sown in succession every 3-4 weeks during the growing season to ensure a continuous supply of fresh leaves. Depending on soil temperature and moisture, the seeds should germinate within 10-14 days.

Dill requires minimal maintenance once established, as it is relatively drought-tolerant and self-seeding. Water the plants consistently during dry spells, ensuring the soil remains moist but not soggy. Dill has few pest issues, although aphids and caterpillars can occasionally be a problem, in which case they can be controlled using organic methods.

Harvest dill leaves as needed throughout the growing season, preferably in the morning when the plant's aromatic oils are most concentrated. Dill seeds can be harvested when they turn brown and become fragrant, usually a few weeks after blooming. Enjoy this herb's unique flavour and visual appeal to your garden and kitchen.

Fennel (Foeniculum vulgare dulce)

To successfully grow fennel in the UK, choose a location with well-draining soil that receives full sun, as fennel prefers a minimum of six hours of sunlight per day. Fennel grows best in fertile, loamy soil with a slightly acidic to neutral pH between 6.0 and 7.5, so amend the soil with compost or organic matter if necessary to improve its fertility and structure.

Sow fennel seeds directly outdoors in spring or early summer once the risk of frost has passed, spacing them about 30-45 cm (12-18 inches) apart. Fennel can also be started indoors and transplanted outdoors when the seedlings are about 10-15 cm (4-6 inches) tall. The seeds should germinate within 10-14 days, depending on soil temperature and moisture.

Fennel requires moderate maintenance once established. Water the plants consistently, ensuring the soil remains moist but not waterlogged. If you're growing fennel for its edible bulb (Florence fennel), it's crucial to keep the soil consistently moist, as fluctuations in moisture can cause the bulbs to split. Fennel has few pest issues, although aphids and caterpillars can occasionally be a problem, in which case they can be controlled using organic methods.

Harvest fennel leaves as needed throughout the growing season, preferably in the morning when the plant's aromatic oils are most concentrated. For bulb fennel, harvest the bulbs when they reach the desired size, typically about 7-10 cm (3-4 inches) in diameter. Fennel seeds can be harvested when they turn brown and become fragrant, usually a few weeks after the flowers have bloomed. Enjoy the unique flavour and visual appeal that this herb brings to your garden and kitchen.

Ginger (Zingiber officinale)

To successfully grow ginger in the UK, it's best to plant it in a container, as the country's climate is not ideal for growing ginger directly in the ground. This approach allows you to move the plant indoors during colder months and control its growing conditions more effectively. Ginger thrives in well-draining, rich, loamy soil with a slightly acidic to neutral pH between 6.0 and 7.0. Amend the soil with compost or organic matter to improve its fertility and structure.

Start by sourcing a healthy, plump ginger rhizome from a garden centre or an organic grocery store. Soak the rhizome in water for a few hours before planting. Plant the ginger rhizome in late winter or early spring, placing it about 2.5 to 5 cm (1-2 inches) deep in a pot filled with well-draining soil. Ensure the pot is at least 30 cm (12 inches) in diameter, as ginger roots can spread out considerably.

Place the pot in a warm, sheltered spot that receives indirect sunlight, as ginger prefers temperatures between 22 to 25°C (72-77°F) and can be sensitive to direct sunlight. Water the plant consistently, ensuring the soil remains moist but not waterlogged. Ginger has few pest issues, although aphids, spider mites, and mealybugs can occasionally be a problem, in which case they can be controlled using organic methods.

Harvest ginger rhizomes as needed, approximately 8-10 months after planting, when the leaves start to die back. Use a small hand trowel or your fingers to gently remove the outer parts of the rhizome, taking care not to damage the central portion, which can continue to grow. Enjoy this plant's unique flavour and visual appeal to your garden and kitchen.

Lemon Balm (Melissa officinalis)

Lemon balm thrives in the United Kingdom's climate, but you need to choose a location with well-draining soil that receives partial to full sun, as lemon balm can tolerate some shade but prefers a minimum of four hours of sunlight per day. Lemon balm grows best in fertile, loamy soil with a neutral to slightly acidic pH between 6.0 and 7.5, so amend the soil with compost or organic matter if necessary to improve its fertility and structure.

Sow lemon balm seeds indoors in late winter or early spring using seed trays filled with well-draining seed compost. Alternatively, you can purchase young lemon balm plants from a garden centre and transplant them outdoors after the risk of frost has passed. Space the plants about 45-60 cm (18-24 inches) apart, ensuring they have enough room to grow and spread.

Lemon balm requires moderate maintenance once established, as it can be quite vigorous and may become invasive if left unchecked. Water the plants consistently, ensuring the soil remains moist but not waterlogged. Lemon balm has few pest issues, although aphids can occasionally be a problem, in which case they can be controlled using organic methods.

Harvest lemon balm leaves as needed throughout the growing season, preferably in the morning when the plant's aromatic oils are most concentrated. The leaves can be used fresh or dried in various culinary, medicinal, and cosmetic applications, including teas, salads, and skin care products.

Lemongrass (Cymbopogon citratus)

Lemongrass, native to Southeast Asia, is a key ingredient in many Asian and Caribbean dishes, providing a fresh, tangy, lemony flavour. With its tall, slender green leaves and attractive appearance, lemongrass adds an exotic touch to any garden or indoor space, making it a valuable addition to a gardener's plant collection.

It's best to plant Lemongrass in a container, as the country's climate is not ideal for growing it directly in the ground. This approach allows you to move the plant indoors during colder months and control its growing conditions more effectively. Lemongrass thrives in well-draining, fertile, loamy soil with a slightly acidic to neutral pH between 6.0 and 7.5. Amend the soil with compost or organic matter to improve its fertility and structure.

Start by sourcing healthy, fresh lemongrass stalks from a garden centre or an organic grocery store. Plant the stalks in late spring or early summer, placing them about 2.5 cm (1 inch) deep in a pot filled with well-draining soil. Ensure the pot is at least 30 cm (12 inches) in diameter, as lemongrass roots can spread out considerably.

Place the pot in a warm, sheltered spot that receives full sun, as lemongrass prefers a minimum of six hours of sunlight daily and temperatures between 20-30°C (68-86°F). Water the plant consistently, ensuring the soil remains moist but not waterlogged. Lemongrass has few pest issues, although spider mites and aphids can occasionally be a problem, in which case they can be controlled using organic methods.

Harvest lemongrass stalks as needed, approximately 3-4 months after planting, when the plant is well-established and has developed a strong root system. Use a sharp knife or pruning shears to cut the stalks near the base of the plant, leaving at least 5 cm (2 inches) above the soil to encourage regrowth. Enjoy this plant's unique flavour and visual appeal to your garden and kitchen.

Lemon Verbena (*Aloysia triphylla*)

Growing lemon verbena is a delightful and rewarding experience for gardeners, as this fragrant and versatile herb offers exceptional culinary and medicinal benefits. Lemon verbena is cherished for its lemon-scented leaves, which have a range of applications, including teas, desserts, and potpourri. With its slender, pointed green leaves and delicate white or pale purple flowers, lemon verbena adds an elegant touch to any garden, making it a valuable addition to a gardener's herb collection.

To grow lemon verbena in the UK, it's best to plant it in a container, as the country's climate is not ideal for growing this tender perennial directly in the ground. This approach allows you to move the plant indoors during colder months and control its growing conditions more effectively. Lemon verbena thrives in well-draining, fertile, loamy soil with a neutral to slightly acidic pH between 6.0 and 7.5. Amend the soil with compost or organic matter to improve its fertility and structure.

Start by sourcing healthy, young lemon verbena plants from a garden centre or nursery, as growing from seed can be challenging. Plant the lemon verbena in late spring or early summer after the risk of frost has passed. Ensure the pot is at least 30 cm (12 inches) in diameter, as lemon verbena can grow up to 1.5-3 meters (5-10 feet) tall, depending on the variety.

Place the pot in a warm, sheltered spot that receives full sun, as lemon verbena prefers a minimum of six hours of sunlight per day and temperatures between 15-25°C (59-77°F). Water the plant consistently, ensuring the soil remains moist but not waterlogged. Lemon verbena has few pest issues, although aphids and spider mites can occasionally be a problem, in which case they can be controlled using organic methods.

Harvest lemon verbena leaves as needed throughout the growing season, preferably in the morning when the plant's aromatic oils are most concentrated. The leaves can be used fresh or dried in various culinary, medicinal, and cosmetic applications, including teas, infused oils, and skin care products.

Lovage (Levisticum officinale)

Lovage is well-suited to the UK's temperate climate. Lovage is valued for its celery-like flavour and aroma, which can be found in its leaves, stems, and seeds, making it a versatile addition to various culinary dishes such as soups, salads, and stews. With its vibrant green foliage, umbels of small yellow flowers, and its ability to grow up to 1.5-2.5 meters (5-8 feet) tall, lovage adds a striking presence to any garden, making it a valuable addition to a gardener's herb collection.

To successfully grow lovage in the UK, choose a location with well-draining soil that receives full sun to partial shade, as lovage can tolerate some shade but prefers a minimum of four hours of sunlight per day. Lovage grows best in fertile, loamy soil with a neutral to slightly acidic pH between 6.0 and 7.5, so amend the soil with compost or organic matter if necessary to improve its fertility and structure.

Sow lovage seeds indoors in late winter or early spring using seed trays filled with well-draining seed compost. Alternatively, you can purchase young lovage plants from a garden centre and transplant them outdoors after the risk of frost has passed. Space the plants about 60-90 cm (24-36 inches) apart, ensuring they have enough room to grow and spread.

Lovage is relatively low maintenance once established, as it is drought-tolerant and has few pest issues. Water the plants consistently, ensuring the soil remains moist but not waterlogged. Keep an eye out for aphids and caterpillars, which can occasionally be a problem, and treat them using organic methods if necessary.

Harvest lovage leaves, stems, and seeds as needed throughout the growing season. The leaves and stems can be used fresh or dried in various culinary dishes, while the seeds can be dried and used as a spice. Lovage is also thought to have medicinal properties, such as aiding digestion and alleviating respiratory issues.

Marjoram (Origanum majorana)

This aromatic and versatile herb thrives in the UK’s temperate climate. Marjoram is prized for its sweet, slightly spicy flavour and aroma, which make it a popular addition to various culinary dishes such as soups, sauces, and meat dishes. With its delicate green foliage and clusters of small white or pale pink flowers, marjoram adds an elegant touch to any garden, making it a valuable addition to a gardener's herb collection.

Choose a location with well-draining soil that receives full sun, as marjoram prefers a minimum of six hours of sunlight per day. Marjoram grows best in fertile, loamy soil with a neutral to slightly alkaline pH between 6.5 and 7.5, so amend the soil with compost or organic matter if necessary to improve its fertility and structure.

Sow marjoram seeds indoors in late winter or early spring, using seed trays filled with well-draining seed compost. Alternatively, you can purchase young marjoram plants from a garden centre and transplant them outdoors after the risk of frost has passed. Space the plants about 20-30 cm (8-12 inches) apart, ensuring they have enough room to grow and spread.

Marjoram is relatively low maintenance once established, as it is drought-tolerant and has few pest issues. Water the plants consistently, ensuring the soil remains moist but not waterlogged. Keep an eye out for aphids and spider mites, which can occasionally be a problem, and treat them using organic methods if necessary.

Harvest marjoram leaves and flowers as needed throughout the growing season, preferably in the morning when the plant's aromatic oils are most concentrated. The leaves and flowers can be used fresh or dried in various culinary dishes, and marjoram is also thought to have medicinal properties, such as aiding digestion and soothing anxiety.

Oregano (Origanum vulgare)

Origanum vulgare thrives in our country's temperate climate. Oregano is prized for its robust, earthy flavour and aroma, making it a popular addition to various culinary dishes, particularly Mediterranean and Italian cuisine. With its small, oval-shaped leaves and clusters of tiny white or pink flowers, oregano adds a charming touch to any garden, making it a valuable addition to a gardener's herb collection.

To successfully grow oregano in the UK, choose a location with well-draining soil that receives full sun, as oregano prefers a minimum of six hours of sunlight per day. Oregano grows best in fertile, loamy soil with a neutral to slightly alkaline pH between 6.5 and 7.5, so amend the soil with compost or organic matter if necessary to improve its fertility and structure.

Sow oregano seeds indoors in late winter or early spring using seed trays filled with a well-draining seed compost. Alternatively, you can purchase young oregano plants from a garden centre and transplant them outdoors after the risk of frost has passed. Space the plants about 30-45 cm (12-18 inches) apart, ensuring they have enough room to grow and spread.

Oregano is relatively low maintenance once established, as it is drought-tolerant and has few pest issues. Water the plants consistently, ensuring the soil remains moist but not waterlogged. Keep an eye out for aphids and spider mites, which can occasionally be a problem, and treat them using organic methods if necessary.

Harvest oregano leaves as needed throughout the growing season, preferably in the morning when the plant's aromatic oils are most concentrated. The leaves can be used fresh or dried in various culinary dishes, and oregano is also thought to have medicinal properties, such as aiding digestion and acting as an antioxidant.

Parsley (Petroselinum hortense, P. crispum)

Parsley is valued for its mild, slightly peppery flavour and attractive, dark green leaves, which make it a popular garnish and addition to various culinary dishes, such as soups, salads, and sauces. With its finely divided, curly or flat leaves and clusters of small, greenish-yellow flowers, parsley adds a fresh touch to any garden, making it a valuable addition to a gardener's herb collection.

To successfully grow parsley in the UK, choose a location with well-draining soil that receives full sun to partial shade, as parsley can tolerate some shade but prefers a minimum of four hours of sunlight per day. Parsley grows best in fertile, loamy soil with a neutral to slightly acidic pH between 6.0 and 7.0, so amend the soil with compost or organic matter if necessary to improve its fertility and structure.

Sow parsley seeds indoors in late winter or early spring, using seed trays filled with a well-draining seed compost. Keep in mind that parsley seeds can take a while to germinate, sometimes up to 3-4 weeks. Alternatively, you can purchase young parsley plants from a garden centre and transplant them outdoors after the risk of frost has passed. Space the plants about 20-30 cm (8-12 inches) apart, ensuring they have enough room to grow and spread.

Parsley is relatively low maintenance once established, as it has few pest issues. Water the plants consistently, ensuring the soil remains moist but not waterlogged. Keep an eye out for aphids and caterpillars, which can occasionally be a problem, and treat them using organic methods if necessary.

Harvest parsley leaves as needed throughout the growing season, starting from the outer leaves and working inwards. The leaves can be used fresh or dried in various culinary dishes, and parsley is also thought to have medicinal properties, such as aiding digestion and supporting kidney health.

Peppermint (Menta piperita)

Peppermint is prized for its cool, refreshing flavour and aroma, making it a popular addition to various culinary dishes, beverages, and medicinal applications. With its bright green, toothed leaves and spikes of small, pale purple flowers, peppermint adds a lively touch to any garden, making it a valuable addition to a gardener's herb collection.

Choose a location with well-draining soil that receives full sun to partial shade, as peppermint can tolerate some shade but prefers a minimum of four hours of sunlight per day. Peppermint grows best in fertile, loamy soil with a neutral to slightly acidic pH between 6.0 and 7.0, so amend the soil with compost or organic matter if necessary to improve its fertility and structure.

Plant peppermint from cuttings or small root sections taken from an established plant, as it rarely grows true from seed. Alternatively, you can purchase young peppermint plants from a garden centre and transplant them outdoors after the risk of frost has passed. Space the plants about 45-60 cm (18-24 inches) apart, ensuring they have enough room to grow and spread. Consider planting peppermint in a container or a designated garden area, as it tends to spread aggressively and may become invasive if not controlled.

Peppermint is relatively low maintenance once established, as it is hardy and has few pest issues. Water the plants consistently, ensuring the soil remains moist but not waterlogged. Keep an eye out for aphids and spider mites, which can occasionally be a problem, and treat them using organic methods if necessary.

Harvest peppermint leaves as needed throughout the growing season, preferably in the morning when the plant's aromatic oils are most concentrated. The leaves can be used fresh or dried in various culinary dishes, beverages, and medicinal applications, such as teas, desserts, and soothing digestive remedies.

Rosemary (Rosmarinus officinalis)

Rosemary has a strong, pine-like flavour and fragrance, making it a popular addition to various culinary dishes, particularly Mediterranean cuisine. With its narrow, needle-like leaves and spikes of small, blue flowers, rosemary adds a touch of Mediterranean charm to any garden, making it a valuable addition to a gardener's herb collection.

Plant rosemary in well-draining soil that receives full sun, as rosemary prefers a minimum of six hours of sunlight daily. Rosemary grows best in light, sandy soil with a neutral to slightly alkaline pH between 6.5 and 7.5, so amend the soil with grit or sand if necessary to improve its drainage and structure.

Plant rosemary from cuttings taken from an established plant, or purchase young rosemary plants from a garden centre and transplant them outdoors after the risk of frost has passed. Space the plants about 90 cm (36 inches) apart, ensuring they have enough room to grow and spread. In colder regions, consider planting rosemary in a container or near a south-facing wall to provide additional warmth and protection during winter.

Rosemary is relatively low maintenance once established, as it is drought-tolerant and has few pest issues. Water the plants consistently, ensuring the soil remains moist but not waterlogged, and allow the soil to dry out slightly between waterings. Keep an eye out for aphids and spider mites, which can occasionally be a problem, and treat them using organic methods if necessary.

Harvest rosemary leaves and sprigs as needed throughout the growing season, preferably in the morning when the plant's aromatic oils are most concentrated. The leaves can be used fresh or dried in various culinary dishes, and rosemary is also thought to have medicinal properties, such as improving memory and promoting relaxation.

Sage (Salvia officinalis)

Sage offers an earthy, slightly peppery flavour and fragrance, making it a popular addition to various culinary dishes, particularly poultry, stuffing, and Mediterranean cuisine. With its grey-green, velvety leaves and spikes of small, purplish-blue flowers, sage adds a touch of elegance to any garden, making it a valuable addition to a gardener's herb collection.

Plant sage in well-draining soil that receives full sun, as sage prefers a minimum of six hours of sunlight daily. Sage grows best in light, sandy or loamy soil with a neutral to slightly alkaline pH between 6.5 and 7.5, so amend the soil with grit, sand, or organic matter if necessary to improve its drainage and structure.

Sow sage seeds indoors in late winter or early spring using seed trays filled with a well-draining seed compost. Alternatively, you can purchase young sage plants from a garden centre and transplant them outdoors after the risk of frost has passed. Space the plants about 60-90 cm (24-36 inches) apart, ensuring they have enough room to grow and spread.

Sage is relatively low maintenance once established, as it is drought-tolerant and has few pest issues. Water the plants consistently, ensuring the soil remains moist but not waterlogged, and allow the soil to dry out slightly between waterings. Keep an eye out for aphids, spider mites, and whiteflies, which can occasionally be a problem, and treat them using organic methods if necessary.

Harvest sage leaves as needed throughout the growing season, preferably in the morning when the plant's aromatic oils are most concentrated. The leaves can be used fresh or dried in various culinary dishes, and sage is also thought to have medicinal properties, such as alleviating digestive problems and soothing sore throats.

Savory (Satureja hortensis, S. montana)

Growing savory, which includes both summer savory (Satureja hortensis) and winter savory (Satureja montana), can be a gratifying and rewarding experience for UK gardeners, as these aromatic and versatile herbs thrive in the country's temperate climate. Savory is known for its peppery, slightly bitter flavour and aroma, making it a popular addition to various culinary dishes, such as beans, soups, and poultry. With their small, narrow leaves and delicate clusters of tiny white or pink flowers, both summer and winter savory add an appealing touch to any garden, making them valuable additions to a gardener's herb collection.

Choose a location with well-draining soil that receives full sun, as savory prefers a minimum of six hours of sunlight daily. Savory grows best in light, sandy or loamy soil with a neutral to slightly alkaline pH between 6.5 and 7.5, so amend the soil with grit, sand, or organic matter if necessary to improve its drainage and structure.

Sow seeds indoors in late winter or early spring using seed trays filled with well-draining seed compost. Sow winter savory seeds directly outdoors in spring after the risk of frost has passed. Alternatively, you can purchase young savory plants from a garden centre and transplant them outdoors. Space the plants about 30-45 cm (12-18 inches) apart, ensuring they have enough room to grow and spread.

Savory is relatively low maintenance once established, as it is drought-tolerant and has few pest issues. Water the plants consistently, ensuring the soil remains moist but not waterlogged, and allow the soil to dry out slightly between waterings. Keep an eye out for aphids and spider mites, which can occasionally be a problem, and treat them using organic methods if necessary.

Harvest savory leaves as needed throughout the growing season, preferably in the morning when the plant's aromatic oils are most concentrated. The leaves can be used fresh or dried in various culinary dishes, and savory is also thought to have medicinal properties, such as aiding digestion and providing relief from insect bites and stings.

Tarragon (Artemisia dracunculus var. sativa)

Tarragon is celebrated for its distinct anise-like flavour and aroma, making it a popular addition to various culinary dishes, particularly in French cuisine where it is used in sauces, dressings, and as a seasoning for fish, poultry, and vegetables. With its slender, glossy green leaves and small, pale greenish-yellow flowers, tarragon adds a touch of sophistication to any garden, making it a valuable addition to a gardener's herb collection.

To successfully grow tarragon in the UK, choose a location with well-draining soil that receives full sun to light shade, as tarragon prefers a minimum of four to six hours of sunlight per day. Tarragon grows best in light, sandy or loamy soil with a neutral to slightly alkaline pH between 6.5 and 7.5, so amend the soil with grit, sand, or organic matter if necessary to improve its drainage and structure.

French tarragon is almost exclusively propagated by root division or stem cuttings, as its seeds are often sterile. Obtain a young tarragon plant or a cutting from an established plant, and transplant it outdoors after the risk of frost has passed. Space the plants about 45-60 cm (18-24 inches) apart, ensuring they have enough room to grow and spread.

Tarragon is relatively low maintenance once established, as it is drought-tolerant and has few pest issues. Water the plants consistently, ensuring the soil remains moist but not waterlogged, and allow the soil to dry out slightly between waterings. Keep an eye out for aphids and powdery mildew, which can occasionally be a problem, and treat them using organic methods if necessary.

Harvest tarragon leaves as needed throughout the growing season, preferably in the morning when the plant's aromatic oils are most concentrated. The leaves can be used fresh or dried in various culinary dishes, and tarragon is also thought to have medicinal properties, such as aiding digestion and promoting appetite.

Thyme (Thymus spp.)

Thyme is known for its earthy, slightly sweet flavour and fragrance, making it a popular addition to various culinary dishes, such as stews, soups, and roasted meats. With its small, evergreen leaves and tiny, tubular flowers in shades of white, pink, or purple, thyme adds a charming touch to any garden, making it a valuable addition to a gardener's herb collection.

Plant thyme in a location with well-draining soil that receives full sun, as it prefers a minimum of six hours of sunlight per day. Thyme grows best in light, sandy or loamy soil with a neutral to slightly alkaline pH between 6.5 and 7.5, so amend the soil with grit, sand, or organic matter to improve drainage and structure.

Sow thyme seeds indoors in late winter or early spring, using seed trays filled with a well-draining seed compost. Alternatively, you can purchase young thyme plants from a garden centre and transplant them outdoors after the risk of frost has passed. Space the plants about 30-45 cm (12-18 inches) apart, ensuring they have enough room to grow and spread.

Thyme is relatively low maintenance once established, as it is drought-tolerant and has few pest issues. Water the plants consistently, ensuring the soil remains moist but not waterlogged, and allow the soil to dry out slightly between waterings. Keep an eye out for aphids, spider mites, and whiteflies, which can occasionally be a problem, and treat them using organic methods if necessary.

Harvest thyme leaves as needed throughout the growing season, preferably in the morning when the plant's aromatic oils are most concentrated. The leaves can be used fresh or dried in various culinary dishes, and thyme is also thought to have medicinal properties, such as promoting relaxation and aiding digestion.

Turmeric (Curcuma longa)

Growing turmeric (Curcuma longa) can be an exciting and rewarding experience for UK gardeners. This tropical and versatile plant can be cultivated in containers or greenhouses. Turmeric is known for its warm, slightly bitter flavour and vibrant orange colour, making it a popular ingredient in various culinary dishes, particularly Indian and Asian cuisine. With its large, tropical-looking green leaves and striking white or pink flowers, turmeric adds a touch of the exotic to any garden, making it a valuable addition to a gardener's plant collection.

Plant turmeric rhizomes, which can be purchased online or from a nursery, in pots or containers filled with a rich, well-draining potting mix. Alternatively, turmeric can be planted directly into the ground if you have access to a greenhouse or polytunnel. Plant the rhizomes about 5 cm (2 inches) deep, with the buds facing upward, and space them about 30-45 cm (12-18 inches) apart, ensuring they have enough room to grow and spread.

Turmeric is relatively low maintenance once established, but it does require consistent warmth and humidity, making it essential to protect the plants from cold temperatures and drafts. Water the plants consistently, ensuring the soil remains consistently moist but not waterlogged. Keep an eye out for pests such as aphids and red spider mites, which can occasionally be a problem, and treat them using organic methods if necessary.

Harvest turmeric rhizomes in the autumn or winter, when the leaves turn yellow and die back, approximately 8-10 months after planting. The rhizomes can be used fresh, dried, or powdered in various culinary dishes. Turmeric is also thought to have numerous health benefits due to its anti-inflammatory and antioxidant properties.

CHAPTER 9

MANAGING PESTS AND DISEASES

Managing Home Vegetable Garden Pests

Here are 20 tips for managing home vegetable garden pests:

Rotate crops: Crop rotation can help to reduce pest populations by disrupting their life cycles and reducing the availability of host plants.

Choose pest-resistant varieties: Select vegetable varieties resistant to common pests in your area.

Use physical barriers: Use row covers, netting, or other physical barriers to keep pests away from your plants.

Handpick pests: Regularly inspect your plants and handpick any pests, such as caterpillars or slugs.

Use companion planting: Plant certain herbs, flowers, or vegetables that can help to repel pests or attract beneficial insects.

Provide habitat for beneficial insects: Encourage beneficial insects such as ladybirds, lacewings, and hoverflies by planting flowering plants or providing shelter for them.

Use organic pest control: Use organic pest control methods such as neem oil, insecticidal soap, or diatomaceous earth to control pests.

Apply nematodes: Nematodes are microscopic worms that can be applied to the soil to control pests such as slugs and vine weevils.

Use biological control: Introduce natural predators or parasites that can control pest populations, such as releasing ladybirds to control aphids.

Keep garden clean: Keep your garden free of debris and remove fallen fruit or vegetables to reduce pest populations.

Use traps: Use traps, such as pheromone traps, to capture and monitor pest populations.

Apply repellents: Apply natural repellents such as garlic, chili powder, or vinegar to keep pests away from your plants.

Mulch: Use mulch to prevent weed growth and reduce pest habitat.

Water plants correctly: Water plants at the base to avoid creating moist environments that pests may be attracted to.

Use proper spacing: Proper spacing can promote air flow and reduce the spread of disease and pests.

Use compost: Use compost to enrich the soil and promote healthy plant growth, which can help to reduce pest problems.

Use sticky traps: Sticky traps can help to capture flying pests such as whiteflies.

Use bird netting: Use bird netting to prevent birds from eating your vegetables.

Use insect-repelling herbs: Plant basil, mint, and rosemary near your vegetable plants to repel pests.

Monitor and act quickly: Monitor your plants regularly and act quickly at the first signs of pest infestation to prevent the problem from worsening.

Common Pests In Vegetable Gardens

A variety of pests can affect vegetable gardens in the UK. Here is a comprehensive list of common garden pests:

Aphids: Small, soft-bodied insects that suck sap from plants, causing stunted growth and distorted leaves.

Slugs and Snails: Mollusks that feed on tender leaves, stems, and seedlings, causing extensive damage to plants.

Cabbage White Caterpillars: Larvae of the cabbage white butterfly that feed on leaves of brassicas (e.g., cabbage, kale, cauliflower, and broccoli), resulting in significant damage.

Carrot Fly: Larvae of the carrot fly that tunnel into the roots of carrots, parsnips, and other related plants, causing damage and disfiguration.

Colorado Potato Beetle: Beetles that feed on potato leaves, leading to defoliation and reduced yields.

Flea Beetles: Small, jumping beetles that feed on the leaves of brassicas and related plants, creating tiny holes.

Vine Weevil: Larvae feed on the roots of various plants, causing wilting and potentially plant death, while adults feed on the leaves.

Whitefly: Tiny, sap-sucking insects that can cause yellowing and distortion of leaves and transmit plant diseases.

Cutworms: Caterpillars that feed on the stems of young plants near the soil surface, causing them to topple over.

Leaf Miners: Larvae of various insects that tunnel inside leaves, creating discoloured and damaged foliage.

Wireworms: Larvae of click beetles that feed on roots and tubers, causing tunnels and plant damage.

Thrips: Tiny insects that feed on plant sap, causing stippling or silvering of leaves and potentially transmitting plant viruses.

Spider Mites: Microscopic mites that suck plant sap, causing stippling or bronzing of leaves and potential defoliation.

Root Maggots: Larvae of various flies that feed on the roots of plants, causing stunted growth and plant stress.

Nematodes: Microscopic roundworms that can damage plant roots, leading to stunted growth and poor nutrient uptake.

Capsid Bugs: Sap-sucking insects that cause distortion and holes in leaves and can transmit plant diseases.

Sawfly Larvae: Caterpillar-like larvae that feed on the leaves of various plants, causing defoliation and reduced plant vigour.

Scale Insects: Sap-sucking insects that can cause yellowing and distortion of leaves, as well as sooty mould due to the secretion of honeydew.

Red Lily Beetle: Beetles that feed on the leaves, stems, and flowers of lilies and fritillaries, causing severe damage.

Ants: While not directly harmful to plants, ants can farm aphids and protect them from predators, exacerbating aphid infestations.

Effectively managing these pests requires vigilance, regular inspection of plants, and employing a combination of cultural, biological, and chemical control measures tailored to the specific pest and garden conditions.

Notifiable Pests in the UK[4]

Beetles

Potato beetle	*Epitrix*
Colorado potato beetle	*Leptinotarsa decemlineata*
Red-necked longhorn beetle	*Aromia bungii*
Plum weevil	*Conotrachelus nenuphar*
Granulate ambrosia beetle	*Xylosandrus crassiusculus*
Two-lined chestnut borer	*Agrilus bilineatus*
Asian longhorn beetle	*Anoplophora glabripennis*
Emerald ash borer	*Agrilus planipennis*

Bugs

Tomato potato psyllid or North American potato psyllid	*Bactericera cockerelli*
Oak lace bug	*Corythucha arcuata*

---

[4] https://planthealthportal.defra.gov.uk/pests-and-diseases/pest-and-disease-alerts/notifiable-pests/

Spotted lanternfly	*Lycorma delicatula*
Grape phylloxera	*Daktulosphaira vitifoliae*
Flies	
Apple maggot fly	*Rhagoletis pomonella*
Eastern cherry fruit fly	*Rhagoletis cingulata*
Moths	
Guatemalan potato moth	*Tecia solanivora*
False codling moth	*Thaumatotibia leucotreta*
Fall armyworm	*Spodoptera frugiperda*
Wasps	
Oriental chestnut gall wasp	*Dryocosmus kuriphilus*

Aphids

Aphids are small, soft-bodied insects that are common pests of many plant species in the United Kingdom. They feed on plant sap by piercing the leaves, stems, and buds with their needle-like mouthparts, leading to leaf distortion, stunted growth, and reduced yield. Aphids can also transmit viral diseases between plants. They reproduce rapidly, and infestations can quickly become severe. Aphids are attracted to young, succulent growth and are favored by warm, dry conditions.

They can be controlled by various means, including cultural methods such as removing infested plant material, using companion planting or repellent plants, and practicing good sanitation measures. Chemical control measures, such as the use of insecticides or soap sprays, can also be effective. However, it is important to take care to avoid harming beneficial insects, such as bees and ladybirds, which can help control aphids naturally.

Monitoring

Inspect plants carefully for the beginnings of an aphid population development. Mummies, grey-brown bloated parasitized aphids showing wasp parasites in action, and alligator-like larvae of lady beetles and lacewings are examples of natural enemies in action. Yellow sticky boards are also used to monitor aphid numbers, and aphids are drawn to the yellow hue and are frequently visible on the cards before being found on the plant.

Management

Additional treatments may not be necessary if there are many mummies or big populations of ladybird beetles or lacewings in addition to the aphids. Controlling numbers early in the season eliminates the need for spraying. Wash aphids off with water as required early in the day. A forceful jet of water will kill many of them. Aphids on the following vegetable plants should be controlled with insecticides:

- *Beans:* use insecticidal soap, horticultural oil, pyrethrins, or malathion on beans.
- *Cabbage, cauliflower, broccoli, Brussels sprouts, and other cole crops*: spray with insecticidal soap, oil (horticultural), pyrethrins, or malathion when infestations are severe and as needed weekly. Wait seven days before harvesting if using malathion.
- *Cucumber, pumpkin*: insecticidal soap, oil (horticultural), or malathion; spray when vines are dry as needed. Wait one day before harvesting while using malathion.
- *Eggplant*: insecticidal soap or malathion can be used to treat eggplant as needed.
- *Peas*: spray one to three applications weekly with insecticidal soap or malathion. Wait three days before harvesting after using malathion.
- *Pepper*: spray as required with insecticidal soap, oil (horticultural), or malathion. If malathion is used, wait three days before harvesting; if insecticidal soap is used, wait one day.
- *Potato*: spray with malathion as needed once a week.
- *Tomatoes*: spray as needed with insecticidal soap, oil (horticultural), or malathion. Wait at least one day before harvesting.

Asparagus Beetles

Asparagus beetles, also known as common asparagus beetles and spotted asparagus beetles, are destructive pests that attack asparagus plants in the United Kingdom. Adult beetles are approximately 6 to 9 mm long, with black or dark blue bodies and reddish-brown wing covers.

The beetles feed on asparagus foliage and stems, causing defoliation and stunted growth. Females also lay their eggs on the foliage, which hatch into larvae that feed on the spears, causing scarring and damage. Asparagus beetles overwinter in soil and plant debris and emerge in the spring to begin feeding and laying eggs.

Management

Management strategies for asparagus beetles include monitoring plants regularly for signs of infestation, handpicking and removing beetles and eggs, maintaining proper plant spacing and cleanliness, and using insecticides when necessary. Early detection and treatment are crucial to prevent damage to asparagus crops.

Bean Leaf Beetles

Bean leaf beetles, also known as southern corn rootworms or bean beetles, are pests that can cause significant damage to bean plants in the United Kingdom. Adult beetles are approximately 5-7 mm long, with yellowish-green bodies and black markings on their wings. They feed on the foliage, stems, and pods of bean plants, causing defoliation, reduced yield, and stunted growth. The beetles may also transmit bean pod mottle virus, which can lead to severe crop losses. Bean leaf beetles overwinter in soil and plant debris and emerge in the spring to begin feeding and laying eggs.

Management

Management strategies for bean leaf beetles include monitoring plants regularly for signs of infestation, using row covers to exclude beetles, maintaining proper plant spacing and cleanliness, and using insecticides when necessary. Early detection and treatment are essential to prevent significant damage to bean crops.

Brown Marmorated Stink Bug

The Brown Marmorated Stink Bug (BMSB), native to Asia, is a relatively new and serious pest threatening UK crops. Adult stink bugs are approximately 1.7 cm long, shield-shaped, and mottled brown in color, with distinctive antennae and legs. They feed on a wide range of plants, including fruits, vegetables, and ornamentals, by piercing the tissue and sucking out the juices, leading to damage and reduced yield. BMSB also emits a foul odor when disturbed, making them a nuisance for homeowners.

Management

Remove the bugs and place them in a bucket of soapy water. Exterior pesticide sprays may provide some relief from pests where entirely sealing the exterior is impractical or impossible. Applications should include a synthetic pyrethroid and should be sprayed by a qualified pest control operator in the autumn, right before insect gathering. Unfortunately, because sunshine breaks down pesticides, their residual action is reduced and may not kill insects for several days or a week.

Cabbage Loopers

Cabbage loopers are a common pest of vegetable crops in the United Kingdom, particularly in brassica crops such as cabbage, broccoli, and cauliflower. The larvae of the cabbage looper moth feed on the leaves of plants, causing significant damage by chewing large holes in the foliage. The larvae are green, caterpillar-like, and can reach up to 2 inches in length. Adult moths are brownish-gray and about 1 inch in length, with distinctive V-shaped markings on their wings. Cabbage loopers overwinter in the soil and emerge in the spring to lay eggs on the underside of leaves.

Management

- Use a lightweight row cover to keep egg-laying moths at bay in early April. When caterpillars are little, spray with *Bacillus thuringiensis* (Bt), which is most effective. Spray the undersides of leaves, where juvenile caterpillars love to eat.
- On cole crops, look for caterpillars and their feeding damage on both sides of the leaves. Check at least once a week for the first week after planting and more frequently as the season advances.
- Immediately destroy crop debris to eliminate sheltered locations that imported cabbageworm may exploit to survive the winter.
- To destroy the caterpillars, take them up and dump them into a basin of soapy water.
- Adult moths are prevented from depositing eggs on plants by floating row coverings

made of lightweight all-purpose garden cloth.

- Natural enemies of the cabbage looper, imported cabbageworm, and diamondback moth include predators such as parasitic flies and wasps such as *Cotesia glomerata*.

Cabbage Maggots

Cabbage maggots are a significant pest of many vegetable crops, including brassicas like cabbage, broccoli, and cauliflower in the United Kingdom. The larvae of the cabbage maggot fly feed on the roots of plants, causing damage that can lead to wilting, stunted growth, and reduced yield. Infested plants may also be more susceptible to other diseases and pests. Cabbage maggots are attracted to moist soil and organic matter and are most active in the spring and fall. They overwinter in soil as pupae and emerge as adult flies in the spring to mate and lay eggs near the base of host plants.

The eggs hatch into small, white, legless larvae that burrow into the soil to feed on the roots of plants. Cabbage maggots can be difficult to control, and management strategies include practicing crop rotation, using floating row covers to exclude the flies, maintaining proper plant spacing and cleanliness, and applying insecticides when necessary. Early detection and treatment are essential to prevent significant damage to crops.

Management

Managing cabbage maggots in vegetable crops can be challenging, but there are several strategies that can be effective in reducing their impact. One of the most important measures is to practice crop rotation, as this can reduce the build-up of cabbage maggot populations in the soil. It is recommended to avoid planting brassicas in the same spot for at least three years.

Additionally, maintaining proper plant spacing and cleanliness can help reduce the risk of infestation, as cabbage maggots are attracted to moist soil and organic matter. Using floating row covers to exclude adult flies from laying eggs near the base of plants can also be effective. Insecticides can also be used as a last resort, but it is important to choose products that are effective against cabbage maggots and to follow all instructions carefully to avoid harm to beneficial insects and the environment. Regular monitoring of crops is crucial for early detection of infestations and implementing appropriate control measures.

Carrot Rust Fly

Carrot rust fly is a significant pest of carrot crops in the United Kingdom. The adult flies are approximately 4-6 mm long, with black bodies and yellowish-brown heads. They lay their eggs in the soil near the base of host plants, and the larvae feed on the roots, causing stunting, reduced yield, and increased susceptibility to other diseases. Infested roots may also become discolored and develop cracks, making them unmarketable.

Management

Carrot rust fly is most active from May to September, and infestations can occur throughout the growing season. Management strategies for carrot rust fly include using fine mesh netting to exclude adult flies, practicing crop rotation, using resistant cultivars, and using appropriate insecticides when necessary. Cultural control measures, such as removing weeds and plant debris, can also help reduce the risk of infestation. Early detection and treatment are essential to prevent significant damage to carrot crops.

Click Beetle Wireworm

Click beetle wireworms are common pests that can cause significant damage to a wide range of crops in the United Kingdom, including potatoes, carrots, and cereals. Wireworms are the larvae of click beetles and are approximately 2-3 cm long, with hard, cylindrical bodies that are yellowish-brown to dark brown in color. They feed on the roots, stems, and tubers of plants, causing significant damage that can lead to reduced yield and crop losses. Wireworms have a long life cycle and can remain in the soil for several years, making them difficult to control.

Management

Management strategies for click beetle wireworms include practicing crop rotation, deep ploughing to expose the larvae to predators, and using insecticides only when necessary. Cultural control measures, such as maintaining proper plant spacing and cleanliness, can also help reduce the risk of infestation. Early detection and treatment are crucial to prevent significant damage to crops.

Cucumber Beetles

Cucumber beetles are pests that can cause significant damage to cucumber and related crops in the United Kingdom. The adult beetles are approximately 0.5-1 cm long, with yellow or greenish-yellow bodies and black markings. They feed on the foliage and flowers of plants, causing defoliation and reduced yield. The larvae of cucumber beetles feed on the roots and stems of plants, causing further damage. Cucumber beetles can also transmit bacterial wilt disease, which can lead to severe crop losses.

Management

Management strategies for cucumber beetles include using floating row covers to exclude the beetles, handpicking and removing beetles and eggs, maintaining proper plant spacing and cleanliness, and using insecticides when necessary. Cultural control measures, such as removing weeds and plant debris, can also help reduce the risk of infestation. Early detection and treatment are essential to prevent significant damage to crops.

Cutworms

Cutworms are night-flying moth larvae (caterpillars). Adult moths either feed on nectar or do not eat at all, and the harm is only done during the larval stage. The larvae are approximately 2 to 5 cm long, with soft, plump bodies that are gray or brown in color. They feed on the stems and leaves of plants, often severing them at or near the soil surface, causing plants to wilt or die. Cutworms are most active at night and can hide during the day under soil clods or plant debris. There are several species of cutworms that attack vegetable crops, and identification can be challenging.

Management

Cutworms can be deterred from eating on garden plants by wrapping a cardboard collar around the stem and extending it above and below ground level. Cutworm moths deposit their eggs on weeds and grasses, so remove them from your garden. Insect traps and barriers are common and have been on the market for a long time.

Diamondback Moths

Diamondback moths are pests that can cause significant damage to cruciferous vegetable crops, such as cabbage, broccoli, and cauliflower, in the United Kingdom. The adult moths are approximately 8 mm long, with narrow, grayish-brown wings that are diamond-shaped when folded. The larvae of diamondback moths feed on the leaves of plants, causing significant damage by creating small, irregular holes in the foliage. Infested plants may also become stunted and produce fewer and smaller heads. Diamondback moths are most active in the spring and summer, and populations can build up quickly, making them difficult to control.

These nocturnal moths are slender and light brown. The folded wings have a three- white-diamond design. Eggs are creamy-white and small and are placed near leaf veins on the leaf. The hatching caterpillars are light green, tapered at both ends, and grow about 8 mm long, considerably smaller than loopers, and respond when touched.

Management

Management strategies for diamondback moths include practicing crop rotation, using resistant cultivars, and using beneficial insects such as parasitic wasps to control moth populations. Cultural control measures, such as removing weeds and plant debris, can also help reduce the risk of infestation. Early detection and treatment are essential to prevent significant damage to crops.

Flea Beetle

Flea beetles are pests that can cause significant damage to a wide range of vegetable crops in the United Kingdom, including brassicas, such as cabbage and broccoli, and solanaceous crops, such as tomatoes and potatoes. The adult beetles are small, approximately 2-3 mm long, and are usually shiny black or metallic in color. They feed on the leaves of plants, causing small, round holes that can coalesce into larger areas of damage. Infested plants may also become stunted and produce fewer and smaller fruits or vegetables. Flea beetles are most active in the spring and summer, and populations can build up quickly, making them difficult to control

Management

Frequent cultivation has been reported to ‘drive’ flea beetles off plants. Large numbers of flea beetles can be captured by placing a box with the inner walls coated with insect-trapping stickers that can be passed over infested plants to capture flea beetles as they jump off plants. Cultural control measures, such as removing weeds and plant debris, can also help reduce the risk of infestation. Early detection and treatment are essential to prevent significant damage to crops.

Imported Cabbage Worm

Imported cabbage worm is a significant pest of brassica crops, such as cabbage, broccoli, and cauliflower, in the United Kingdom. The adult moths are white and have a wingspan of approximately 2.5 cm. They lay their eggs on the undersides of leaves, and the larvae feed on the foliage, causing significant damage by creating large, irregular holes. Infested plants may also become stunted and produce fewer and smaller heads. Imported cabbage worm is most active in the spring and summer, and populations can build up quickly, making them difficult to control.

Management

Management strategies for imported cabbage worm include practicing crop rotation, using resistant cultivars, and using beneficial insects such as parasitic wasps to control moth populations. Cultural control measures, such as removing weeds and plant debris, can also help reduce the risk of infestation. Early detection and treatment are essential to prevent significant damage to crops.

Japanese Beetle

Japanese beetle is a pest that can cause significant damage to a wide range of vegetable and ornamental plants in the United Kingdom. The adult beetles are approximately 1 cm long, with metallic green bodies and copper-colored wings. They feed on the foliage and flowers of plants, causing significant defoliation and reduced yield. The larvae of Japanese beetles, known as white grubs, feed on the roots of plants, causing further damage. Japanese beetle is most active in the summer months, and populations can build up quickly, making them difficult to control.

Management

As irritating as it may appear, handpicking and squashing or drowning these pests is the most effective remedy accessible to the amateur grower. Fill a receptacle with soapy water, such as a coffee can, and flick the beetles into it. Later, cover it and throw it away. The technique is simple since the beetles travel slowly and do not conceal, and early attempts result in a greatly diminished population. The effectiveness of other Japanese beetle management strategies varies.

A variety of natural predators eats Japanese beetles. Among birds, only starlings consume beetles, while numerous species consume larvae in the spring. Assassin bugs and Tiphia wasps are two helpful insects that destroy Japanese beetle larvae.

Leafhoppers

Leafhoppers (LH) have sucking mouthparts that pierce plant tissues. They extract plant sap (similar to a mosquito taking blood). This results in a stippled or speckled pattern of colour loss in the areas where the LH was supplied. The adult insects are approximately 3-4 mm long, with wedge-shaped bodies that are green, brown, or yellow in color. They feed on the leaves of plants, causing significant damage by piercing the plant tissues and sucking out the sap. This can lead to stunted growth, reduced yield, and in severe cases, plant death. Leafhoppers are most active in the summer months, and populations can build up quickly, making them difficult to control. LH are also major virus and disease vectors, such as Aster yellows, curly top of sugar beets and other crops, yellow dwarf potatoes, etc.

Management

To date, LH predators and parasites seldom give satisfactory control, especially where the LH is a disease carrier. Cultural control measures may relieve LH damage depending upon LH species, crop and companion crops, etc.

Leafminers

Leafminers are pests that can cause significant damage to a wide range of vegetable and ornamental plants in the United Kingdom. The adult insects are small, approximately 2-3 mm long, and are usually black or gray in color. They lay their eggs on the undersides of leaves, and the larvae mine into the leaves, causing significant damage by creating serpentine tunnels. Infested leaves may become discolored and distorted, and in severe cases, plants may lose leaves and become stunted. Leafminers are most active in the spring and summer months, and populations can build up quickly, making them difficult to control.

Management

- Check young seedlings for leaf mines regularly, especially if leafminers have already invaded your garden. The majority of mines appear on the first genuine leaves.
- Vegetable leafminers are generally kept under control by their natural enemies, and no management is required.
- When spinach leafminers attack the leaves of a root crop, such as beets, it is not required to cure them. However, treatment may be required if it occurs on spinach or another leafy green.
- To protect the plants from insects, use fine-mesh netting row coverings.
- Use a material that will not block sunshine and rain from reaching the plants (e.g. cheesecloth).
- Apply in locations where there hasn't been a leafminer problem in at least a year.
- If leafminer problems have been noted in the previous year, this netting will not assist since pupae that survived the winter are still inside the row cover and can infest plants.

Mexican Bean Beetle

Mexican bean beetle is a pest that can cause significant damage to beans, peas, and other legumes in UK gardens. The adult beetles are approximately 6 mm long, with a distinctive yellow-orange color and 16 black spots on their wings. They feed on the leaves and pods of plants, causing significant defoliation and reduced yield. The larvae of Mexican bean beetle are yellow and spiny and feed on the undersides of leaves, causing further damage. Mexican bean beetle is most active in the summer months, and populations can build up quickly, making them difficult to control.

Management

Management strategies for Mexican bean beetle include using insecticides, practicing crop rotation, and using physical barriers such as netting to exclude the beetles. Insecticides should be applied according to label instructions and should be chosen based on their efficacy against

Mexican bean beetle. Cultural control measures, such as removing weeds and plant debris, can also help reduce the risk of infestation. Early detection and treatment are essential to prevent significant damage to crops. One effective way to manage Mexican bean beetle is to remove infested plants and destroy them, reducing the population of the pest in the garden. Crop rotation can also help reduce the risk of infestation, as Mexican bean beetle tends to overwinter in soil near legumes. Using resistant cultivars can also be effective in reducing the impact of Mexican bean beetle on garden crops.

Onion Maggot

Onion maggot is a pest that can cause significant damage to onions, garlic, and other allium crops in UK gardens. The adult flies are small, approximately 5-6 mm long, and resemble small houseflies. They lay their eggs in the soil near onion plants, and the larvae feed on the roots of the plants, causing significant damage by creating tunnels and causing rot. Infested plants may become stunted and produce smaller bulbs. Onion maggot is most active in the spring and summer months, and populations can build up quickly, making them difficult to control.

Management

Management strategies for onion maggot include practicing crop rotation, using physical barriers such as netting to exclude the flies, and using beneficial insects such as parasitic wasps to control populations. Insecticides should be applied according to label instructions and should be chosen based on their efficacy against onion maggot. Cultural control measures, such as removing weeds and plant debris, can also help reduce the risk of infestation. Early detection and treatment are essential to prevent significant damage to crops. One effective way to manage onion maggot is to plant allium crops later in the season when onion maggot populations are lower. Planting allium crops in well-drained soil can also help reduce the risk of infestation, as onion maggot prefers moist soil.

Sap Beetles

Sap beetles are pests that can cause significant damage to a wide range of vegetable and fruit crops in the United Kingdom. The adult beetles are small, approximately 2-3 mm long, and are usually brown or black in color. They feed on damaged or overripe fruits and vegetables, such as tomatoes, sweet corn, and strawberries, causing further damage and creating entry points for other pests and diseases. Infested produce may become soft and rot, reducing yield and quality. Sap beetles are most active in the summer months, and populations can build up quickly, making them difficult to control.

Management

Management strategies for sap beetles include using insecticides, practicing good sanitation practices such as promptly removing damaged or overripe produce, and using physical barriers such as netting to exclude the beetles. Insecticides should be applied according to label instructions and should be chosen based on their efficacy against sap beetles. Cultural control measures, such as removing weeds and plant debris, can also help reduce the risk of infestation. Early detection and treatment are essential to prevent significant damage to crops. One effective way to manage sap beetles is to promptly remove any damaged or overripe produce from the garden and to properly dispose of it, reducing the attraction and breeding of sap beetles in the area.

Research conducted by UK universities has also shown that trap crops can be an effective way to manage sap beetles. These crops are planted near susceptible crops and are designed to attract the beetles away from the main crop. Trap crops can be planted earlier in the season to allow for a head start in attracting the beetles, and they should be removed and destroyed before the beetles have a chance to move on to the main crop. Additionally, the use of beneficial insects such as parasitic wasps and ground beetles can help to control sap beetle populations. These insects prey on sap beetles, reducing their numbers and preventing significant damage to crops.

Scale

Scale insects of diverse species damage numerous fruits and ornamental plants around the country. They adhere as little bumps on branches, twigs, and the undersides of leaves. Cottony cushion scale is thick, white, and coated with a waxy or fuzzy material, but some are flattened and brown.

The leaves of affected plants become yellow, and the plant's general vitality suffers. Plants that are severely affected may perish within a few seasons. Under their protective shells, mature females eat, lay eggs, and rear families. Crawlers eat by sucking plant secretions from eggs. Crawlers develop a shell-like coat and lose their legs as they age. Each year, there may be numerous generations.

Management

Research conducted by UK universities has also shown that the use of horticultural oils can be an effective way to manage scale pests. These oils are applied to the plant's foliage, and they work by smothering the pests and their eggs. Horticultural oils should be applied according to label instructions and during the recommended times of the year. Additionally, the use of insecticidal soaps can be effective in controlling scale pests, as they work by disrupting the pests' outer membrane, causing dehydration and death.

Slugs and Snails

Slugs and snails are among the most common pests in UK gardens and can cause significant damage to a wide range of plants, especially those with soft foliage. Identifying these pests is relatively easy, as they leave a slimy trail on plants and the surrounding soil. Slugs and snails are most active during wet and humid conditions and tend to feed during the night, making them difficult to detect.

Management

Management strategies for slugs and snails include using physical barriers, such as copper tape or mesh, to exclude the pests from garden beds and containers. Creating a dry and less humid environment around plants can also help to reduce slug and snail populations. This can be achieved by using irrigation methods that limit soil moisture, such as drip irrigation or soaker hoses. Encouraging natural predators, such as hedgehogs, toads, and birds, can also help to control slug and snail populations.

Chemical control measures are also available and include the use of slug and snail baits and molluscicides. These products should be used according to label instructions and should be placed in areas where slugs and snails are known to be active. Cultural control measures, such as removing plant debris and weeds, can also help reduce the risk of infestation. Regular inspection of plants and prompt removal of any infested plant parts can help to prevent significant damage to crops.

Spider mites

Spider mites are a common pest in UK gardens, and they can cause significant damage to a wide range of plants, especially those with delicate foliage. Identifying spider mites can be challenging, as they are very small and often go unnoticed until they have caused significant damage. Signs of infestation include yellow or brown speckling on the plant's leaves, as well as webbing on the plant surface.

Management

Management strategies for spider mites include using insecticidal soaps or horticultural oils, which work by suffocating the pests and their eggs. These products should be applied according to label instructions and should be targeted to the areas where the mites are active. The use of beneficial insects, such as predatory mites or ladybirds, can also help to control spider mite populations. Cultural control measures, such as removing weeds and plant debris, can also help reduce the risk of infestation.

Preventative measures are also effective in managing spider mites. Regularly inspecting plants and maintaining good plant health can help to prevent spider mites from infesting the garden. Avoiding the use of chemical fertilizers and overwatering can also help to reduce the risk of infestation, as these conditions can create a hospitable environment for spider mites. If infestation occurs, prompt removal of infested plant parts can help to prevent the pests from spreading to other plants.

Spittlebugs

Spittlebugs, also known as froghoppers, are a common pest in UK gardens, and they can cause significant damage to a wide range of plants. The pests are named for the white foam-like substance that they create on plants, which serves as a protective covering for their eggs and nymphs. Identifying spittlebugs can be relatively easy, as the foam-like substance is often visible on the plant's leaves and stems.

Management

Management strategies for spittlebugs include using insecticidal soaps or horticultural oils, which work by smothering the pests and their eggs. These products should be applied according to label instructions and should be targeted to the areas where the spittlebugs are active. Cultural control measures, such as removing weeds and plant debris, can also help reduce the risk of infestation.

Preventative measures are also effective in managing spittlebugs. Regularly inspecting plants and maintaining good plant health can help to prevent spittlebugs from infesting the garden. Avoiding over-fertilizing and overwatering can also help to reduce the risk of infestation, as these conditions can create a hospitable environment for spittlebugs. If infestation occurs, prompt removal of infested plant parts can help to prevent the pests from spreading to other plants.

It's worth noting that spittlebugs are generally considered to be a minor pest and often do not require any control measures. However, if significant damage is occurring or if the pests are present in large numbers, management strategies should be implemented.

Squash Bugs

Squashbugs, also known as stinkbugs, are a common pest in UK gardens, and they can cause significant damage to a wide range of plants, including squash, pumpkins, and cucumbers. Identifying squashbugs can be relatively easy, as they are shield-shaped and have a distinctive brown or gray color. The pests feed on plant sap and can cause wilting, yellowing, and stunted growth in plants.

Management

- To help prevent squash bug damage, maintain healthy, robust plants with adequate fertilizer and watering.
- Adult squash bugs are tough to destroy, so remove them from the plant as soon as possible.
- Drop nymphs and adults into a bucket of soapy water to destroy them. This is only feasible if only a few plants are impacted.
- Squash bugs may be difficult to remove because they hide under leaves and move swiftly when disturbed.
- Crush any eggs that have been adhered to the undersides or stems of leaves.
- Lay down boards or pieces of newspaper to trap squash bugs. Squash bugs will congregate under the boards at night, which you may gather and eliminate in the morning.

Squash Vine Borers

Squash vine borers are a common pest in UK gardens, and they can cause significant damage to squash and pumpkin plants. The pests are larvae of a type of moth that lays its eggs at the base of the plant, and the larvae burrow into the stem, causing wilting and eventually killing the plant. Identifying squash vine borers can be challenging, as they are often hidden within the plant stem.

Management

Beginning in the last week of June, check your squash for the presence of adult borers. Adult squash vine borers can be detected using one of two ways.

- Keep an eye out for their behavior in the garden. These moths are easily identified due to their distinctive black/orange colour and a pretty loud buzzing noise while they fly.
- For trapping, use a yellow-coloured container (pan, bucket, bowl) filled with water and a drop of dish soap (break surface tension). Adult squash vine borers are drawn to yellow, and they'll fly to the container and become stuck when they autumn into the water. Set traps by late June, monitoring them at least once a day.
- Make a meticulous strategy for your planting timetable – plant squash vine borers-resistant vine crops such as butternut squash, cucumbers, melons, and watermelons.
- In early July, sow a second crop of summer squash. These plants will grow after the adult borers have laid eggs and will be unharmed.
- Pull and remove any plants that have been destroyed by squash vine borers as soon as possible.
- Place floating row covers over your vine crops as plants begin to vine (or, for non-vining types, in late June or early July) or when squash vine borer adults are first detected.
- Maintain the barriers for about two weeks after the first adult borer is spotted.
- Secure the row coverings so that adults cannot move beneath them.

- Row coverings should not be used if cucurbits were planted in the same region the previous year because squash vine borers spend the winter in the soil near their host plants. When the adults emerge the following summer, they may become trapped behind the row cover rather than kept out.

Threelined Potato Beetles

A threelined potato bug is similar to a striped cucumber, except they eat on different plants. The threelined potato beetle is about 6 mm long and has cream to reddish- yellow wing coverings and three black bands along its back.

Even if you observe a lot of threelined potato bugs in one region, they are typically not a concern. If you encounter these beetles in your garden and wish to get rid of them, handpick them and place them in a bucket of soapy water.

Thrips

Thrips are drawn to flower pollen, although both immatures and adults mostly feed on plant tissue. Thrips eat by extracting plant juices with their rasping/sucking mouthparts. Feeding damage shows on the leaf surface as coarse stippling. Thrips populations in large numbers inflict considerable plant damage, resulting in a silvery or scratchy look on leaf surfaces. Thrips also eat on floral tissue, causing marginal necrosis and petal browning.

Blue adhesive cards are more effective than yellow sticky cards at attracting thrips and should be put right near beans, and this will draw thrips to the fava beans, increasing the likelihood of thrips eating on them. Remove the blooms from fava beans to encourage thrips to feed on the leaves rather than the flowers. Plants should be kept in the greenhouse for at least three weeks.

Management

Thrips control is critical because they can act as disease vectors. Total eradication is typically not attainable, especially given the possibility of pesticide resistance in thrips populations. To manage thrips numbers, growers should employ a combination of cultural, chemical, and biological management measures. To avoid resistance, pesticides should be alternated. Plants infected with TOSPO viruses should be removed to limit the risk of viral transmission.

Tomato Hornworms

Tomato hornworms are massive caterpillars with horn-like tails. Their preferred plant is tomato, which they can fully defoliate, although they have also been detected on potatoes, eggplant, and pepper. Many plants, such as horsenettle, jimsonweed, and nightshade, act as alternative hosts. Caterpillars in large numbers may defoliate plants fast in home gardens. Tomato hornworm caterpillars begin munching on the top leaves of the plants. The caterpillars blend in with the foliage and may go unnoticed until most of the damage has been done. They produce dark green or black droppings that are easily visible while feeding. Older tomato hornworms may wreak havoc on several leaves and fruit. The final caterpillar stage eats almost as much as all the younger stages combined.

Management

- During the summer, inspect plants for tomato hornworms at least twice a week.
- Weeds should be removed to minimize the number of places where worms can lay eggs.
- After harvest, till the soil to kill burrowing caterpillars and pupae.
- Picking hornworms off plants is the most efficient control method, and their enormous size makes them easier to discover. To kill them, immerse them in soapy

water.

- The tomato hornworm has several natural predators, including general predatory insects such as lady beetles and green lacewings, prey on the eggs, and juvenile caterpillars.
- When caterpillars are little, use *Bacillus thuringiensis* (Bt).
- If you come across a caterpillar with what seems to be white rice grains stuck to its body, do not remove it. The "grains" are the larvae of a parasitic wasp that feeds on hornworms. Allow the parasitized caterpillar to remain in the garden so that the pupae it carries can develop into new wasps to help manage other hornworms.

Whitefly

Whiteflies are a common pest in UK gardens, known for their small, winged, moth-like appearance and their tendency to infest various plants. In order to identify and manage these pests effectively, gardeners should first familiarise themselves with the whitefly's characteristics, which include their size (approximately 1-2mm in length), colour (white or pale yellow), and their habit of congregating on the underside of leaves.

Management

To manage whitefly infestations, it is recommended that gardeners employ an integrated approach, combining cultural, biological, and chemical control methods. Cultural practices include regular inspection of plants, removing heavily infested leaves, and using reflective mulches to deter whiteflies. Biological control can involve the introduction of natural predators such as ladybirds, lacewings, and parasitic wasps, which can help keep whitefly populations in check. If required, chemical control methods using approved insecticides, such as those containing neem oil or pyrethrum, can be used as a last resort. Always follow label instructions and ensure chemicals are used responsibly to minimize any potential harm to beneficial organisms or the environment.

Plants that Attract Beneficial Insects

Plants that attract beneficial insects such as lady beetles, lacewings, parasitic wasps, and minute pirate bugs are anise, aster, basil, black locust, bee balm, canola, caraway, common knotweed, coneflower, coriander, cosmos, cowpea, crimson clover, daisy, dill, fennel, flowering buckwheat, hairy vetch, lovage, marigold, mint, nasturtium, oregano, parsley, poppy, Queen

Anne's lace, sage, salvia, spearmint, sweet alyssum, sweet fennel, subterranean clover, tansy, wallflower, white sweet clove, wild buckwheat, wild mustard, yarrow, and zinnia.

Animal Garden Pests

Birds

Many birds are beneficial to gardeners because they eat dangerous insects and weed seeds. However, we label them as pests when they prey on our crops. Blackbirds, starlings, and even robins have been observed pulling up delicious corn seedlings, munching on blossoming cherries, peaches, and blueberries, and digging holes in lawns in search of insects. The extent of the damage will vary based on the year's weather and local food supplies. Birds will attack many different fruits and vegetables, such as tomatoes and melons, seeking food and moisture in dry years.

Management

Any fear device will work for a few days, but birds are intelligent and adapt quickly. Hanging metal pie tins, reflecting Mylar tape, and giant fear eye balloons (that mimic the scary eyes of predator birds) are all good visual scare tactics. Radios and intermittent cannon exploders are also handy noisemakers. Commercial bird repellents, as well as homemade hot pepper spray sprayed to preferred fruits, are effective. On the other hand, exclusion is the most effective method of controlling bird damage. When erected two to three weeks before the fruit matures, bird netting protects the tree fruit and berries. To deter birds, wrap ripening corn ears with paper bags and place floating row covers over growing seedlings.

Squirrels

Squirrels are a common sight in British gardens, and although they can be endearing to watch, they can also pose a challenge for vegetable gardeners. These agile creatures are known to dig up bulbs, steal fruits, and nibble on tender shoots, causing damage to a variety of plants. Their inquisitive nature and appetite for fresh produce can result in frustration for those trying to cultivate a thriving vegetable garden.

Management

To manage squirrels in your vegetable garden, a few measures can be taken. Firstly, consider using protective barriers such as fine mesh or chicken wire to cover your plants or raised beds, ensuring the barrier is well-secured and extends below the soil surface to deter digging. Another option is to install a squirrel-proof bird feeder, as squirrels are often attracted to the seeds and nuts intended for birds. Additionally, try to eliminate any sources of standing water, as squirrels require water just as much as they require food. Motion-activated sprinklers can serve a dual purpose in this regard, scaring off squirrels while keeping your garden watered. Lastly, plant a diverse range of crops, as this can make it more difficult for squirrels to target specific plants. While it is challenging to completely squirrel-proof your garden, these strategies can help minimize their impact on your vegetable plot.

Mice, Voles, and Rats

These rodents, which range in size from the tiniest house mouse to the biggest Norway rat, dwell everywhere people do. Rats and mice are only active at night, but voles can be observed scurrying around at any time of day or night. These critters like digging and burrowing, making them important pests of subterranean garden plants. Mice and vole activity is indicated by partially consumed potatoes or carrots. They eat newly sowed seeds and most flower bulbs (except daffodils). Spring melting frequently shows chewed bark from the base of young tree trunks.

Management

The first line of defense is to make the environment hostile to mice by eliminating food, water, and shelter. Seal any entrances to buildings, clean up pet food bowls, and store rubbish in locked containers. The old-fashioned trap is the most effective family control. Place a snap or live trap on mouse pathways, baited with peanut butter or bacon. Delay adding fluffy mulches like straw in the garden until late in the season. Mice enjoy wintering in this material because it allows them free access to your plants under the snow. When used as intended, ammonium-based repellents can be effective against rodents.

Rabbits

These lovely, fuzzy critters can do a lot of damage to your garden and landscape. Rabbit and hare species abound across the country, and as the saying goes, they breed like... well, you know. They dwell in tunnel networks known as warrens and do not go far to feed. Peter Rabbit's cuisine includes young shoots of peas, beans, lettuce, flowers, tulips, clover, and deciduous tree bark. Fortunately, after plants have grown past the seedling stage or trees have developed strong bark, they are typically protected from bunny assaults. Look for cleanly cut leaves and stems to identify rabbit damage from a bug or other animal damage.

Management

Rabbits can be deterred, trapped, and fenced out. Install an area of alfalfa or clover apart from the garden to keep rabbits away from cherished crops. In the winter, use tree guards to protect young trees. Remove brush piles and tall grasses from areas where rabbits may hide in your garden. Although some gardeners employ repellents such as human or dog hair, chili powder, blood meal, fish emulsion, and commercial treatments, a fence is the most dependable approach to keep rabbits out of the garden.

Diseases

Alternaria

Alternaria disease is a group of fungal infections caused by species belonging to the Alternaria genus, which affect a wide range of plants, including vegetables, fruits, and ornamental plants. Commonly observed in the United Kingdom, these infections are characterized by dark, necrotic spots or concentric rings on leaves, fruits, and stems. The lesions can expand, leading to leaf drop, fruit rot, and defoliation, resulting in reduced yield and overall plant health. Alternaria disease is often exacerbated by warm, humid conditions, and the spores can spread through the air, water, or contaminated equipment. Implementing effective cultural practices, such as crop rotation, proper sanitation, and maintaining optimal plant spacing for air circulation, can help reduce the prevalence and impact of Alternaria disease in plants.

Management

- If symptoms emerge only on a few plants, remove contaminated plants as soon as they appear. Ensure that the entire plant, not just the leaves, is removed. Remove diseased leaves from all plants if they are afflicted.
- If you come into contact with sick leaves, thoroughly wash your hands before dealing with healthy Brassica plants. After contacting sick plants, wash and sterilize your pruning equipment.

- Purchase clean seed from trusted sources.
- Only preserve seeds from healthy plants if you want to save them.
- Think about heat-treating your seed.
- Remove or bury any leftovers in your garden.
- Allow three years before replanting Brassica plants in the same spot.
- If this disease has been an issue for you, avoid using cover crops in the Brassica family, such as tillage radish.
- Increase airflow by keeping plants at a reasonable distance apart. Broccoli spacing should be 10–18 inches apart in rows 18–36 inches apart.
- Keep an eye out for weeds in the Brassica family, including shepherd's purse, black mustard, and field mustard. Remove them from your garden to avoid serving as a host for black rot.
- Each time you start seeds, clean and sterilize the trays.

Angular Leaf Spot

Angular leaf spot, caused by the bacterium Pseudomonas syringae pv. lachrymans, is a disease that primarily affects cucurbits, including cucumbers, melons, and squash. Commonly observed in the United Kingdom, the disease is characterized by water-soaked, angular lesions on the leaves, which are generally confined by the leaf veins. As the infection progresses, the lesions may turn necrotic and develop a yellow halo, leading to defoliation and reduced plant health. Angular leaf spot can also cause lesions on fruits and stems, impacting yield and quality. The disease is favored by cool, wet conditions and can spread through rain, irrigation water, and contaminated equipment.

Management

Use a two-year rotation at the very least. Plant resistant cultivars and seed stock from arid areas. Drip irrigation is preferable to overhead watering. When the plants are damp, avoid working in the garden. To prevent the spread of infection, destroy sick plants as well as those nearby.

Anthracnose

Anthracnose disease, caused by a group of fungi within the Colletotrichum genus, affects a wide range of plants, including fruits, vegetables, and ornamental plants in the United Kingdom. The disease is characterized by the development of dark, sunken lesions on leaves, stems, and fruits, often with a concentric ring pattern. As the infection progresses, these lesions can coalesce, leading to defoliation, fruit rot, and reduced plant health. Anthracnose is favored by warm, wet, and humid conditions, and the spores can spread through rain splash, irrigation water, or contaminated equipment.

Management

Compost enriches the soil, which helps plants withstand the assault. Get disease-free seed and cultivate resistant cultivars. Working with plants when they are damp is not a good idea. Irrigate using drip rather than overhead sprinklers. Rotate crops at least once a year (a two-to-three-year rotation is better). Keep ripening fruits away from the dirt. When used as stated on the product label, copper fungicides are effective as a preventative. It's better not to rely too much on this form of management since copper may accumulate in the soil to dangerous levels for earthworms and bacteria.

Black Rot

Black rot, caused by the bacterium Xanthomonas campestris pv. campestris, is a devastating disease affecting brassicas, including cabbage, cauliflower, broccoli, and Brussels sprouts, commonly found in the United Kingdom. This disease is characterized by V-shaped, yellow to brown lesions along the leaf margins that gradually expand inwards, eventually leading to necrosis and leaf drop. In advanced stages, black rot can cause blackening of the veins, wilting, and even plant death. The bacterium thrives in warm, wet conditions and can spread through rain splash, irrigation water, contaminated seeds, and equipment.

Management

Plant disease-free seeds and transplants. Remove diseased plants. Irrigation systems that moisten the tops of plants should be avoided. Give a two-year gap before planting susceptible plants.

Blight (Bacterial)

Bacterial blight, caused by various strains of the bacterium Pseudomonas syringae, is a disease that affects a wide range of plants, including vegetables, fruits, and ornamentals in the United Kingdom. The disease is characterized by water-soaked lesions on leaves, stems, and fruits, which can expand and become necrotic. In severe cases, bacterial blight can lead to defoliation, reduced yield, and overall plant decline. The bacterium thrives in cool, wet conditions and can spread through rain splash, irrigation water, or contaminated equipment.

Management

For beans, use a three-year crop rotation. When the plants are damp, avoid working in the garden. Save no seeds from diseased plants. When used as indicated on the product label, copper fungicides are effective as a preventative but harm the soil biota.

Blight (Early)

Early blight, caused by the fungus Alternaria solani, is a common disease affecting solanaceous plants, such as potatoes and tomatoes, in the United Kingdom. The disease is characterized by the appearance of small, dark brown lesions on leaves, which often display a concentric ring pattern resembling a target. As the infection progresses, the lesions can expand and cause defoliation, reduced yield, and overall plant decline. Early blight can also affect the fruits, resulting in dark, sunken spots. The fungus favors warm, wet conditions and can spread through rain splash, irrigation water, or contaminated equipment.

Management

Plant in well-drained soil with sufficient air circulation. Rotate crops and remove any stray potato or tomato plants. When watering, avoid wetting the leaves. Amend the soil with compost and fertilize plants sparingly to preserve plant vitality. Ensure that your seed potatoes and tomato transplants are disease-free. Tomato plants with early blight gradually lose their leaves, but ripe tomatoes can typically be harvested unless the infection is severe. At the first indication of the illness, use a copper-based fungicide as instructed on the product label.

Blight (Late)

Late blight, caused by the oomycete Phytophthora infestans, is a destructive disease that predominantly affects solanaceous plants, such as potatoes and tomatoes, in the United Kingdom. The disease is characterized by the rapid development of water-soaked, dark brown lesions on leaves, which can lead to extensive defoliation and plant death. Late blight can also infect fruits and tubers, causing them to rot. The pathogen thrives in cool, wet, and humid conditions and can spread rapidly through rain splash, irrigation water, wind, or contaminated equipment. Due to its ability to cause devastating crop losses, late blight management is crucial.

Management

Fertilize sparingly, as excess nitrogen promotes the illness. Avoid overhead watering using a sprinkler system (wet foliage). To prevent the spread of the disease, use a flame weeder to remove diseased plants. To avoid infecting tubers, wait a week after potato plants die before harvesting at the end of the season. Use a flame weeder to eliminate plant remnants before digging tubers for an early harvest.

Club Root

Club root, caused by the soil-borne protist Plasmodiophora brassicae, is a widespread and persistent disease affecting brassicas, such as cabbage, cauliflower, and broccoli, in the United Kingdom. The disease is characterized by the formation of swollen, distorted, and sometimes club-like roots, leading to poor nutrient and water uptake, wilting, stunted growth, and potentially plant death. The pathogen thrives in wet, acidic soils and can persist in the soil for many years, making it challenging to control.

Management

Management strategies for club root include the use of resistant cultivars, raising the soil pH to at least 7.0 through the addition of lime, practicing crop rotation with non-host plants, maintaining proper plant spacing for air circulation, and implementing good sanitation measures, such as cleaning equipment and footwear to avoid spreading the pathogen between plots.

Leaf Spot (Bacterial)

Bacterial leaf spot, caused by various species of bacteria, such as Xanthomonas and Pseudomonas, is a common disease affecting a wide range of plants, including vegetables, fruits, and ornamentals in the United Kingdom. The disease is characterized by the appearance of small, water-soaked lesions on leaves, which can expand, turn necrotic, and develop a yellow halo. In severe cases, bacterial leaf spot can cause defoliation, reduced yield, and overall plant decline. The bacteria thrive in warm, wet conditions and can spread through rain splash, irrigation water, or contaminated equipment.

Management

Use a three- to four-year crop rotation. Destroy any volunteer tomato and pepper plants and any contaminated fruits. Only buy transplants that have been verified as disease-free. Plants should be watered and fertilized regularly. Allow enough space between plants and support vines to allow proper air circulation. Avoid overhead watering and working around damp plants to keep the illness from spreading. While the weather is conducive to disease spread, spray actively aerated compost tea every seven to ten days.

Leaf Spot (Septoria)

Septoria leaf spot, caused by the fungus Septoria species, is a common disease affecting a wide range of plants, including vegetables, fruits, and ornamentals in the United Kingdom. The disease is characterized by the appearance of small, circular or angular spots on leaves, which can expand and merge, causing leaf yellowing, necrosis, and defoliation. Septoria leaf spot is favored by warm, humid conditions and can spread through rain splash, irrigation water, or contaminated equipment.

Management

Management strategies for septoria leaf spot include the use of resistant cultivars, practicing crop rotation, maintaining proper plant spacing for air circulation, implementing good sanitation measures, and applying appropriate fungicides when conditions are conducive to disease development. Proper disposal of infected plant debris is also essential to prevent the spread of the disease.

Mildew (Downy)

Downy mildew, caused by various species of fungi within the Peronospora genus, is a common disease affecting a wide range of plants, including vegetables, fruits, and ornamentals in the United Kingdom. The disease is characterized by the appearance of yellow or white patches on leaves, which are covered with a fuzzy, mold-like growth on the undersides. As the infection progresses, the patches can turn brown or purple, leading to defoliation, reduced yield, and overall plant decline. Downy mildew is favored by cool, humid conditions and can spread through wind, rain splash, irrigation water, or contaminated equipment.

Management

Management strategies for downy mildew include the use of resistant cultivars, practicing crop rotation, maintaining proper plant spacing for air circulation, implementing good sanitation measures, and applying appropriate fungicides when conditions are conducive to disease development. Prompt detection and treatment are essential to prevent the spread of the disease. To limit disease transmission, organic gardeners might use actively aerated compost tea.

Mildew (Powdery)

Powdery mildew, caused by various species of fungi within the Erysiphales order, is a common disease affecting a wide range of plants, including vegetables, fruits, and ornamentals in the United Kingdom. The disease is characterized by the appearance of white or grayish powdery patches on leaves, stems, and fruits, which can cause leaf curling, yellowing, and reduced photosynthesis. In severe cases, powdery mildew can cause defoliation, reduced yield, and overall plant decline. The fungus thrives in warm, dry conditions and can spread through wind, water, or contaminated equipment.

Management

Management strategies for powdery mildew include the use of resistant cultivars, maintaining proper plant spacing for air circulation, implementing good sanitation measures, such as removing infected plant debris and cleaning equipment, and applying appropriate fungicides when conditions are conducive to disease development. Early detection and treatment are essential to prevent the spread of the disease.

Wilt (Bacterial)

Bacterial wilt, caused by the bacterium Ralstonia solanacearum, is a serious disease affecting a wide range of plants, including vegetables, fruits, and ornamentals in the United Kingdom. The disease is characterized by wilting and yellowing of leaves, which can rapidly progress to plant death. The bacterium enters the plant through the roots and spreads throughout the vascular system, leading to blockage and wilting of the entire plant. Bacterial wilt is favored by warm, moist conditions and can spread through contaminated soil, irrigation water, or infected plant material.

Management

Management strategies for bacterial wilt include the use of resistant cultivars, practicing crop rotation, maintaining proper plant spacing for air circulation, implementing good sanitation measures, such as cleaning equipment and tools, and avoiding planting in infected soil. There are no effective chemical control measures for bacterial wilt, so prevention and early detection are essential to reduce the risk of spread.

Wilt (Verticillium and Fusarium)

Wilt disease, caused by various species of fungi, such as Verticillium and Fusarium, is a common disease affecting a wide range of plants, including vegetables, fruits, and ornamentals in the United Kingdom. The disease is characterized by wilting and yellowing of leaves, which can gradually spread throughout the plant. The fungi enter the plant through the roots and colonize the vascular system, leading to blockage and reduced water and nutrient uptake. Wilt diseases are favored by warm, moist conditions and can persist in the soil for many years. They can spread through contaminated soil, water, or infected plant material.

Management

Management strategies for wilt diseases include the use of resistant cultivars, practicing crop rotation, maintaining proper plant spacing for air circulation, implementing good sanitation measures, such as removing infected plant debris and cleaning equipment, and applying appropriate fungicides when conditions are conducive to disease development. Early detection and treatment are essential to prevent the spread of the disease.

Mould (Grey)

Grey mould, caused by the fungus Botrytis cinerea, is a common disease affecting a wide range of plants, including vegetables, fruits, and ornamentals in the United Kingdom. The disease is characterized by the appearance of fuzzy, grayish-brown mold on leaves, flowers, fruits, and stems. As the infection progresses, the mold can spread, leading to plant tissue decay and rot. Grey mould is favored by cool, moist conditions and can spread through wind, rain splash, irrigation water, or contaminated equipment.

Management

Management strategies for grey mould include the use of resistant cultivars, maintaining proper plant spacing for air circulation, implementing good sanitation measures, such as removing infected plant debris and cleaning equipment, and applying appropriate fungicides when conditions are conducive to disease development. Early detection and treatment are essential to prevent the spread of the disease.

Scab (Potato)

Potato scab, caused by the bacterium Streptomyces scabies, is a common disease affecting potato crops in the United Kingdom. The disease is characterized by the formation of rough, corky, scab-like lesions on the surface of the potato tubers. Although unsightly, potato scab rarely affects the quality or edibility of the potato. The bacterium thrives in alkaline soils and can survive in the soil for several years.

Management

Management strategies for potato scab include maintaining soil pH below 5.2, practicing crop rotation, avoiding excessive irrigation and fertilization, and using certified seed potatoes. Soil amendments, such as the addition of organic matter, can also help reduce the severity of the disease. There are no effective chemical control measures for potato scab, so prevention and cultural control measures are essential. Consider growing potatoes in buckets.

Viruses

There are several plant-specific viruses that may affect your garden crops. Below is an inexhaustive list of some of the most common vegetable viruses.

1. Tomato spotted wilt virus (TSWV)
2. Cucumber mosaic virus (CMV)
3. Tobacco mosaic virus (TMV)
4. Potato virus Y (PVY)
5. Bean yellow mosaic virus (BYMV)
6. Lettuce mosaic virus (LMV)
7. Pepper mild mottle virus (PMMoV)
8. Beet mosaic virus (BMV)
9. Zucchini yellow mosaic virus (ZYMV)
10. Squash mosaic virus (SqMV)
11. Watermelon mosaic virus (WMV)
12. Cucumber green mottle mosaic virus (CGMMV)
13. Broad bean mottle virus (BBMV)
14. Pea seed-borne mosaic virus (PSbMV)
15. Carrot motley dwarf virus (CMDV)
16. Onion yellow dwarf virus (OYDV)
17. Turnip mosaic virus (TuMV)
18. Cauliflower mosaic virus (CaMV)
19. Spinach latent virus (SpLV)
20. Alfalfa mosaic virus (AMV)

Symptoms vary depending on the virus, but may include mottling, streaking, puckering, or curling leaves. Cucumber mosaic virus, for example, infects cucurbits, tomatoes, and peppers, causing green and yellow mottling of foliage, curled leaves, stunted plants, and fruits with light splotches warty pimples. Many viruses are transmitted from plant to plant by sucking insects like aphids and leafhoppers as they eat.

Management

Control disease-carrying insects. Infected plants should be removed and burned. When available, select resistant kinds. Purchase virus-free seed potatoes. Weeds that carry viruses must be controlled.

Plant Problems and Possible Causes

Rapid leaf drop:

- Extreme temperature or light changes
- Root loss from transplanting
- Overwatering
- Underwatering

Gradual leaf drop:

- Insufficient light
- Insufficient fertilizer
- Overwatering
- Underwatering

Wilting of the entire plant:

- Exposure to cold
- Excess fertilizer
- Overwatering
- Underwatering

Loss of leaf colour:

- Excess light

- Insufficient light
- Insufficient fertilizer
- Overwatering
- Underwatering
- Spider mite damage

Spotted leaves:

- Leaf scorch
- Sunburn
- Cold water on leaves (particularly African violets)
- Bacterial or fungal disease
- Air pollution
- Overwatering
- Spider mite damage

Leaf tips turning brown:

- Low humidity
- Incorrect potting mix pH
- Air pollution
- Poor water quality (fluoride, sodium)
- Excess fertilizer
- Overwatering
- Underwatering

Stunted plants:

- Excess fertilizer
- Overwatering
- Underwatering
- Root-bound

- Insufficient light intensity
- Insufficient fertilizer

Leaf droop or curl:

- Air pollution
- Underwatering
- Aphids

Pale and spindly new growth:

- Insufficient fertilizer
- Insufficient light
- Underwatering

Wilted or blackened new growth:

- Cold or hot drafts
- Sunburn
- Temperature too warm
- Temperature too cold
- Excess fertilizer
- Underwatering

White spots on leaves:

- Spider mites

Cottony masses on stems:

- Mealybugs and some scale species

Dark bumps on leaves or stems:

- Armoured scales

Sticky spots under the leaves:

- Honeydew excreted by aphids, mealy bugs, scale, or white flies

CHAPTER 10

MONTHLY TASKS

January

- Plan your vegetable garden: Sketch out a design for your garden, including the layout, spacing, and what crops you want to grow.
- Order seeds and supplies: Research and purchase seeds, fertilizers, and other necessary supplies for the upcoming growing season.
- Clean and maintain tools: Check your gardening tools for wear and tear, sharpen blades, and clean handles.
- Prepare seed trays and propagators: Clean and sterilize seed trays and propagators to prevent diseases.
- Start indoor seedlings: Sow seeds for slow-growing crops such as peppers, tomatoes, and aubergines indoors.
- Chit potatoes: Lay seed potatoes in a tray with the "eyes" facing up to encourage sprouting before planting.
- Inspect stored vegetables: Check stored vegetables for signs of rot, mold, or pests and remove any affected items.
- Prune fruit trees and bushes: Prune apple and pear trees, currant and gooseberry bushes to maintain shape and encourage healthy growth.
- Apply organic matter: Spread well-rotted manure or compost over empty beds to improve soil fertility.
- Create a compost heap: Start a new compost heap or turn existing ones to speed up decomposition.
- Build raised beds: Construct raised beds to improve drainage and soil quality.
- Plant bare-root fruit trees and bushes: Plant dormant fruit trees and bushes, such as raspberries, currants, and gooseberries.
- Harvest winter vegetables: Pick hardy winter vegetables like Brussels sprouts,

kale, and leeks.

- Protect tender plants: Cover tender plants, such as artichokes and chard, with fleece or cloches to protect them from frost.
- Check for pests: Inspect plants for pests like aphids and slugs and take appropriate measures to control them.
- Test soil pH: Test your soil's pH levels and make any necessary adjustments to create the optimal growing environment.
- Install water butts: Set up water butts to collect rainwater for use during drier months.
- Improve garden paths and structures: Repair or create new paths and trellises to make gardening tasks easier and more efficient.
- Force rhubarb: Cover rhubarb crowns with a forcing jar or bucket to encourage early, tender growth.
- Plan crop rotation: Plan a crop rotation schedule to prevent soil depletion and reduce the risk of pests and diseases.

February

- Finalize your garden plan: Review your layout and make any necessary adjustments to ensure a successful growing season.
- Continue ordering seeds and supplies: Purchase any additional seeds, fertilizers, or equipment needed for the upcoming growing season.
- Start indoor seedlings: Sow seeds indoors for crops like onions, leeks, celery, and early brassicas (cabbage, cauliflower, and broccoli).
- Chit potatoes: Continue chitting seed potatoes in a cool, frost-free environment.
- Plant bare-root fruit trees and bushes: If you didn't plant them in January, there's still time to plant dormant fruit trees and bushes.
- Plant shallots and garlic: Plant shallot sets and garlic cloves in well-drained soil.
- Prune grapevines: Prune grapevines before the sap starts to rise, to prevent "bleeding."

- Prepare seedbeds: Rake over beds to create a fine tilth and remove any weeds or debris.
- Apply organic matter: If you haven't already, spread well-rotted manure or compost over empty beds to improve soil fertility.
- Mulch perennial vegetables: Add a layer of mulch around perennial vegetables like asparagus and artichokes to help conserve moisture and suppress weeds.
- Heat greenhouse or polytunnel: If you have a greenhouse or polytunnel, use a heater to maintain a suitable temperature for seedlings and tender plants.
- Maintain tools: Continue to clean and maintain your gardening tools to keep them in good working order.
- Sow peas and broad beans: Plant peas and broad beans in pots or directly into the soil, depending on local conditions.
- Rotate compost heaps: Turn your compost heaps to speed up decomposition and ensure an even breakdown.
- Plant Jerusalem artichokes: Plant tubers in a sunny spot with well-drained soil.
- Check stored vegetables: Inspect stored vegetables for signs of rot or pests and remove any affected items.
- Protect tender plants: Continue to protect tender plants from frost using fleece, cloches, or other suitable materials.
- Harvest winter vegetables: Harvest any remaining winter vegetables, such as parsnips, kale, and Brussels sprouts.
- Check for pests and diseases: Inspect your plants for signs of pests and diseases, and treat them accordingly.
- Clean bird feeders and baths: Clean and refill bird feeders and baths to help support local wildlife.

March

- Prepare garden beds: Remove any weeds or debris, and rake the soil to create a fine tilth in preparation for planting.

- Test soil pH: Test your soil's pH levels and make any necessary adjustments to create the optimal growing environment.
- Apply organic matter: Spread well-rotted manure or compost over empty beds to improve soil fertility, if you haven't done so already.
- Plant onion sets and shallots: Plant onion sets and shallot sets in well-drained soil in a sunny location.
- Sow early potatoes: Plant early potato varieties in prepared trenches or containers.
- Plant summer-flowering bulbs: Plant bulbs such as gladioli and lilies for a colorful display later in the year.
- Sow seeds outdoors: Direct sow hardy vegetables like peas, carrots, beetroot, lettuce, and radishes.
- Start indoor seedlings: Continue sowing seeds indoors for crops like tomatoes, peppers, cucumbers, and courgettes.
- Transplant seedlings: Carefully transplant seedlings that have outgrown their containers into larger pots or trays.
- Harden off seedlings: Gradually expose indoor seedlings to outdoor conditions to prepare them for planting out.
- Plant bare-root fruit trees and bushes: If you haven't done so yet, plant dormant fruit trees and bushes.
- Prune fruit trees: Finish pruning fruit trees like apples, pears, and cherries to encourage healthy growth.
- Maintain tools: Clean and maintain your gardening tools to ensure they are in good working order.
- Set up supports: Install supports like stakes, cages, and trellises for climbing vegetables, such as peas and beans.
- Rotate compost heaps: Turn compost heaps to speed up decomposition and ensure an even breakdown.
- Water and feed plants: Provide adequate water and nutrients to your growing plants as needed.

- Protect young plants from pests: Use barriers or organic methods to protect your seedlings and young plants from slugs, snails, and other pests.
- Install water butts: Set up water butts to collect rainwater for use during drier months.
- Harvest spring vegetables: Begin harvesting spring vegetables like spring onions, asparagus, and early radishes.
- Keep an eye on frost: Monitor weather forecasts and protect tender plants from late frosts with fleece, cloches, or other suitable materials.

April

- Sow seeds outdoors: Begin sowing seeds outdoors for crops like carrots, beetroot, radishes, lettuce, and spinach, as well as peas and broad beans.
- Plant potatoes: Plant your chitted potatoes, ensuring adequate spacing and depth for optimal growth.
- Plant onion sets and shallots: Plant onion sets and shallots, if you haven't already, in well-drained soil.
- Transplant seedlings: Harden off and transplant seedlings of brassicas, leeks, and onions into their final growing positions.
- Sow herbs: Sow herbs like parsley, chives, and coriander directly into the soil or in pots.
- Sow greenhouse crops: Sow greenhouse crops like tomatoes, peppers, cucumbers, and aubergines, if you haven't already, and maintain proper temperature and humidity.
- Plant asparagus crowns: Plant asparagus crowns in well-prepared beds with good drainage.
- Earth up potatoes: As potato plants grow, "earth up" by covering the stems with soil to protect the developing tubers from sunlight.
- Thin seedlings: Thin out seedlings of direct-sown vegetables to give them adequate space to grow.
- Apply organic mulch: Mulch around fruit trees and bushes to conserve moisture,

suppress weeds, and improve soil structure.

- Water wisely: Water plants as needed, especially during dry spells, and prioritize seedlings and newly transplanted plants.
- Continue rotating compost heaps: Turn your compost heaps to speed up decomposition and ensure an even breakdown.
- Install supports: Put up supports for climbing plants like peas, beans, and tomatoes.
- Protect against pests: Watch for pests like aphids, slugs, and snails, and take appropriate measures to control them.
- Feed fruit trees and bushes: Apply a balanced fertilizer to fruit trees and bushes to encourage healthy growth and fruit production.
- Harden off tender plants: Gradually acclimatize tender plants, like tomatoes and peppers, to outdoor conditions before planting them out.
- Harvest early crops: Harvest early crops like radishes, spring onions, and spinach as they become ready.
- Plant summer bulbs: Plant summer-flowering bulbs, like gladioli and lilies, in well-drained soil.
- Maintain paths and structures: Keep paths and structures, like trellises and raised beds, in good condition.
- Enjoy your garden: Spend time in your garden, appreciating the beauty and tranquility it offers, and make notes on any adjustments or improvements for the coming months.

May

- Plant out tender vegetables: Harden off and transplant tender vegetables like tomatoes, peppers, aubergines, and cucumbers into their final growing positions.
- Sow beans: Sow runner beans and French beans directly into the soil or start them in pots for transplanting later.
- Sow additional crops: Sow seeds outdoors for crops like sweetcorn, pumpkins, courgettes, and squash.

- Successional sowings: Make successional sowings of fast-growing crops like radishes, lettuce, and spinach to ensure a continuous harvest.
- Plant out herbs: Plant out herbs like basil, parsley, and dill or sow directly into the soil or pots.
- Earth up potatoes: Continue earthing up potatoes to protect the developing tubers from sunlight and prevent them from turning green.
- Water consistently: Ensure consistent watering, focusing on seedlings, transplants, and plants in containers or greenhouses.
- Apply organic mulch: Continue to mulch around vegetables and fruit plants to suppress weeds and conserve moisture.
- Feed tomatoes: Start feeding tomato plants with a high-potassium fertilizer to encourage fruit production.
- Support climbing plants: Install supports for climbing plants like beans, peas, and cucumbers.
- Thin seedlings: Thin out seedlings of direct-sown vegetables to provide adequate space for growth.
- Protect fruit from birds: Install netting over fruit bushes and trees to protect ripening fruit from birds.
- Harvest early crops: Continue harvesting early crops like radishes, spring onions, and spinach as they become ready.
- Monitor for pests and diseases: Regularly inspect your plants for signs of pests and diseases, and treat them accordingly.
- Weed control: Keep on top of weeding to prevent competition for nutrients, water, and sunlight.
- Ventilate greenhouses and polytunnels: Open vents and doors on warm days to regulate temperature and humidity, and prevent overheating.
- Pinch out tomato side shoots: Remove side shoots from tomato plants to encourage a strong central stem and larger fruit.
- Cut back spring-flowering perennials: Trim back spring-flowering perennials, like chives and mint, to encourage new growth.

- Harden off winter brassicas: Gradually acclimatize winter brassica seedlings, like kale and Brussels sprouts, before planting them out in the garden.
- Enjoy your garden: Take time to appreciate the progress of your garden, take photos, and note any changes or improvements you would like to make in the coming months.

June

- Plant out winter brassicas: Transplant winter brassica seedlings, like kale, Brussels sprouts, and winter cabbage, into their final growing positions.
- Successional sowings: Continue making successional sowings of fast-growing crops like lettuce, radishes, and beetroot to ensure a continuous harvest.
- Harvest early potatoes: Begin harvesting early potato varieties as soon as the foliage starts to die back.
- Plant out leeks: Transplant leek seedlings into their final growing positions, ensuring they are well-spaced and adequately watered.
- Sow fast-growing herbs: Sow fast-growing herbs like coriander, dill, and parsley directly into the soil or pots.
- Feed fruiting vegetables: Apply a high-potassium fertilizer to fruiting plants like tomatoes, peppers, and aubergines to encourage better yields.
- Pinch out tomato side shoots: Continue removing side shoots from tomato plants to encourage a strong central stem and larger fruit.
- Water consistently: Water plants regularly, especially during dry spells, focusing on seedlings, transplants, and plants in containers or greenhouses.
- Protect plants from pests: Monitor plants for pests like aphids, slugs, and snails, and take appropriate measures to control them.
- Support climbing plants: Check and adjust supports for climbing plants like beans, peas, and cucumbers, tying in growth as necessary.
- Harvest ripe fruits: Pick ripe fruits, like strawberries, raspberries, and currants, regularly to encourage further production.
- Thin out fruit on fruit trees: Thin out crowded clusters of fruit on apple and pear

trees to allow remaining fruit to grow larger and prevent branches from breaking.

- Mulch around plants: Maintain a layer of organic mulch around vegetables and fruit plants to suppress weeds and conserve moisture.
- Ventilate greenhouses and polytunnels: Ensure proper ventilation in greenhouses and polytunnels on warm days to prevent overheating and maintain optimal growing conditions.
- Weed control: Stay on top of weeding to prevent competition for water, nutrients, and sunlight.
- Harvest salad crops: Pick salad leaves, like lettuce and spinach, regularly to encourage new growth and prolong the harvesting period.
- Maintain garden paths and structures: Keep garden paths and structures, like trellises and raised beds, in good condition and free from debris.
- Prune fruit bushes: Prune summer-fruiting raspberry canes after they have finished fruiting, and tie in new growth on blackberries and hybrid berries.
- Net brassicas: Cover brassicas with fine netting to protect them from pests like cabbage white butterflies and pigeons.
- Enjoy your garden: Take time to appreciate your garden's beauty and productivity, and make notes on any changes or improvements you would like to make in the coming months.

July

- Successional sowings: Continue making successional sowings of fast-growing crops like lettuce, radishes, and beetroot to ensure a continuous harvest.
- Harvest potatoes: Harvest maincrop potatoes when the foliage begins to die back, and allow them to dry before storing.
- Water consistently: Water plants regularly, especially during dry spells, focusing on seedlings, transplants, and plants in containers or greenhouses.
- Feed fruiting vegetables: Continue to apply a high-potassium fertilizer to fruiting plants like tomatoes, peppers, and aubergines to encourage better yields.
- Pinch out tomato side shoots: Keep removing side shoots from tomato plants to

encourage a strong central stem and larger fruit.

- Harvest ripe fruits: Pick ripe fruits, like cherries, plums, and blueberries, regularly to encourage further production.
- Support climbing plants: Check and adjust supports for climbing plants like beans, peas, and cucumbers, tying in growth as necessary.
- Protect plants from pests: Monitor plants for pests like aphids, slugs, and snails, and take appropriate measures to control them.
- Prune fruit trees: Summer prune fruit trees like apples and pears to maintain shape, encourage fruiting spurs, and allow sunlight to ripen the fruit.
- Mulch around plants: Maintain a layer of organic mulch around vegetables and fruit plants to suppress weeds and conserve moisture.
- Ventilate greenhouses and polytunnels: Ensure proper ventilation in greenhouses and polytunnels on warm days to prevent overheating and maintain optimal growing conditions.
- Harvest salad crops: Continue to pick salad leaves like lettuce and spinach, as well as other crops like peas, beans, and courgettes, regularly to encourage new growth and prolong the harvesting period.
- Weed control: Stay on top of weeding to prevent competition for water, nutrients, and sunlight.
- Maintain garden paths and structures: Keep garden paths and structures, like trellises and raised beds, in good condition and free from debris.
- Deadhead flowers: Remove spent flowers from plants like sweet peas and marigolds to encourage further blooms.
- Net brassicas: Keep brassicas covered with fine netting to protect them from pests like cabbage white butterflies and pigeons.
- Check stored produce: Inspect stored produce for signs of rot or pests and remove any affected items.
- Plan autumn garden: Begin planning your autumn garden, considering which crops to plant and where to plant them based on crop rotation principles.
- Enjoy your garden: Take time to appreciate your garden's beauty and productivity, and make notes on any changes or improvements you would like to

make in the coming months.

August

- Harvest vegetables: Continue to harvest ripe vegetables such as tomatoes, cucumbers, courgettes, beans, peas, and salad leaves.
- Successional sowings: Make successional sowings of fast-growing crops like lettuce, radishes, and spring onions to ensure a continuous harvest.
- Sow autumn and winter vegetables: Sow seeds for autumn and winter vegetables like spinach, turnips, Swiss chard, and winter salad leaves.
- Water consistently: Keep watering plants regularly, especially during dry spells, focusing on seedlings, transplants, and plants in containers or greenhouses.
- Feed fruiting vegetables: Continue applying a high-potassium fertilizer to fruiting plants like tomatoes, peppers, and aubergines to encourage better yields.
- Harvest ripe fruits: Pick ripe fruits like raspberries, blackberries, and early apple varieties as they become ready.
- Protect plants from pests: Monitor plants for pests like aphids, slugs, and snails, and take appropriate measures to control them.
- Support climbing plants: Check and adjust supports for climbing plants like beans and cucumbers, tying in growth as necessary.
- Ventilate greenhouses and polytunnels: Ensure proper ventilation in greenhouses and polytunnels on warm days to prevent overheating and maintain optimal growing conditions.
- Prune fruit bushes: Prune summer-fruiting raspberries, gooseberries, and currants after they have finished fruiting, removing old canes or branches.
- Mulch around plants: Maintain a layer of organic mulch around vegetables and fruit plants to suppress weeds and conserve moisture.
- Weed control: Stay on top of weeding to prevent competition for water, nutrients, and sunlight.
- Deadhead flowers: Remove spent flowers from plants like sweet peas and marigolds to encourage further blooms.

- Plant autumn onion sets: Plant onion sets for an early crop next year, ensuring they have adequate space and are in a well-drained area.
- Harvest potatoes: Continue to harvest maincrop potatoes as the foliage dies back, and allow them to dry before storing.
- Maintain garden paths and structures: Keep garden paths and structures, like trellises and raised beds, in good condition and free from debris.
- Net brassicas: Keep brassicas covered with fine netting to protect them from pests like cabbage white butterflies and pigeons.
- Check stored produce: Inspect stored produce for signs of rot or pests and remove any affected items.
- Collect seeds: Collect seeds from your favorite plants to store for next year's sowing.
- Enjoy your garden: Take time to appreciate your garden's beauty and productivity, and make notes on any changes or improvements you would like to make in the coming months.

September

- Dig onions and garlic after tops autumn over naturally and necks begin to dry.
- Plant radishes, green onion sets, lettuce and spinach for autumn harvest.
- Thin autumn crops, such as lettuce and carrots, that were planted earlier.
- Harvest crops such as tomatoes, peppers, eggplants, melons and sweet potatoes before frost, or cover plants with blankets, newspaper, etc. (but not plastic) to protect them from light frost.
- Mature green tomatoes can be ripened indoors. Individually wrap fruits in newspaper, or leave them on the vine, pulling the entire plant out of the garden. Store in a cool location – about 13–16°C.
- Harvest winter squash when mature (skin is tough) with deep, solid colour, but before hard frost. Some cultivars will show an orange blush when mature.
- Plant, transplant or divide peonies, daylilies, iris and phlox only if you can apply irrigation during dry spells.

- Save plants such as coleus, wax begonias, impatiens or fuchsia for indoor growing over winter. Dig plants and cut them back about halfway, or take cuttings of shoot tips, and root them in moist vermiculite, soil mix or perlite.
- Watch for garden chrysanthemums to bloom as days grow shorter. Some may have bloomed earlier this summer, which will decrease the number of autumn blooms.
- Plant spring-flowering bulbs beginning in late September. Planting too early can cause bulbs to sprout top growth before winter. However, allow at least four to six weeks before the ground freezes for good root formation.
- Dig tender bulbs, such as cannas, caladiums, tuberous begonias and gladiolus, before frost. Allow to air dry, and store in dry peat moss or vermiculite.
- Choose the mild weather during this period to plant or transplant the following: beets, broccoli, cabbage, carrots, collards, lettuce, mustard, onions, radishes, spinach and turnips. Plant your second planting of autumn crops such as collards, turnips, cabbage, mustard and kale.
- Refurbish mulch to control weeds, and start adding leaves and other materials for the compost pile. Store your manure under cover to prevent leaching of nutrients.
- Water deeply and thoroughly to prevent drought stress. Pay special attention to new transplants.
- Harvest mature green peppers and tomatoes before frost gets them – it may not come until November, but be ready.
- Harvest herbs and dry them in a cool, dry place.

October

- Harvest root crops and store in a cold (0°C), humid location. Storing produce in perforated plastic bags is a convenient, easy way to increase humidity.
- Harvest Brussels sprouts as they develop in the axils of the leaves from the bottom of the stem. Brussels sprouts will continue to develop up the stem.
- Harvest pumpkins and winter squash before frost, but when rind is hard and fully coloured. Store in a cool location until ready to use.
- Harvest gourds when stems begin to brown and dry. Cure at 21 - 24°C for two to four

weeks.

- Harvest mature, green tomatoes before frost and ripen indoors in the dark. Warmer temperatures lead to faster ripening.
- Asparagus top growth should not be removed until foliage yellows. Let foliage stand over winter to collect snow for insulation and moisture.
- Remove plant debris from the garden to protect next year's plantings from insect and disease buildup. Compost plant refuse by alternating layers of soil, plant material, and manure or commercial fertilizer.
- Have garden soil tested for fertilizer needs every three to five years.
- Incorporate organic matter in autumn to avoid the rush of garden activities and waterlogged soil in spring. Soils prepared in the autumn tend to warm faster and allow earlier planting in spring.
- Dig tender garden flower bulbs for winter storage. Gladiolus corms should be dug when leaves begin turning yellow. Caladiums, geraniums and tuberous begonias should be lifted before killing frost. Dig canna and dahlia roots after a heavy frost. Allow to air dry, then pack in dry peat moss or vermiculite, and store in a cool location.
- Complete planting of spring-flowering bulbs.

November

- If frost hasn't taken your garden yet, continue harvesting.
- Harvest mature green tomatoes before frost, and ripen indoors in the dark. Store at 13–21°C. The warmer the temperature, the faster they ripen.
- Harvest root crops and store them in a cold (0°C), humid location. Use perforated plastic bags as an easy way to increase humidity.
- Remove crop and weed plant debris from the garden and add to the compost pile. This will help reduce the carryover of diseases, insects and weeds to next year's garden.
- Fall tilling, except in erosion-prone areas, helps improve soil structure and usually leads to soils warming and drying faster in the spring. This allows crops to be planted

earlier.

- Apply mulch to strawberries to prevent winter injury or death to their crowns. Wait until temperatures have hit -5°C to be sure plants are dormant. If mulch is applied too soon the plant's crown can rot.
- Dig and store tender flowering bulbs, and keep in a protected location.
- Complete planting of spring-flowering bulbs.
- Why not get started early for next year?
- Spread manure, rotted sawdust and leaves over the garden and plow them under; you'll be surprised at the difference this organic matter will make in the fertility, physical structure and water-holding capacity of the soil.
- Take a soil sample to allow plenty of time to get the report back. Lime applied now will be of more benefit next year than if it is applied in the spring before planting. Always apply Dolomitic limestone in order to get both calcium and magnesium.
- Save those leaves for the compost heap.
- Take an 'inventory.' Maybe you had too much of some vegetables and not enough of others – or maybe there were some unnecessary 'skips' in the supply. Perhaps some insect, disease or nematode problem got the upper hand. Make a note about favorite varieties. Start planning next year's garden now!
- You're wise to order flower and vegetable seeds in December or January, while the supply is plentiful. Review the results of last year's garden and order the more successful varieties.
- You may have seeds left over from last year. Check their viability by placing some in damp paper towels and observing the germination percentage. If the percentage is low, order new ones.
- Before sending your seed order, draw a map of the garden area and decide the direction and length of the rows, how much row spacing is needed for each vegetable, whether or not to plant on raised beds, and other details. That way, you won't order too many seeds. This same advice applied to the flower garden. Try new cultivars, add more colour, change the colour scheme, layer the colours by having taller and shorter plants – don't do it the same way year after year.
- Look around for tools you do not have and hint for these for Christmas presents.

December

- To protect newly planted or tender perennials and bulbs, mulch with straw, chopped leaves or other organic material after plants become dormant.
- Store leftover garden chemicals where they will stay dry, unfrozen and out of the reach of children, pets and unsuspecting adults.
- Once the plants are completely dormant and temperatures are consistently below freezing, apply winter mulch to protect strawberries and other tender perennials. In most cases, 5 to 10 mm of organic material such as straw, pine needles, hay or bark chips will provide adequate protection.
- Check produce and tender bulbs in storage, and discard any signs of decay, such as mould or softening. Shrivelling indicates insufficient relative humidity.
- Clean up dead plant materials, synthetic mulch and other debris in the vegetable garden, as well as in the flowerbeds, rose beds and orchards.
- Make notes for next year's garden.

ADDENDUM

A	
Abiotic disease	A condition caused by nonliving, nonparasitic, or noninfectious agents.
Abscisic acid (ABA)	Is considered a 'stress hormone.' It is a signaling molecule that induces stomatal closure under drought or extreme temperature stress conditions.
Absorption	The intake of water and other materials through root or leaf cells.
Accumulated thermal units	Number of heat units in a growing season. An ATU is the Celsius value per day, accumulated across a season.
Acid soil	Soil with pH below 7 on a pH scale of 1 to 14. The lower the pH, the more acid the soil. (See also pH.)
Actinomycete	A group of microorganisms, intermediate between bacteria and true fungi. Generally, produce a characteristic branched mycelium, and these organisms are responsible for the earthy smell of compost (Goemin).
Action or damage threshold	The level of a pest population at which control is initiated.
Active ingredient	The chemical in a pesticide formulation that kills the target pest.

Acute toxicity	An injury that occurs soon after exposure to a pesticide.
Additive	When added to a pesticide, a substance reduces the surface tension between two unlike materials (e.g. spray droplets and a plant surface), thus improving adherence. Also called an adjuvant or surfactant.
Adventitious bud	A bud that develops in locations where buds usually do not occur. An example would be buds found on root pieces used for propagation; roots do not have buds.
Adventitious root	A root that forms at any place on the plant other than the primary root system.
Aerated static pile	Forced aeration method of composting in which a freestanding composting pile is aerated by a blower moving air through perforated pipes located beneath the pile.
Aeration or aerification	The practice involving removal of cores or turf plugs and soil with the purpose of reducing compaction and improving air flow.
Aerobic	An adjective describing an organism or process that requires oxygen (for example, an aerobic organism).
After-ripening	The seed maturation process that must be completed before germination can occur.
Aggregate	Soil aggregates are groups of soil particles that bind to each other more strongly than to adjacent particles. The space between the aggregates provides pore space for retention and exchange of air and water.
Aggregation	The process by which individual particles of sand, silt, and clay cluster and bind together to form soil peds.
Agriculture	The science or practice of farming.

Agronomy	The science of land cultivation, soil management, and crop production.
Air drainage	The downward flow of air through the soil caused by gravity; also, as cold air is heavier than warm air, it flows downhill and often fills hollows which become frost pockets.
Alkaline soil	Soil with pH above 7 on a pH scale of 1 to 14. The higher the reading, the more alkaline the soil.
Alternate leaf arrangement	Leaves are attached at alternating points from one side of the stem to the other.
Ambient air temperature	The temperature of the air near the compost pile or plants.
Amendment	An addition to soil or compost to enhance its characteristics.
Ammonium	A form of nitrogen that is commonly found in the soil. An ion of nitrogen and hydrogen. Ammonium is readily converted to and from ammonia depending on conditions in the compost pile.
Anaerobic	An adjective describing an organism or process that does not require air or free oxygen.
Anatomy	The study of a living organisms' structure.
Angiosperm	Flowering plants. Plants that have a highly evolved reproductive system. Seeds enclosed in an ovary such as a fruit, grain, or pod.
Anion	Negatively charged ion, for example, chloride.
	Anion exchange capacity (AEC). The sum total of exchangeable anions that a soil can absorb expressed in

Anion exchange	meq/100g (milliequivalents per 100 grams) soil.
Annuals	Plants that reproduce by seed and live for a single year.
Antagonists	Organisms that release toxins or otherwise change conditions so that activity or growth of the pest organism is reduced.
Anther	The pollen-bearing part of a flower's male sexual organ. The filament supports the anther; together they are referred to as the stamen.
Anthracnose	Plant disease characterized by black or brown dead areas on leaves, stems, or fruits.
Anvil pruner	A pruning tool that cuts a branch between one sharpened blade and a flat, anvil-shaped piece of metal. Has a tendency to crush rather than make a smooth cut.
Apex	The tip of a stem or root.
Aphids	Small soft-bodied insects with long, slender mouth parts with which they pierce stems and leaves to suck out plant fluids.
Arboretum	An area devoted to specimen plantings of trees and shrubs.
Archaea	Microorganisms that are similar to bacteria in size and simplicity of structure but radically different in their molecular organization.
Asexual propagation	Reproduction of a plant using its own vegetative parts. (See also Vegetative propagation.)
Aspect	Direction of exposure to sunlight.

Aspergillus fumigatus	Species of a fungus with spores that cause allergic reactions in some individuals. It can also cause complications for people with existing respiratory health problems.
Assimilation	Building of cell matter from inorganic (minerals) and organic (carbohydrates and sugars) materials.
ATP (adenosine triphosphate)	A molecule that is used in a number of metabolic reactions in plant cells to carry out cellular work.
Available water supply	Soil water that is available for plant uptake. Excludes water bound tightly to soil particles.
Axil	The upper angle formed by a leaf stalk (petiole) and the internodes above it on a stem.
Axillary bud	An embryonic shoot which lies at the junction of the stem and petiole of a plant. As the apical meristem grows and forms leaves, it leaves behind a region of meristematic cells at the node between the stem and the leaf, an undeveloped shoot or flower at the node. Also called the lateral bud.
Azotobacter	A type of bacteria found in compost piles that can fix atmospheric nitrogen into a form plants can use.
B	
Bacillus thuringiensis.	A bacterium used as a biological control agent for many insects and pests.
Bacterium	A group of microorganisms having single-celled or noncellular bodies. Bacteria generally appear as a spheroid, rod-like, or curved entity but occasionally appear as sheets, chains, or branched filaments.
Balled-and-burlapped	A plant dug with soil. The root ball is enclosed with

	burlap or a synthetic material.
Bare-root	A plant with little or no soil around its roots; deciduous plants and small evergreens are commonly sold bare-root.
Bed planting	Growing vegetables in closely spaced rows that grow together at crop maturity.
Bedding	Dry absorbent material used to provide a dry lying surface for livestock. Bedding material, such as sawdust and straw, absorb moisture from livestock waste, the soil, and the environment
Beneficial fungi	Fungi used in controlling organisms that attack desirable plants.
Beneficial insect	Insects that are beneficial for crop production because they pollinate plants, attack insect pests or serve other useful purposes.
Berry	The fleshy fruit of cane fruits, bush fruits, and strawberries.
Biennial	A plant that lives for two years. It produces leaves in the first and flowers in the second.
Biennial bearing	Producing fruit in alternate years.
Binomial	A biological species name consisting of two names: the genus name and specific epithet.
Biochar	Charcoal that participates in biological processes and has beneficial properties for both soils and compost.
Biodegradable plastic mulch	Plastic mulch that degrades in the environment.
Biological control	Any activity of one species that reduces the adverse

	effects of another.
Biosolids	A by-product of wastewater treatment sometimes used as a fertilizer, also known as municipal sewage sludge.
Blanch	To exclude light from plants or parts of plants to render them white or tender. Often done to cauliflower, endive, celery, and leeks. Also used to promote adventitious root formation on stems.
Blend, seed	A combination of two or more cultivars of the same species, for example Rebel and Falcon tall fescue.
Blight	Rapid death of leaves and other plant parts.
Blossom-end rot	A calcium deficiency in tomato and pepper fruit that causes the tip of the fruit to blacken and rot.
Blotch	A blot or spot (usually superficial and irregular in shape) on leaves, shoots, or fruit.
Bolting	The formation of a seed stalk instead of an edible portion of the plant.
Bone meal	Ground-up animal bones that are an excellent source of phosphate, calcium and trace elements.
Botanical insecticide	An insecticide, such as rotenone or pyrethrum, derived from a plant. Most botanicals biodegrade quickly. Most, but not all, have low toxicity to mammals.
Botanical maturity	In fruits, refers to a final stage of development when the fruit is still on the plant and cell enlargement and the accumulation of carbohydrates and other flavor constituents are complete.
Botany	The science that studies all phases of plant life and growth.

Botrytis	A fungal disease promoted by cool, moist weather. Also known as gray mold or fruit rot.
Bramble	A spiny cane bush with berry fruits (e.g. raspberries and blackberries).
Branch	A subsidiary stem arising from a plant's main stem or from another branch.
Broadcast	(1) To sow seed by scattering it over the soil surface. (2) To apply a pesticide or fertilizer uniformly to an entire, specific area by scattering or spraying it.
Broadleaf evergreen	A non-needled evergreen.
Broadleaves	Dicot weeds that have meristems at the terminal end of their branches.
Brown rot	Soft rot of fruit covered by gray to brown mold.
BTU	British thermal unit. Amount of heat required to raise the temperature of 1 pound of water 1°F.
Bud	A small protuberance on a stem or branch, sometimes enclosed in protective scales, containing an undeveloped shoot, leaf, or flower.
Buffer capacity	The maximum amount of either strong acid or strong base that can be added before a change of one pH unit occurs.
Bulb	A below-ground stem (e.g. a tulip) that is surrounded by fleshy scale-like leaves that contain stored food.
Bunchgrass, bunch-type growth	Plant development in the absence of rhizome and stolon production; a non-spreading grass.
C	

C	Chemical symbol for carbon.
Cabbageworms	Caterpillars that attack cole crops.
Calcium carbonate	A compound found in limestone, ashes, bones, and shells; the primary component of lime.
Callus	Tissue that forms over wounds.
Calorie	Amount of heat required to raise the temperature of 1 cubic centimeter of water 1°C.
Cantaloupe	A muskmelon of the round-to-oval, firm fleshed, no sutured, heavy-netted type.
Capillary action	The force by which water molecules bind to the surfaces of soil particles and to each other, thus holding water in fine pores against the force of gravity.
Carbon dioxide (CO_2)	An inorganic gaseous compound of carbon and oxygen. Carbon dioxide is produced by the oxidation of organic carbon compounds during composting.
Carbon-to-nitrogen ratio	The ratio of the weight of organic carbon (C) to that of total nitrogen (N) in (C:N ratio) an organic material.
Casaba	A somewhat rounded melon with a smooth rind and white flesh.

Cation	An atom or molecule with a positive charge (ammonium, NH4+).
Cation exchange capacity (CEC)	The ability of clay and humus to attract and exchange positive ions.
Causal organism	The organism (pathogen) that produces a given disease.

Cellulose	A long chain of tightly bound sugar molecules that constitutes the chief part of the cell walls of plants.
Chelate	A complex organic substance that holds micronutrients, usually iron, in a form available for absorption by plants.
Chemical insect control	The use of chemicals, or insecticide, to control insect populations.
Chemical oxygen demand (COD)	A measure of the oxygen-consuming capacity of inorganic and organic matter present in water or wastewater. It is expressed as the amount of oxygen consumed from a chemical oxidant in a specified test. It does not differentiate between stable and unstable organic matter and thus does not necessarily correlate with biochemical oxygen demand.
Chilling injury	A description of plant damage to tropical and sub-tropical species, caused by temperatures that are cold but not freezing, generally ranging from 1°C to 15°C.
Chlorophyll	The green pigment in plants responsible for trapping light energy for photosynthesis.
Chloroplast	A specialized component of certain cells. Contains chlorophyll and is responsible for photosynthesis.
Clay	The smallest type of soil particle (less than 0.002mm in diameter).
Clear plastic mulches	Plastic mulch that is clear and allows light to penetrate.
Climber	A plant that climbs on its own by twining or using gripping pads, tendrils, or some other method to attach itself to a structure or another plant. Plants that must be trained to a support are properly called trailing plants, not climbers.

Cloche	A netted, plastic, glass, or Plexiglas plant cover is used to warm the growing environment and protect plants from frost.
Clone	A plant group whose members have all been derived from a single individual through constant propagation by vegetative (asexual) means, e.g. by buds, bulbs, grafts, cuttings, or laboratory tissue culture.
C:N ratio	The ratio of carbon to nitrogen in organic materials. Materials with a high C:N ratio (high in carbon) are good bulking agents in compost piles, while those with a low C:N ratio (high in nitrogen) are good energy sources.
Cold composting	A slow composting process that involves simply building a pile and leaving it until it decomposes. This process may take months or longer. Cold composting does not kill weed seeds or pathogens.

Cold frame	A plastic-, glass-, or Plexiglas-covered frame or box that relies on sunlight as a source of heat to warm the growing environment for tender plants.
Cole crops	A group of vegetables belonging to the cabbage family; plants of the genus Brassica, including cauliflower, broccoli, cabbage, turnips, and Brussels sprouts.
Collar	A swollen area at the base of a branch where it connects to a trunk. Contains special tissue that prevents decay from moving downward from the branch into the trunk. The place to make a proper pruning cut. (See also Shoulder ring.)

Compaction	Pressure that squeezes soil into layers that resist root penetration and water movement. Often the result of foot or machine traffic.
Companion planting	The practice of growing two or more types of plants in combination to discourage disease and insect pests.
Compatible	Different varieties or species that set fruit when cross-pollinated or that make a successful graft union when intergrafted.
Complementary	In landscaping, use of opposite colours on the colour wheel such as red and green, orange and blue, and yellow and violet.
Complete fertilizer	A fertilizer that contains all three macronutrients (N, P, K).
Complete metamorphosis	A type of insect development in which the insect passes through the stages of egg, larva, pupa, and adult. The larva usually is different in form from the adult. (See also Simple metamorphosis.)
Compost	The product created by the breakdown of organic waste under conditions manipulated by humans. Used to improve both the texture and fertility of garden soil. (See also Humus.)
Composting	Biological degradation of organic matter under aerobic conditions to a relatively stable humus-like material called compost.
Compost amendment	An ingredient in a mixture of composting raw material included to improve the overall characteristics of the mix. Amendments often add carbon, dryness, or porosity to the mix.

Compound bud	More than one bud on the same side of a node. Usually, unless growth is extremely vigourous, only one of the buds develops, and its branch may have a very sharp angle of attachment. If it is removed, a wider angled shoot usually is formed from the second (accessory) bud. Ashes and walnuts are examples of plants that typically have compound buds.
Contact herbicide	A chemical that will harm a plant when it comes into contact with green plant tissue.
Contamination	An introduction into the environment (water, air, or soil) of microorganisms, chemicals, wastes, or wastewater in a concentration that makes the environment unfit for its intended use.
Cool-season Vegetables	Vegetables that have optimum growth at temperatures between 15°C and 24°C.

Corm	A below-ground stem that is solid, swollen, and covered with reduced, scale-like leaves (for example, in crocus).
Cormel	A small, underdeveloped corm, usually attached to a larger corm.
Cornicle	A short, blunt horn or tube (sometimes button like) on the top and near the end of an aphid’s abdomen. Emits a waxy liquid that helps protect against enemies.
Corolla	Part of a flower; all of the petals together.
Cover crop	(1) A crop planted to protect the soil from erosion. (2) A crop planted to improve soil structure or organic matter

	content.
Crawler	An early stage of insect development (nymph) that is mobile.
Creeping growth habit	Plant development at or near the soil surface that results in lateral spreading by rhizomes, stolons, or both.
Crop rotation	The practice of growing different types of crops in succession on the same land chiefly to preserve the productive capacity of the soil by easing insect, disease, and weed problems.
Crop seed	Any seed grown for profit, often including undesirable grassy weeds, such as orchard grass.
Cross-pollination	The fertilization of an ovary on one plant with pollen from another plant, producing an offspring with a genetic makeup distinctly different from that of either parent. (See also Pollinizer.)
Cultipack	To firm and pulverize (a seedbed) with a corrugated roller.
Cultivar	A cultivated variety of a species. Propagation of cultivars results in little or no genetic change in the offspring, which preserves desirable characteristics.
Cultivation	In turf, the working of the soil without the destruction of the turf.
Cultural insect control	Controlling an insect population by maintaining good plant health and by crop rotation and/or companion crops.
Cutting	One of several forms of asexual propagation.

Cyme	A flower stalk on which the florets start blooming from the top of the stem and progress toward the bottom.
Cyst	The swollen, egg-containing female body of certain nematodes. Can sometimes be seen on the outside of infected roots.
D	
Damping off	Stem rot near the soil surface leading to either failed seed emergence or to the plant's autumning over after emergence.
Day-neutral plant	A cultivar or species capable of flowering without regard to day length. (See also Short-day plant, Long-day plant.)
Deadhead	To remove individual, spent flowers from a plant for the purpose of preventing senescence and prolonging blooming. For effective results, the ovary behind the flower must be removed as well.
Deciduous	A plant that sheds all of its leaves annually.
Decomposers	The microorganisms and invertebrates that accomplish composting.
Decomposition	The breakdown of organic materials by microorganisms.
Defoliation	The unnatural loss of a plant's leaves, generally to the detriment of its health. Can be caused by several factors such as high wind, excessive heat, drought, frost, chemicals, insects, or disease.

Degradability	The term describes the ease and extent that a substance is decomposed by the composting process. Material that breaks down quickly and/or entirely during composting is highly degradable. Material that resists biological decomposition is considered poorly degradable or even nondegradable.
Denitrification	An anaerobic biological process that converts nitrogen compounds to nitrogen gas or nitrous oxide. The conversion of nitrates into atmospheric nitrogen by soil microbes in waterlogged soils.
Density	The weight or mass of a substance per unit of volume.
Depredation	Causing damage or loss.
Dermal exposure	Pesticide or allergens absorbed through the skin.
Desiccation	Excessive dryness or loss of moisture resulting in drying out the plant tissues.
Determinate	A plant growth habit in which stems stop growing at a certain height and produce a flower cluster at the tip. Determinate tomatoes, for example, are short, early fruiting, have concentrated fruit set, and may not require staking. (See also Indeterminate.)
Diatomaceous earth	The fossilized remains of diatoms (a type of tiny algae) used to kill insect pests, snails, and slugs.
Dieback	Progressive death of shoots, branches, or roots, generally starting at the tips.
Differentiation	A change in composition, structure, and function of cells and tissues during growth.
Dioecious	Plants that have male and female flowers occurring on separate plants (e.g. holly).

Direct seeding (direct sowing)	Planting seeds into garden soil rather than using transplants.
Distorted growth	Twisted or misformed growth.
Diurnal	Active during the day.
Division	The breaking or cutting apart of a plant's crown for the purpose of producing additional plants, all genetically identical to the parent plant.
DNA	Deoxyribonucleic acid is the genetic information that dictates all cellular processes. DNA is organized into chromosomes and is responsible for all characteristics of the plant.

Dolomitic limestone	Lime that supplies both calcium and magnesium.
Dormancy	An annual period which causes the resting stage of a plant or ripe seeds during which nearly all manifestations of life come to an almost complete standstill.
Dormant	Resting or not growing. A deciduous tree is dormant in the winter.
Dormant oil	An oil applied during the dormant season to control insect pests and diseases.
Double digging	A process whereby the gardener works the topsoil and also loosens the subsoil.
Double worked	Grafted twice, i.e. grafted to an intermediate stock.
Downy	Leaf textures that are covered with very short, weak, and soft hairs.

Downy mildew	Known best by its common name, downy mildew is caused by the oomycete. It is an obligate parasite of vascular plants, meaning that it cannot survive outside of a living host. It does not produce overwintering oospores, but survives from year to year on living plants. These organisms are distinctly different from the powdery mildews.
Drainage	Movement of water away from the surface of a garden either down into the soil or by flow across the surface.
Dried blood	Blood of animals that is collected from slaughterhouses. It contains high levels of nitrogen.
Drip line	An imaginary line on the ground directly beneath the outermost tips of a plant's foliage. Rain tends to drip from leaves onto this line.
Dwarfed	Restricted plant size without loss of health and vigour. (See also Bonsai.)
E	
E. coli	A bacteria associated with animal wastes that can cause serious health problems.
Ear	The female flower of corn that produces seed after pollination.
Ecology, plant	The study of the complex relationships of plants in biological communities.
Economic threshold	The level at which pest damage justifies the cost of control. In home gardening, the threshold may be aesthetic rather than economic.

Ecosystem services	Provisioning services such as food and water; regulating services such as flood and disease control; cultural services such as spiritual, recreational, and cultural benefits; and supporting services such as nutrient cycling that maintain the conditions for life on earth.
Elytra	Hardened opaque outer wings of a beetle.

Endemic	Belonging exclusively or confined to a particular place.
Endoskeleton	The internal body support found in most animals outside of the insect kingdom.
Endosperm	The tissue surrounding the embryo of flowering plant seeds that provides nutrition to the developing embryo, or the food- storage area in a seed for the growing embryo.
Endotoxin	Metabolic products of gram-negative bacteria are part of the cell wall. They will remain in the bacteria after they have died.
Enzyme	Any of numerous complex proteins produced by living cells to catalyze specific biochemical reactions.
Epidemic	A widespread and severe outbreak of a disease.
Ethylene	Is the only hormone that is a gas. It speeds aging of tissues and enhances fruit ripening.
Evergreen	A plant that never loses all its foliage at the same time.
Excise	To remove or extract, as an embryo from a seed or ovule.
Exfoliating	Peeling off in shreds or thin layers, as in bark from a

	tree.
Exoskeleton	An insect's outer body support.
Exotic	Of foreign origin or character; not native; introduced from abroad, but not fully naturalized
F	
F1 Hybrids	Cultivars resulting from a cross between two different true breeding (referred to as inbred) parents.
Fallow	To keep land unplanted during one or more growing seasons.
Family	A sub-order in the classification of plants.
Feeder roots	Fine roots and root branches with a large absorbing area (root hairs.) Responsible for taking up the majority of a plant's water and nutrients from the soil.
Fertility (soil)	The presence of minerals necessary for plant life.
Fertilizer	Any substance added to the soil (or sprayed on plants) to supply those elements required in plant nutrition.
Fibrous root	A root system that branches in all directions, often directly from the plant's crown, rather than branching in a hierarchical fashion from a central root. (See also Taproot.)
Field capacity	The amount of soil moisture or water content held in the soil after excess water has drained away and the rate of downward movement has decreased. This usually takes place two to three days after rain or irrigation in pervious soils of uniform structure and texture.

Fish meal	Ground-up fish. Contains nitrogen and phosphorus.

Flag or Flagging	Loss of turgor and drooping of plant parts, usually as a result of water stress. Can be seen as branch loss in a tree.
Floating row covers	Covers, usually of a cloth-like material, placed over growing plants and used to protect the plants growing beneath from undesirable pests and climate.
Flower bud	A type of bud that produces one or more flowers.
Foliar fertilization/feeding	Fertilization of a plant by applying diluted soluble fertilizer, such as fish emulsion or kelp, directly to the leaves.
Force	To bring a plant into early growth, generally by raising the temperature or transplanting it to a warmer situation. Tulips and paper whites are examples of plants that often are forced.
Forced aeration	Can be either negatively (vacuum) or positively forced (blowers) supply of air through a composting pile.
Form	(1) A naturally occurring characteristic different from other plants in the same population. (2) The growth habit (shape) of a plant.
Frass	The excrement of insect larvae.
Friable	A soil that is easy to work with.
Frost pocket	A low-lying area where frost occurs late in the season.
Frost-free date	The average last day of frost for a specific area.
Fruit	The enlarged ovary that develops after fertilization

	occurs.
Fruiting habit	The location and manner in which fruit is borne on woody plants.
Fumigation	The application of a toxic gas or other volatile substance to disinfect soil or a container, such as a grain bin.
Fungicide	A compound toxic to fungi.
Fungus (Fungi)	A plant organism that lacks chlorophyll, reproduces via spores, and usually has filamentous growth. It is possible for them to form long filaments known as hyphae. Hyaline bodies can be formed by the hyphae growing together.
G	
Genetically modified	A plant or animal that has had genetic material introduced to its genome from other organisms through artificial means.
Genus	A subdivision of family in the classification of plants. Plants of the same genus share similarities mostly in flower characteristics and genetics. Plants in one genus usually cannot breed with plants of another genus.
Germination	The processes that begin after planting a seed that lead to the growth of a new plant.
Girdled roots	A root system that has outgrown its pot to the extent that the roots are encircling the inside of the pot, restricting nutrient uptake.

Gourd	A fruit with a hard outer rind that is used for decoration.

Grasses	A category of weed that are monocots, have narrow leaves and a growing point at or just below the soil surface.
Gravitational water	Water in excess of a soil's capacity. Drains downward to groundwater.
Green cone	An enclosed composting unit often used for composting food waste.
Green manure	An herbaceous crop plowed under while green to enrich the soil.
Greensand	A ground rock material that contains potassium and trace elements.
Grinding	Operation that reduces the particle size of material. Grinding implies that particles are broken apart primarily by smashing and crushing rather than tearing or slicing.
Groundcover	Plants used for holding soil, controlling weeds, and providing leaf texture.
Growing season	The period between the beginning of growth in the spring and the cessation of growth in the autumn.
Growth regulator	A compound applied to a plant to alter its growth in a specific way. May be a natural or synthetic substance. (See also Hormone.)
H	
Habit	The growth, shape, and form of a plant.
Half-hardy	Plants able to withstand some cold, damp weather but will be damaged by frost.

HAPs	Hazardous Air Pollutants. There are 188 HAPs on EPA's list, including at least 29 HAPs that have been quantified in composting air emissions. The kinds and quantities of HAPs tend to be a function of feedstocks, with biosolids composting having the most carefully and thoroughly studied air emission profiles.
Hardening off	(1) The process of gradually exposing seedlings started indoors to outdoor conditions before transplanting. (2) The process of gradual preparation for winter weather.
Hardpan	An impervious layer of soil or rock that prevents root growth and downward drainage of water.
Hardy	Frost or freeze tolerant. In horticulture, this term does not mean tough or resistant to insect pests or disease.
Head	(1) To cut off part of a shoot or limb rather than remove it completely at a branch point. (2) The part of a tree from which the main scaffold limbs originate.
Heavy Soil	A soil that contains a high proportion of clay and is poorly drained.
Heeling in	The temporary burying of a newly dug plant's roots to prevent their drying until a new planting site is prepared. Nurseries heel in bareroot berries, trees, and shrubs.
Heirloom cultivars	Cultivars that are more than 100 years old and whose seeds are passed down from generation to generation.
Herbicide	A chemical used to kill undesirable plants.
Herbicide, contact	Herbicide that injures only those portions of a plant with which it comes into contact.

Hill planting	Planting multiple seeds together in clumps.
Honeydew	1. A sticky substance excreted by aphids and some other insects. 2. A round melon with smooth rind and green flesh.
Hormone	A naturally occurring compound that alters plant growth in a specific manner. (See also Growth regulator.)
Horticultural oil	An oil made from petroleum products, vegetable oil, or fish oil used to control insect pests and diseases. Oils work by smothering insects and their eggs and by protectively coating buds against pathogen entry.
Horticulture	The science of growing fruits, vegetables, flowers, and other ornamental plants.
Host plant	A plant that is invaded by a parasite.
Hotbed	An enclosed bed for propagating or protecting plants. Has a source of heat to supplement solar energy.
Hot caps	Individual structures placed over a vegetable plant that warm the temperature and protect the plant against frost.
Hot composting	A fast composting process that produces finished compost in four to eight weeks. High temperatures are maintained by mixing balanced volumes of energy materials and bulking agents, by keeping the pile moist, and by turning it frequently to keep it aerated.
Humus	The dark or black carbon-rich, relatively stable residue resulting from the decomposition of organic matter.
	The results of a cross between two different species or well- marked varieties within a species. Hybrids grown

Hybrid	in a garden situation will not breed true to form from their own seed.
Hydrogen sulfide (H_2S)	A gas with the characteristic odor of rotten eggs produced by anaerobic decomposition.
Hydrolysis	The word literally means unbinding by water. It is when water is involved in breaking chemical bonds. In plant biology the process results in complex compounds reduced to monomers.
Hydrophobic	Having little or no affinity for water.
Hydroponics	A method of growing plants without soil. Plants usually are suspended in water or polymers, and plant nutrients are supplied in dilute solutions.

Hygroscopic	Attracts and retains water.
Hypha (or hyphae)	A single filament of a fungus. A fine threadlike structure of cell formed by fungi affecting a plant.
I	
Imbibition	The portion of the germination process that involves the absorption of water, causing the seed to swell, and that triggers cell enzyme activity, growth, and the bursting of the seed coat.
Immobilization	The process by which soil microorganisms use available nitrogen as they break down materials with a high C:N ratio, thus reducing the amount of nitrogen available to plants.
Immune	A plant that does not become diseased by a specific pathogen. (See also Resistance, Tolerant.)

Incompatible	Kinds or varieties of a species that do not successfully cross- pollinate or intergraft.
Incubation	A period of development during which a pathogen changes to a form that can penetrate or infect a new host plant.
Infection	The condition reached when a pathogen has invaded plant tissue and established a parasitic relationship between itself and its host.
Infiltration	The movement of water into soil.
Inoculation	The introduction of a pathogen to a host plant's tissue.
Inoculum	Any part of the pathogen that can cause infection.
Inorganic	Being or composed of matter other than plant or animal.
Insectary plant	A plant that attracts beneficial insects.
Insecticidal soap	A specially formulated soap that is only minimally damaging to plants, but kills insects. Usually works by causing an insect's outer shell to crack, resulting in its interior organs drying out.
Insecticide	A chemical used to control, repel, suppress, or kill insects.
Insectivore	An animal or plant that feeds mainly on insects. Any of various small, usually nocturnal mammals of the order Insectivora that feed on insects and other invertebrates.
Integrated control	An approach that attempts to use several or all available methods for control of a pest or disease.
Integrated insect control	The use of a variety of insect control methods,

	beginning with simpler.
Integrated pest management (IPM)	A method of managing pests that combines cultural, biological, mechanical, and chemical controls, while taking into account the impact of control methods on the environment.
Intensive gardening	The practice of maximizing use of garden space, for example, by using trellises, intercropping, succession planting, and raised beds.

Intercropping/Interplanting	The practice of mixing plants to break up pure stands of a single crop.
Interiorscape	An interior planting, usually referring to professional designs installed in commercial buildings.
Internode	The area of the stem that is between the nodes.
Interstem/interstock	The middle piece of a graft combination made up of more than two parts, i.e. the piece between the scion and the rootstock. Often has a dwarfing effect.
Invasive	Growing vigourously and outcompeting other plants in the same area; difficult to control.
Ion	An electrically charged particle. In soils, an ion refers to an electrically charged element or combination of elements resulting from the breaking up of an electrolyte in solution.
IR mulches	Mulches that allow infrared radiation to penetrate through the mulch but reflects photosynthetically active radiation.

Isolation	The separation of a pathogen from its host by culturing on a nutrient medium or on an indicator plant.
J	
Joint	A node; the place on a stem where a bud, leaf, or branch forms.
Juvenile stage	(1) The early or vegetative phase of plant growth characterized by the inability to flower. (2) The first stage of an insect's life cycle after the egg, either a larva or a nymph. (3) The immature stage of an organism.
K	
K	The symbol for Potassium also referred to as Potash
L	
Land application	Application of manure, sewage sludge, municipal wastewater, and industrial waste to land either for ultimate disposal or for reuse of the nutrients and organic matter for their fertilizer value.
Larva	(larvae is plural) The immature form of an insect that undergoes complete metamorphosis. Different from the adult in form, a caterpillar for example. The newly hatched, wingless, often wormlike form of many insects before metamorphosis.
Layering	A method of stimulating adventitious roots to form on a stem. There are two primary methods of layering. In ground layering, a low-growing branch is bent to the ground and covered by soil. In air layering, moist rooting medium is wrapped around a node on an above-ground stem.

Leaching	The downward movement of water and nutrients from the soil surface to the water table due to gravity.
Leaf-axil	The area between the leaf or petiole and the stem.

Lesion	Alocalisedarea of discoloured or dead tissue.
Life cycle	The successive stages of growth and development of an organism.
Lignen	A substance that forms the woody cell walls of plants and the cementing material between them. Lignin is resistant to decomposition.
Light soil	A soil that contains a high proportion of sand.
Lime	A rock powder consisting primarily of calcium carbonate. Used to raise soil pH (decrease acidity).
Litter, poultry	Dry absorbent bedding material, such as straw, sawdust, and wood shavings, spread on poultry barn floors to absorb waste. The manure-bedding combination from the barn is referred to as litter.
Living mulches	Any plant that is used to cover an area of soil and add nutrients, enhance soil porosity, decrease weeds, and prevent soil erosion.
Loam	A soil with roughly equal proportions of sand, silt, and clay particles.
Long-day plant	A plant requiring more than 12 hours of continuous daylight to stimulate a change in growth, e.g. a shift from the vegetative to reproductive phase. (See also Short-day plant, Day-neutral plant.)

M	
Macroclimate	The overall climate of a particular region.
Macronutrient	Collectively, primary and secondary nutrients.
Macropore	A large soil pore. Macropores include earthworm and root channels and control a soil's permeability and aeration. In a substrate, the larger spaces (or pores) that lies between component particles that hold air.
Mandible	The first pair of jaws on insects: stout and tooth-like in chewing insects, needle or sword-shaped in sucking insects. The lateral (left and right) upper jaws of biting insects.
Manure	The fecal and urinary excretion of livestock and poultry. Sometimes referred to as livestock waste. This material may also contain bedding, spilled feed, water, or soil. It may also include waste not associated with livestock excrete, such as milking center wastewater, contaminated milk, hair, feathers, or other debris.
Maturity	(1) In fruit, ripeness, usually the state of development that results in maximum quality. (2) The flowering phase of plant growth.
Maximum temperature	The warmest temperature that germination occurs for seed of a particular vegetable.
Mechanical insect control	Manual removal of insects and eggs from infested plants

Mesic	Characterized by, relating to, or requiring a moderate amount of moisture

Metamorphosis	The process by which an insect develops. The term is a combination of two Greek words: meta meaning 'change' and morphe meaning 'form.' Metamorphosis is a marked or abrupt change in form or structure, like a caterpillar turning into a butterfly. (See also Complete metamorphosis, Simple metamorphosis.)
Microclimate	Climate affected by landscape, structures, or other unique factors in a particular immediate area. The specific environmental conditions of your garden site.
Micronutrient	A nutrient, usually in the parts per million range, used by plants in small amounts, less than 1 part per million (boron, chlorine, copper, iron, manganese, molybdenum, zinc, and nickel).
Microorganism	An organism that requires magnification to be seen.
Micropore	A fine soil pore, typically a fraction of a millimeter in diameter. Micropores are responsible for a soil's ability to hold water. In a substrate, the smaller spaces (or pores) between component particles that are occupied by water or air.
Microscopic	Organisms so small that they can be seen only with the aid of a microscope.
Minimum Temperature	Coolest temperature that seed germination or growth occurs for a particular vegetable.
Mixed buds	Buds that produce both shoots and flowers.
Mixed fertilizer	A fertilizer that contains at least two of the three macronutrients (N, P, K).
Mixture, seed	A combination of seeds of two or more species, for example Kentucky bluegrass and perennial ryegrass.

Moisture content	The fraction or percentage of a substance made up of water. Moisture content equals the weight of the water part divided by the total weight (water plus dry matter part). Moisture content is sometimes reported on a dry basis. Dry-basis moisture content equals the weight of the water divided by the weight of the dry matter.
Monomers	Natural monomers are amino acid from proteins and monosaccharides from carbohydrates amongst others.
Morphology	The study of the origin and function of plant parts.
Mosaic	Non-uniform foliage colouration with a more or less distinct intermingling of normal green and light green or yellowish patches.
Mottle	An irregular pattern of light and dark areas.
Mulch	Any material placed on the soil surface to conserve soil moisture, moderate soil temperature, and/or control weeds.
Mushroom	The fruiting structure of certain families of fungi characterized by gills.
Muskmelon	A melon that has a musky aroma and salmon- to orange- coloured flesh when mature. It has a netted rind with deep sutures.
Mutation	A genetic change within an organism or its parts that changes its characteristics. Also called a bud sport or sport.
Mycelia	Masses of fungal threads (hyphae) that make up the vegetative body of a fungus.

Mycology	The study of fungi.
Mycorrhizae	Beneficial fungi that infect plant roots and increase their ability to take up nutrients from the soil.
N	
N	The symbol for Nitrogen, A primary plant nutrient, especially important for foliage and stem growth.
Native plant	A plant indigenous to a specific habitat or area.
Naturalize	(1) To design a garden with the aim of creating a natural scene. Planting generally is done randomly, and space is left for plants to spread at will. (2) The process whereby plants spread and fill in naturally.
Necrosis or necrotic tissue	Death of cells resulting in necrotic or dead tissue.
Nematicide	A material that kills or protects against nematodes.
Nematode	Microscopic roundworms that live in soil and living tissue, as well as water, and survive as eggs or cysts.
Netted veins	Having branched veins that form a network, as the leaves of most dicotyledonous plants.
Nitrate-nitrogen	A negatively charged ion made up of nitrogen and oxygen (NO_3^-). Nitrate is a water-soluble and mobile form of nitrogen. Because of its negative charge, soil particles are not firmly held and leached away.
Nitrification	The biochemical oxidation of ammonia nitrogen to nitrate.
Nitrifier	A microbe that converts ammonium to nitrate.
Nitrogen	A primary plant nutrient, especially important for

	foliage and stem growth.
Nitrogen cycle	The sequence of biochemical changes undergone by nitrogen as it moves from living organisms, to decomposing organic matter, to inorganic forms, and back to living organisms.
Nitrogen fixation	The conversion of atmospheric nitrogen into plant-available forms by rhizobia bacteria living on the roots of legumes.
Nitrogen, quick release	Readily available sources of nitrogen that exhibit fast turf greening, short residual, and high burn potential, such as ammonium nitrate.

Nitrogen, slow release	Slowly available sources of nitrogen that exhibit slow turf green- up, long residual, and low burn potential, such as IBDU, urea formaldehyde.
Nocturnal	Active at night.
Node	The area of the stem that bears a leaf or a branch. A joint where leaves, roots, branches, or stems arise.
Nomenclature	The assigning of names in the classification of plants.
Nonpoint source	A relatively small, nonspecific source of pollutants that, when added to other sources, may pose a significant threat to the environment. (See also Point source.)
Nonselective pesticide	A pesticide that kills most plants or animals.
Nonviable	Not alive; nonviable seeds may look normal but will not grow.
Noxious weed	Weeds that government agencies want to prevent from

	establishing in a particular area.
N-P-K	Acronym for the three major plant nutrients contained in manure, compost, and fertilizers. N stand for nitrogen, P for phosphorus, and K for potassium.
Nutrient	Any substance, especially in the soil, that is essential for and promotes plant growth. (See also Macronutrient, Micronutrient.)
Nutrient-holding capacity	The ability to absorb and retain nutrients is available to the roots of plants.
Nymph	The immature form of those insects that do not pass through a pupal stage. Nymphs usually resemble the adults, but are smaller, lack fully developed wings, and are sexually immature but eat the same food, and reside in the same environment.
O	
Offset	A new shoot that forms at the base of a plant or in a leaf axil.
Open-pollinated seed	Seed produced from natural, random pollination so that the resulting plants are varied.
Opposite leaf arrangement	Two leaves are attached at the same point on the stem, but on opposite sides.
Optimum temperature	The temperature at which the greatest or most rapid seed germination occurs for a particular vegetable.

Organic	(1) Relating to, derived from, or involving the use of food produced with the use of feed or fertilizer of plant or animal origin without employment of synthetically formulated fertilizers, growth stimulants, antibiotics, or pesticides. (2) Being or composed of plant or animal matter. (3) A labeling term that refers to an agricultural product produced in accordance with government standards.
Organic fertilizer	A natural fertilizer material that has undergone little or no processing. Can include plant, animal, and/or mineral materials.

Organic matter	Any material originating from a living organism (peat moss, plant residue, compost, ground bark, manure, etc.). Chemical substances of animal or vegetable origin containing hydrocarbons and their derivatives.
Organic pesticide	Pesticides derived from plant or animal sources.
Organic production	The production of food using accepted naturally occurring materials.
Organism	A living being.
Ornamental plant	A plant grown for beautification, screening, accent, specimen, colour, or other aesthetic reasons.
Osmosis	Passage of materials through a membrane from an area of high concentration to an area of lower concentration.
Outer seed coat	The protective outer shell for the seed.
	The part of a flower containing ovules that will develop into seeds upon fertilization. Along with the style and

Ovary	stigma, it makes up the pistil (female sexual organ).
Over mulching	Applying too much mulch.
Ovule	Within the ovary, a tissue/structure that will develop into a seed after fertilization.
Oxidative respiration	The chemical process by which sugars and starches are converted to energy. In plants, known as respiration.
Oxygen starvation	Roots cannot get the oxygen they need.
P	
P	The chemical symbol for phosphorus. A primary plant nutrient, especially important for flower production. In fertilizer, usually expressed as phosphate.
Paper Mulches	Mulches made from newspaper or paper fibers.
Parasite	An organism that lives in or on another organism (host) and derives its food from the latter.
Parasitic seed plant	A plant that lives parasitically on other seed plants. An example is mistletoe.
Parent material	The underlying geological material (generally bedrock or a superficial or drift deposit) in which soil horizons form.
Passive Composting	Air movement through composting windrows and piles occurs by natural forces, including convection, diffusion, wind, and the tendency of warm air to rise (thermal buoyancy).
Pathogen	Any organism capable of producing disease or infection. Often found in waste material, most pathogens are killed by the high temperatures of the composting process.

Pathology	The study of plant diseases.

Peat	Unconsolidated soil material consisting mainly of organic matter accumulated under excessive moisture conditions. The organic matter is not decomposed or is only slightly decomposed.
Peat moss	The partially decayed remains of sphagnum moss.
Ped	A cluster of individual soil particles.
Perennial	A plant that lives more than two years and produces new foliage, flowers, and seeds each growing season.
Perlite	Lightweight volcanic material often used in soil less media.
Permanent wilting point	The point at which a wilted plant can no longer recover.
Permeability	The rate at which water moves through a soil.
Persistent	(1) Adhering to a position instead of autumning, whether dead or alive, e.g. flowers or leaves. (2) A pesticide that retains its chemical properties in the soil for a long time.
Pest	Plants, fungi, bacteria, nematodes, insects and animals that occur in a place they are not wanted.
Pesticide	A chemical that kills undesirable plants, plant diseases, insects or other pests.
Petals	Highly coloured portions of the flower, inside the sepals, that protect the inner reproductive structures. Often attract insects with their colour or may contain osmophores which are scent structures both of which

	facilitate pollination.
pH	The acidity or alkalinity of a solution on a scale of 0–14, with a value of 7 signifying neutral, values below 7 signifying acidic, and values above 7 signifying alkaline. Relates to the concentrations of hydrogen (H+) ions in the soil. pH values are logarithmic (factors of 10).
Phosphate	The form of phosphorus listed in most fertilizer analyses.
Phosphorus (P)	A primary plant nutrient, especially important for flower production. In fertilizer, usually expressed as phosphate.
Photodegradable mulch	Mulch that contains chemicals that cause the plastic to degrade when exposed to ultraviolet radiation.
Photoperiod	The amount of time a plant is exposed to light.
Photosynthate	A food product (sugar or starch) created through photosynthesis.
Photosynthesis	(1) The process in which green plants convert light energy from the sun into chemical energy in order to produce carbohydrates. (2) Formation of carbohydrates from carbon dioxide and a source of hydrogen (as water) in the chlorophyll- containing tissues of plants exposed to light.
Phototropism	The phenomenon of plants growing toward the direction of a light source.

	The study dealing with the functioning of plants, their mechanisms of response, and their physical and

Physiology	biochemical processes.
Phytoplasm	Microscopic, single-celled organisms that lack distinct cell walls and that cause destructive diseases in plants.
Phytotoxic	An adjective describing a substance that has a toxic effect on plants. Immature or anaerobic compost may contain phytotoxins (acids or alcohols) harmful to seedlings or sensitive plants.
Pinch	To remove a growing tip from a stem, thus causing axillary shoots or buds to develop. (See also Deadhead, Shear.)
Plant cages	Structures made from cloth or plastic that keeps out migrating insects while allowing sunlight, rain and wind to enter. They generally do not protect against cool temperatures.
Plant classification	The scientific grouping and naming of plants by characteristics.
Plant disease	Any lasting change in a plant's normal structure or function that deviates from its healthy state.
Plant nutrition	A plant's need for and use of basic chemical elements. (See also Macronutrient, Micronutrient.)
Plant pathology	The study of diseases in plants: what causes them, what factors influence their development and spread, and how to prevent or control them.
Plant tissue culture	Plant material grown in vitro under sterile conditions in an artificial medium. A primary means of rapidly increasing the number of plants from a single mother

	plant.
Plug	A 5 to 10 cm lawn, either round or square, with soil around their roots.
Pollen	A plant's male sex cells, which are held on the anther for transfer to a stigma by insects, wind, or some other mechanism.
Pollen tube	A slender tube growing from the pollen grain that carries the male gametes and delivers them to the ovary.
Pollination	The first step in fertilization; the transfer of pollen from anther to a stigma.
Pollinator	An agent such as an insect that transfers pollen from a male anther to a female stigma.
Potash	The form of potassium listed in most fertilizer analyses.
Potassium	A primary plant nutrient, especially important for developing strong roots and stems. In fertilizers, usually expressed as potash. It is the K in N-P-K.
Powdery mildew	Fine, white to gray, powdery fungal coating on leaves, stems, and flowers.
Predator	An animal that eats another animal.
Preemergence	A product applied before crops or weeds emerge from the soil.
Preharvest interval	The amount of time that must elapse (legally) after application of a pesticide before harvest takes place.

Preplant	A product applied before a crop is planted.
Primary growth	Growth that occurs via cell division at the tips of stems and roots.
Primary nutrient	A nutrient required by plants in a relatively large amount (nitrogen, phosphorus, and potassium).
Processed fertilizer	A fertilizer that is manufactured or refined from natural ingredients to be more concentrated and more available to plants.
Production	Nursery or greenhouse growing area used before plants are put up for retail sales.
Propagate	To start new plants by seeding, budding, grafting, dividing, etc.
Protozoa	Any of a diverse group of eukaryotes, of the kingdom Protista, that are primarily unicellular, existing singly or aggregating into colonies.
Prune	To remove plant parts to improve a plant's health, appearance, or productivity.
Pupa	The stage between larva and adult in insects that go through complete metamorphosis.
Pupae	An insect in the non-feeding stage between the larva and adult, during which it typically undergoes complete transformation within a protective cocoon or hardened case. Only insects that undergo complete metamorphosis have pupal stages.
Q	
	A regulation forbidding sale or shipment of plants or plant parts, usually to prevent disease, insect,

Quarantine	nematode, or weed invasion in an area.
Quick-release fertilizer	A fertilizer that contains nutrients in plant-available forms such as ammonium and nitrate. Fertilizer is readily soluble in water.
Quiescent	In a state or period of inactivity or dormancy.
R	
Raised bed	Mound the soil up in the planting area above the surrounding soil level. May have a frame around the edges.
Raking, power	Removal of debris with rapidly rotating vertical tines or brush.
Receptacle	The base of the flower stalk that holds the sexual organs of a flower.
Regulatory insect	Term used to describe insects that have an unknown impact in a new environment to which they may be moved.
Relative humidity	The percentage of moisture saturating the air at a given temperature. The ratio of water vapor in the air to the amount of water the air could hold at the current temperature and pressure.
Repotting (or 'transplanting')	The process of moving previously potted plants into new containers, usually of larger size.
Resistance	The ability of a host plant to prevent or reduce disease development by retarding multiplication of the pathogen within the host.

Respiration	The process of burning sugars to use as energy for plant growth. The process by which carbohydrates are converted into energy. This energy builds new tissues, maintains the chemical processes, and allows growth within the plant.
Rhizobia bacteria	Bacteria that live in association with roots of legumes and convert atmospheric nitrogen to plant-available forms, a process known as nitrogen fixation.
Rhizome	A stem that forms the main axis of the plant. An underground creeping stem that can produce roots and shoots at each node. (adj. rhizomatous)
Rhizosphere	The thin layer of soil immediately surrounding plant roots.
Rogue/Roguing	To uproot and destroy diseased plants.
Rootbound	A condition in which a plant's root system has outgrown its pot resulting in root constriction. Typically, the roots begin to encircle the pot's outer edge. Further growth is prevented until the plant is removed from the container.
Root cutting	An asexual method of propagation that involves removing a section of root from a two- to three-year-old plant during the dormant season and placing it into growing medium.
Root hair	Thin hair-like structure that grows from the epidermis of the region of maturation of the root. This structure absorbs water and nutrients from the soil.
Root knots	Swelling and deformation of roots.
Root pruning	The cutting or removal of some of a plant's roots.

Root/stem rot	Soft and disintegrated roots and lower portions of the stem; sometimes results in death of the plant.
Rootstock	The portion of a plant used to provide the root system and sometimes the lower part of the stem for a grafted plant.
Rot	Decomposition and destruction of tissue.
Rotation (rotate)	The practice of growing different plants in different locations each year to prevent the buildup of soil borne diseases and insect pests.
Row cover	A sheet of synthetic material used to cover plants in order to retain heat and exclude insect pests.

Row planting	Growing vegetables in single or double rows with aisles between each row.
Runner	See Stolon. (Examples of runners are strawberries and spider plants.)
Rust	Fruiting structure of certain family of fungi. Raised pustules on leaves, stems, and fruits; contain yellow-orange or rust-coloured spore masses.
S	
Sand	Soil particles ranging in size between 0.2 to 2 mm.
Sanitation	The removal and disposal of infected plant parts; decontamination of tools, equipment, hands, etc. Removing sources of pests so as few pests as possible get into your garden.
Saprophytes	Organisms that live on dead or dying organic matter and obtain their energy by breaking plant and animal

	material down.
Sapwood	The newly formed lighter outer wood located just inside the vascular cambium of a tree trunk and active in the conduction of water.
Scab	Slightly raised, rough areas on fruits, tubers, leaves, or stems.
Scabrous	Leaf textures that are rough to the touch; texture of sandpaper.
Scale	A type of insect pest.
Scout/Scouting	Assessing pest pressure and plant performance. The first step in any IPM plan. Regularly checking crops for pests and damage symptoms; looking in your garden to determine if pests are a problem.
Secondary growth	Growth that increases the girth of stems or roots without elongating them. Secondary growth is seen in some dicots but not in monocots.
Secondary nutrient	A nutrient needed by plants in a moderate amount: calcium, magnesium, and sulfur. (See also Macronutrient, Primary nutrient.)
Secondary root	A type of root system that forms after the primary root emerges from a seed and branches outward.
Seed	Matured ovule that occurs as, or in, mature fruits.
Seed, certified	A seed lot inspected to meet minimum standards and to ensure trueness to type for a given cultivar.
Seed coat	The protective outer layer of a seed that provides protection for the enclosed embryo.

Seed coat impermeability	Caused by a hard seed coat that is impermeable to water, preventing the seed from germinating.
Seed dormancy	An adaptive feature of some plants to keep the seeds from germinating until conditions exist that favor seedling survival.

Seed scarification	Involves breaking, scratching, or softening the seed coat so that water can enter and begin the germination process.
Selective pesticide	A pesticide that kills only certain kinds of plants or animals; for example, 2,4-D kills broadleaf lawn weeds but leaves grass largely unharmed.
Self-fertile	A plant that produces seed with its own pollen.
Self-fruitful	A plant that bears fruit through self-pollination.
Self-pollination	Pollination that can occur when the anther and stigma are in the same flower or if the anther and stigma are in different flowers on the same plant or in different flowers on different plants of the same species, variety, or cultivar.
Self-sterile	A plant that needs pollen from another species, variety, or cultivar (e.g. cross-pollination).
Self-unfruitful	A plant that requires another variety for pollination. (See also Pollinizer.)
Separation	A term applied to a form of propagation by which plants that produce bulbs or corms multiply.
Sexual propagation	The deliberate, directed reproduction of plants using seeds or spores. (See also Asexual propagation.)

Shear	To cut back a plant (as opposed to selective pruning or deadheading). Often used to regenerate plants with many small stems, where dead-heading would be too time consuming.
Shoot	One season's branch growth. The bud scale scars (ring of small ridges) on a branch mark the start of a season's growth.
Short-day plant	A plant requiring more than 12 hours of continuous darkness to stimulate a change in growth, e.g. a shift from the vegetative to reproductive phase. (See also Long-day plant, Day-neutral plant.)
Shredding	An operation that reduces the particle size of material and increases the surface area.
Side-dress	The process of applying soil amendments or fertilizers next to an emerged vegetable crop.
Sign	The part of a pathogen seen on a host plant; the physical evidence of something that has attacked a plant.
Silt	Soil particles between 0.002 and 0.05 mm in size.
Simple metamorphosis	A type of insect development involving three stages: egg, nymph, and adult. The nymph usually resembles the adult. (See also Complete metamorphosis.)
Slow-release fertilizer	A fertilizer material that must be converted into a plant-available form by soil microorganisms.
Soft pinch	To remove only the succulent tip of a shoot, usually with the fingertips.
Soft rot	The water-soaked appearance of cells that don't get enough oxygen.

Soil	A natural, biologically active mixture of weathered rock fragments and organic matter at the earth's surface.
Soil conditioner	A soil additive that improves the soil's resistance to erosion, increases its permeability to air and water, improves its texture, its resistance to surface compaction, and improves tilth.
Soil horizons	A soil horizon is a layer generally parallel to the soil crust, whose physical characteristics differ from the layers above and beneath. Each soil type usually has three or four horizons. Horizons are defined in most cases by obvious physical features, chiefly colour and texture.
Soilless mix or substrate	Components used in potting mixes that are not true soils, such as vermiculite, perlite, peat, bark, sand, gravel, sphagnum moss used in container growing mixes but no real soil.
Soil salinity	A measure of the total soluble salts in a soil.
Soil solution	The solution of water and dissolved minerals found in soil pores.
Soil structure	The combination or arrangement of primary soil particles into secondary particles, units, or peas. Compost helps bind primary soil particles to improve the structure of the soil.
Soil texture	How coarse or fine a soil is. Texture is determined by the proportions of sand, silt, and clay in the soil.
Soluble salt	A mineral (salt) often remaining in soil from irrigation water, fertilizer, compost, or manure applications.

Sonic repeller	A sonic wave-emitting unit said to disrupt the activities of small mammals or insects but not proven to be effective.
Sori	A cluster of sporangia borne on the underside of a fern frond.
Species	A group of individual plants interbreeding freely and having many (or all) characteristics in common.
Species-specific	Limited to effecting one species or a certain group of species.
Specimen	An individual plant with outstanding characteristics (leaves, flowers, or bark), generally used as a focal point in a landscape.
Spines	Are modified leaves, leaflets, petioles or stipules. Blackberries or wintergreen barberry (*Berberis juliane*) have spines.
Spore	(1) The reproductive body of a fungus or other lower plant, containing one or more cells. (2) A bacterial cell modified to survive in an adverse environment. (3) The reproductive unit of ferns.
Sport	See Mutation.
Spot treatment	To apply a pesticide to a small section or area of a crop.
Sprig	A stolon or rhizome used to establish turf.
Spur	Short, stubby stems common on fruit trees such as apples and pears. These spurs produce the flower buds.

Stability of compost	The rate of change or decomposition of compost. Generally, stability refers to the lack of change or resistance to change. A stable compost continues to decompose slowly and has a low oxygen demand. Temperatures are constant.
Starch-based biodegradable mulch	Mulch made from plastic that contains starch, which is degraded by bacteria.
Stem cutting	A section of a stem prepared for vegetative propagation; forms adventitious roots on the stem.
Sterile	(1) Material that is free of disease organisms (pathogens), as in potting medium. (2) A plant that is unable to produce viable seeds.
Stolon	An above-ground creeping stem that can produce roots and shoots at each node. This horizontal stem can be either fleshy or semi-woody.
Stoma, stomate, stomata (plural)	Any pore or opening on the surface of a leaf or stem through which gases (water vapor, carbon dioxide, and oxygen) are exchanged. This pore is an opening into a leaf that is formed by specialized epidermal cells on the underside (and sometimes upper sides) of the leaf.
Strain	A variation within a cultivar or variety.
Stratification	Chilling seed under moist conditions. This method mimics the conditions a seed might endure after it autumns to the ground in the autumn and goes through a cold winter on the ground.
Stylet	A nematode's lance like or needlelike mouthpart. Used to puncture and feed from plant cells.
Subspecies	A major division of a species, more general in

	classification than a cultivar or variety.
Succession	The progression of a plant community to a stable mixture of plants.
Succession planting	(1) The practice of planting new crops in areas vacated by harvested crops. (2) Several smaller plantings made at timed intervals.
Succulent	Leaf textures that are fleshy, soft, and thickened in texture; modified for water storage.
Sucker	A shoot or stem that originates underground from a plant's roots or trunk, or from a root- stock below the graft union. (See also Reversion growth.)
Summer annual	Annual plant in which the seed germinates in the spring, and the plant develops, matures, and produces seed by the end of the growing season.
Summer oil	A light refined horticultural oil used during the growing season to control insect pests and diseases.
Sun scald	Winter or summer injury to the trunk or leaves of plants caused by hot sun and fluctuating temperatures. Typically, sun scalded bark splits and separates from the trunk.

Susceptibility	The condition of a plant in which it is prone to the damaging effects of a pathogen or other factor.
Sustainable gardening	Gardening practices allow plants to thrive with minimal inputs of labor, water, fertilizer, and pesticides.
Symbiotic	Mutually beneficial.

Symptom	A plant's response to an attack by animal or pathogen; a visible reaction of a plant to disease such as wilting, necrosis, abnormal colouration, defoliation, fruit drop, abnormal cellular growth, or stunting.
Synthetic fertilizer	Chemically formulated fertilizers, mainly from inorganic sources.
Synthetic pesticide	Chemically formulated pesticide, mainly from inorganic sources.
Systemic	Spreading internally throughout the plant.
Systemic pesticide	A pesticide that moves throughout a target organism's system to cause its death.
T	
Taproot	A type of root system that grows straight down with few lateral roots.
Tassel	The structure at the tip of the corn plant, which is the male flower.
Taxonomy	Classification or naming of plants or animals.
Tender	Not tolerant of frost and cold temperatures. In horticulture, tender does not mean weak or susceptible to insect pests or diseases.
Tendril	A slender projection used for clinging, usually a modified leaf. Easily seen on vines such as grapes and clematis.
Terminal	The tip (apex), usually of a branch or shoot.
Terminal bud	The bud that is found at the tip of shoots.

Texture of composting mix	Characteristic that describes the available surface area of particles. A fine or raw material texture implies many small particles with a large combined surface area. A course texture implies large particles with less overall surface area.
Thermoperiod	The change in temperature from day to night.
Thermophilic	Heat-loving microorganisms that thrive in and generate temperatures above 40°C.
Thin	(1) To remove an entire shoot or limb where it originates. (2) To selectively remove plants or fruits to allow remaining plants or fruits to develop.
Threshold	The point at which plant aesthetic quality or injury leads a gardener to decide action should be taken.

Tiller	A grass plant shoot arising in the axes of leaves in the unelongated portion of the stem. A shoot that arises from a plant's crown.
Tilth	The state of aggregation of a soil especially in relation to its suitability for crop growth, a measurement of soil workability.
Tissue culture	The process of generating new plants by placing small pieces of plant material onto a sterile medium.
Tolerant	A plant that will produce a normal yield even if faced with challenges like disease, insect pest, shade, or frost. Tolerance is generally specified.
Top-dressing	1) The practice of spreading a thin layer (6 mm) of soil, compost, humus, or a sand and peat mix over the turf or soil. 2) For turf: a sand or prepared soil mix applied to

	the turf to help smooth the surface, enhance establishment, and reduce thatch buildup.
Tracheophytes	Any plant that has elaborate tissues with water- and nutrient- conducting tissue termed 'vascular tissue' including roots, stems and leaves. Some tracheophytes reproduce with seeds and some with spores.
Trailing	Cane berries that are not self-supporting and have low yields.
Transpiration	The loss of water through the leaf stomata. The transpired water comes from the photosynthetic process and also from water in the cells.
Trap Crop	A trap crop is a plant that attracts agricultural creatures, usually insects, away from nearby crops. This form of companion planting can save the main crop from decimation by pests without the use of pesticides.
Tuber	(1) A below-ground stem used for food storage (e. g. potato). (2) For turf: an underground stem modified for food storage that is attached to the root system as found in yellow nutsedge.
Tuberous root	An underground storage organ made up of root tissue. Sprouts only from the point at which it was attached to the stem of the parent plant. Dahlias are an example.
Tuberous stem	A below-ground stem consisting of a swollen hypocotyl, lower epicotyl, and upper primary root (e.g. in tuberous begonias).
Tunicate	A tunicate bulb has a paper-like covering or tunic that protects the scales from drying and from mechanical injury. Examples of tunicate bulbs include: tulips, daffodils, hyacinths, grape hyacinths (muscari), and

	alliums.
Turf	A covering of mowed vegetation, usually a grass.
Turgor or turgor pressure (turgid)	Cellular water pressure; responsible for keeping cells firm.

Twig	A young stem (1 year old or less) that is in the dormant winter stage (has no leaves).
U	
USDA zones	Areas derived by the USDA that indicate average-low winter temperatures. Used as a plant hardiness indicator. Other plant hardiness zones developed by other entities use different numbering systems.
V	
Vaporization	The evaporation of the active ingredient in a pesticide during or after application.
Variegated	Having patches, stripes, or marks of different colours.
Variety	A botanical subdivision within a species.
Vascular pathogen	A disease-causing organism that invades primarily the conductive tissues (xylem or phloem) of the plant.
Vascular system	The internal structure of the stem that transports water, minerals, and sugars throughout the plant.
Vascular tissue	Water, nutrient, and photosynthate-conducting tissue. (See also Xylem, Phloem).
Vector	A living organism that is able to transmit or spread a

	pathogen.
Vegetative propagation	The increase of plants by asexual means using vegetative parts. Normally results in a population of identical individuals. Can occur by either natural means (e.g. bulblets, cormels, offsets, plantlets, or runners) or artificial means (e.g. cuttings, division, budding, grafting, or layering).
Venation	(1) The pattern of veins in leaves. (2) In insects, the arrangement of veins in wings.
Vermicomposting	Composting with worms. Although there are over 6,000 species of worm, only seven have been found suitable for bin composting. One in particular, *Eisenia fetida* (common name: red wiggler), is the most widely used.
Vermiculite	Lightweight expanded mica often used in soil-less media.
Vermin	Noxious or objectionable animals, insects, or other pests, especially small ones such as rats, mice, and flies.
Vernation	The arrangement of new leaves within an older leaf sheath (e.g. on a grass plant).
Viability	A seed's ability to germinate.
Viable	Alive; seeds must be alive in order to germinate.
Vine crop	Crops that produce vines that grow along the ground including watermelon, muskmelon and pumpkins.

Virulent	Capable of causing severe disease.
Virus	An infectious agent composed of DNA or RNA, too small to see with a compound microscope; multiplies only in

	living cells.
VOCs	Volatile Organic Compounds. Organic compounds or substances vaporize at relatively low temperatures, including alcohol, methane, and ammonia. Volatile compounds are rapidly lost from the composting pile environment.
W	
Warm-season vegetables	Vegetables that grow optimally at temperatures between 25°C and 35°C.
Water-holding capacity (WHC)	The ability of a soil's micropores to hold water for plant use.
Watering-in	The initial watering after plants have been potted or repotted into new containers.
Water-soaking	Lesions that appear wet and dark and usually are sunken and or translucent. Often a symptom of bacterial disease.
Weed	A plant growing where it is not wanted.
Weed-and-feed	A combination fertilizer and herbicide sometimes used on lawns.
Weediness	Likelihood of seeds germinating into unwanted plants that must be removed.
Wetting agent	A chemical that aids in liquid-to-surface contact.
Wetwood	Another name for slime flux.
Wheel hoe	An oscillating or stationary hoe blade mounted on a wheel with handles.

Wilt	Loss of cell turgor; drooping and drying plant parts due to interference with the plant's ability to take up water and nutrients.
Wilting point	Point at which the water content within plant cells is low enough that cellular turgor is lost and the plant wilts.
Winter annual	Annual plant in which the seed germinates in the autumn, producing a plant that overwinters, matures, and produces seed the following growing season.
Winter melon	An oscillating or stationary hoe blade mounted on a wheel with handles.
Winter squash	A squash whose fruit are harvested when uniform in colour and rind is hard.
Witches' broom	A plant condition suspected to be caused by genetic mutation or a virus where all adventitious buds in a certain part of the plant start growing, resulting in a lot of tiny stems; abnormal brush-like development of many weak shoots.

X	
Xeric	A plant or landscape that conserves water. Most xeric plants need minimal supplemental water after an establishment period (18 to 24 months after planting) unless there is extreme drought.
Xylem	The principal water conducting tissue of vascular plants.
Y	
Yard Waste	Leaves, grass clippings, yard trimmings, and other

	organic garden debris.
Yield	Refers to both the measure of the yield of a crop per unit area of land cultivation, and the seed generation of the plant itself.
Z	
Zucchini	A summer squash with harvested fruit has a green-coloured skin and is long cylindrical-shaped with little or no taper.

Conversion Tables

LINEAR MEASUREMENT (LENGTH & DISTANCE)				
IMPERIAL	METRIC		METRIC	IMPERIAL
1 inch	25.4 millimeters (mm)		1 millimeter (mm)	0.0384 inch
1 foot (1 foot = 12 inches)	0.3048 meter (m)		1 centimeter (1 cm = 10 mm)	0.3837 inch
1 yard (3 feet)	0.9144 meter (m)		1 meter (1 m = 100	1.0936 yards

			cm)	
1 mile (1760 yards)	1.6093 kilometer (km)		1 kilometer (1 km = 1000 m)	0.6214 miles
AREA MEASUREMENT				
IMPERIAL	METRIC		METRIC	IMPERIAL
1 square inch	6.4516 cm_2		1 square centimeter (cm_2)	0.155 square inches
1 square foot (144 square inches)	92.9 cm_2		1 square meter (1 m_2 = 10,000 cm_2)	1.196 square yards
1 square yard (9 square feet)	0.8361 m_2		1 hectare (1 ha = 10,000 m2)	2.47 acres

1 acre (4840 square yards)	0.040469 hectare		1 square kilometer (1 km_2 = 100 ha)	247.105 acres
1 square mile (640 acres)	259 hectares			
CUBIC MEASUREMENT (VOLUME)				
IMPERIAL	METRIC		METRIC	IMPERIAL
1 cubic inch	16.4 cc or cm_3		1 cubic centimeter (cc or cm_3)	0.0610 cubic inches
1 cubic foot (1728 in.3)	0.0283 m_3		1 cubic meter (1 million cm_3)	1.308 cubic yards
1 cubic yard (27 ft.3)	0.765 m_3			
CAPACITY MEASURE (VOLUME)				
IMPERIAL	METRIC		METRIC	IMPERIAL
1 (imperial) fl. oz. (1/20 imperial pint)	28.41 ml		0.5 liter (5 cm_3)	1.056 US pint
1 (US liquid) fl. oz. (1/16 US pint)	29.57 ml		1 liter (10 cm_3)	2.11 US pints
1 (imperial) pint (20	568.26 ml			

fl. oz.)				
1 (US liquid) pint (16 fl. oz.)	473.18 ml			
1 (imperial) gallon (4 quarts)	4.546 liter			
1 (US liquid) gallon (4 quarts)	3.785 liter			
MASS (WEIGHT)				
IMPERIAL	METRIC		METRIC	IMPERIAL
1 ounce	28.35 gram		1 gram (1,000 mg)	15.43 grain
1 pound (10 ounces)	0.3545 kilogram		1 kilogram (1,000 g)	2.205 pounds
1 ton (2240 lbs)	1.016 tonnes		1 tonne (1,000 kg)	0.984 ton

TEMPERATURE				
FAHRENHEIT	CELCIUS		CELCIUS	FAHRENHEIT
32°F	0.0°C		-20°C	-4°F
40°F	4.4°C		-10°C	14°F
50°F	10.0°C		0°C	32°F
55°F	12.8°C		10°C	50°F
60°F	15.6°C		20°C	68°F
70°F	21.1°C		30°C	86°F
77°F	25.0°C		40°C	104°F
90°F	32.2°C		50°C	122°F
105°F	40.6°C		60°C	140°F
120°F	48.9°C		70°C	158°F
140°F	60.0°C		80°C	176°F
145°F	62.8°C		90°C	194°F
150°F	65.6°C		100°C	212°F
160°F	71.1°C		110°C	230°F

METRIC TO IMPERIAL CONVERSION

Convert	To	Multiply by

Kilometers	Miles	0.62
Kilometers	Feet	3280.8
Meters	Feet	3.28
Centimeters	Inches	0.39
Millimeters	Inches	0.039
Liters	Quarts	1.057
Liters	Gallons	0.264
Milliliters	Cups	0.0042
Milliliters	Ounces	0.0338
Celsius	Fahrenheit	°C x 9/5 + 32 = °F
Kilogram	Tons	0.0011
Kilogram	Pounds	2.2046
Grams	Ounces	0.035
Grams	Pounds	0.002205
Milligrams	Ounces	0.000035

IMPERIAL TO METRIC CONVERSION

Convert	To	Multiply by
Fahrenheit	Celsius	(°F - 32) x 5/9 = °C
Inches	Meters	0.0254
Inches	Centimeters	2.54
Inches	Millimeters	25.4
Feet	Meters	0.3
Yards	Meters	0.91
Yards	Kilometers	0.00091
Miles	Kilometers	1.61
Ounces	Milliliters	29.57
Cups	Milliliters	236.6
Quarts	Liters	0.95
Gallons	Liters	3.785
Ounces	Milligrams	28350
Ounces	Grams	28.35
Pounds	Kilograms	0.454
Tons	Kilograms	907.18

Helpful Weights

I advise keeping your compost at 50% moisture until used (within six months of making it).

A full cubic-yard-sized bin (the size of a standard composting bin) will produce just over 12 cubic feet of compost weighing about 150 pounds – enough to cover 150 square feet of soil an inch deep.

Compost weighs approximately 12.5 pounds per cubic foot (specific gravity 0.2).

A spread of 12mm thick will cover 300 sq. ft. from a single composted pile of 3 cubic feet (cubic yard).

An application of ½ inch is adequate for annual bed maintenance.

EPILOGUE

After following the expert guidance in Your First Vegetable Garden, you have now successfully grown your own delicious and nutritious vegetables. You have learned the importance of choosing the right location, preparing the soil, and selecting the best vegetables for your climate. You have also gained valuable knowledge on how to combat common pests and diseases, ensuring the health and longevity of your garden.

You will be rewarded with abundant fresh produce as you continue to nurture and tend to your garden. The satisfaction and pride that comes with harvesting your own vegetables is unparalleled. You have discovered the joys of gardening and the benefits of growing your own food.

Thank you for choosing Your First Vegetable Garden as your guide on this gardening journey. We hope you continue cultivating your green fingers and that your garden brings you endless enjoyment and nourishment.

If you're looking for more gardening information, we recommend Simplify Gardening (simplifygardening.com and youtube.com/simplifygardening). These resources offer a range of gardening tips and advice for all competency levels. Check them out to continue learning and improving your gardening skills.

Printed in Great Britain
by Amazon

20836391R00201